GRAMMAR AND BEYOND
ESSENTIALS

3

Laurie Blass
Susan Iannuzzi
Alice Savage
with Randi Reppen

CAMBRIDGE
UNIVERSITY PRESS

CAMBRIDGE
UNIVERSITY PRESS

University Printing House, Cambridge CB2 8BS, United Kingdom

One Liberty Plaza, 20th Floor, New York, NY 10006, USA

477 Williamstown Road, Port Melbourne, VIC 3207, Australia

314–321, 3rd Floor, Plot 3, Splendor Forum, Jasola District Centre, New Delhi – 110025, India

103 Penang Road, #05-06/07, Visioncrest Commercial, Singapore 238467

Cambridge University Press is part of the University of Cambridge.

It furthers the University's mission by disseminating knowledge in the pursuit of education, learning and research at the highest international levels of excellence.

www.cambridge.org
Information on this title: www.cambridge.org/9781108697170

20 19 18 17 16 15 14 13 12

Printed in Poland by Opolgraf

A catalogue record for this publication is available from the British Library

ISBN 978-1-108-69717-0 Student's Book with Online Workbook

Additional resources for this publication at www.cambridge.org/essentials

Cambridge University Press has no responsibility for the persistence or accuracy of URLs for external or third-party internet websites referred to in this publication, and does not guarantee that any content on such websites is, or will remain, accurate or appropriate. Information regarding prices, travel timetables, and other factual information given in this work is correct at the time of first printing but Cambridge University Press does not guarantee the accuracy of such information thereafter.

Scope and Sequence

Unit	Theme	Grammar	Topics	Avoid Common Mistakes
PART 1 The Present and Past				
UNIT 1 page 2	First Impressions	Simple Present and Present Progressive	Simple Present vs. Present Progressive (p. 4) Stative Verbs (p. 8) Special Meanings and Uses of Simple Present (p. 12)	Remembering the simple present with stative verbs; avoiding the base form of the verb when using the present progressive
UNIT 2 page 16	Global Marketing	Simple Past and Past Progressive; *Used To*, *Would*	Simple Past vs. Past Progressive (p. 18) Time Clauses with Simple Past and Past Progressive (p. 20) *Used To* and *Would* (p. 24)	Remembering the base form of the verb after *would* and *used to*; remembering the simple past for specific events in the past; remembering the past progressive for background information
PART 2 The Perfect				
UNIT 3 page 28	Success	Present Perfect and Present Perfect Progressive	Present Perfect (p. 30) Present Perfect vs. Simple Past (p. 34) Present Perfect vs. Present Perfect Progressive (p. 37)	Remembering correct subject–verb agreement with present perfect; remembering *been* for the present perfect progressive
UNIT 4 page 42	Nature vs. Nurture	Past Perfect and Past Perfect Progressive	Past Perfect (p. 44) Past Perfect with Time Clauses (p. 49) Past Perfect Progressive (p. 52)	Remembering when to use the past perfect or past perfect progressive
PART 3 The Future				
UNIT 5 page 56	Looking Ahead at Technology	*Be Going To*, Present Progressive, and Future Progressive	*Be Going To*, Present Progressive, and Simple Present for Future (p. 58) *Will* and *Be Going To* (p. 61) Future Progressive (p. 64)	Remembering *be* with *be going to*; remembering when to use the future progressive, the simple present, or the present progressive
UNIT 6 page 68	Business Practices of the Future	Future Time Clauses, Future Perfect, and Future Perfect Progressive	Future Time Clauses (p. 70) Future Perfect vs. Future Perfect Progressive (p. 75)	Avoiding the future form in the time clause; remembering *will* with the future perfect

Unit	Theme	Grammar	Topics	Avoid Common Mistakes
PART 12 Connecting Ideas				
UNIT 26 page 304	Globalization of Food	Conjunctions	Connecting Words and Phrases with Conjunctions (p. 306) Connecting Sentences with Coordinating Conjunctions (p. 310) Reducing Sentences with Similar Clauses (p. 314)	Avoiding *either* when joining ideas with *and*; avoiding *too* after a negative verb
UNIT 27 page 318	Consumerism	Adverb Clauses and Phrases	Subordinators and Adverb Clauses (p. 320) Reducing Adverb Clauses (p. 323) Subordinators to Express Purpose (p. 325)	Remembering to spell *even though* as two words; avoiding *even* in adverb clauses
UNIT 28 page 328	Technology in Entertainment	Connecting Information with Prepositions and Transitions	Connecting Information with Prepositions and Prepositional Phrases (p. 330) Connecting Information with Transition Words (p. 333)	Avoiding *in the other hand*

Appendices

Introduction to Grammar and Beyond Essentials

Grammar and Beyond Essentials is a research-based and content-rich grammar series for beginning to advanced-level students. The series focuses on the most commonly used English grammar structures and practices all four skills in a variety of authentic and communicative contexts. It is designed for use both in the classroom and as a self-study learning tool.

Grammar and Beyond Essentials is Research-Based

The grammar presented in this series is informed by years of research on the grammar of written and spoken English as it is used in college lectures, textbooks, academic essays, high school classrooms, and conversations between instructors and students. This research, and the analysis of over one billion words of authentic written and spoken language data known as the *Cambridge International Corpus*, has enabled the authors to:

- Present grammar rules that accurately represent how English is actually spoken and written

- Identify and teach differences between the grammar of written and spoken English

- Focus more attention on the structures that are commonly used, and less on those that are rarely used, in writing and speaking

- Help students avoid the most common mistakes that English language learners make

- Choose reading topics that will naturally elicit examples of the target grammar structure

- Introduce important vocabulary from the Academic Word List

Special Features of *Grammar and Beyond Essentials*

Realistic Grammar Presentations

Grammar is presented in clear and simple charts. The grammar points presented in these charts have been tested against real-world data from the *Cambridge International Corpus* to ensure that they are authentic representations of actual use of English.

Data from the Real World

Many of the grammar presentations and application sections include a feature called Data from the Real World. Concrete and useful points discovered through analysis of corpus data are presented and practiced in exercises that follow.

Avoid Common Mistakes

Each unit features an Avoid Common Mistakes section that develops students' awareness of the most common mistakes made by English language learners and gives them an opportunity to practice detecting and correcting these errors. This section helps students avoid these mistakes in their own work. The mistakes highlighted in this section are drawn from a body of authentic data on learner English known as the *Cambridge Learner Corpus*, a database of over 35 million words from student essays written by non-native speakers of English and information from experienced classroom teachers.

Academic Vocabulary

Every unit in *Grammar and Beyond Essentials* includes words from the Academic Word List (AWL), a research-based list of words and word families that appear with high frequency in English-language academic texts. These words are introduced in the opening text of the unit, recycled in the charts and exercises, and used to support the theme throughout the unit. By the time students finish each level, they will have been exposed several times to a carefully selected set of level-appropriate AWL words, as well as content words from a variety of academic disciplines.

Series Levels

The following table provides a general idea of the difficulty of the material at each level of *Grammar and Beyond Essentials*. These are not meant to be interpreted as precise correlations.

	Description	TOEFL IBT	CEFR Levels
Level 1	Beginning	20 – 34	A1 – A2
Level 2	Low Intermediate to Intermediate	35 – 54	A2 – B1
Level 3	High Intermediate	55 – 74	B1 – B2
Level 4	Advanced	75 – 95	B2 – C1

Student Components

Student's Book with Online Workbook

Levels 1 through 3 teach all of the grammar points appropriate at each level in short, manageable cycles of presentation and practice organized around a high-interest unit theme. Level 4 focuses on the structure of the academic essay in addition to the grammar rules, conventions, and structures that students need to master in order to be successful college writers. Please see the Tour of a Unit on pages xvi–xix for a more detailed view of the contents and structure of the units.

Online Workbook

The Online Workbook provides extra practice to help you master each grammar point. Automatically-graded exercises give immediate feedback. Each unit offers practice correcting the errors highlighted in the Avoid Common Mistakes section in the Student's Book. Self-Assessment sections at the end of each unit allow students to test their mastery of what they learned. Look for in the Student's Book to see where additional online practice is available.

Quiz Your English app

Quiz Your English is a fun new way to practice, improve, and test your English by competing against learners from all around the world. Learn English grammar with friends, discover new English words, and test yourself in a truly global environment.

- Learn to avoid common mistakes with a special section just for *Grammar and Beyond Essentials* users
- Challenge your friends and players wherever they are
- Watch where you are on the leaderboards

Teacher Resources

Grammar and Beyond Essentials offers a variety of downloadable resources for instructors on eSource: esource.cambridge.org. Contact your Cambridge ESL Specialist (www.cambridge.org/cambridgeenglish/contact) to find out how to access the site.

Teacher's Manual

- Suggestions for applying the target grammar to all four major skill areas, helping instructors facilitate dynamic and comprehensive grammar classes
- An answer key and audio script for the Student's Book
- Teaching tips, to help instructors plan their lessons
- Downloadable communicative activities to add more in-class speaking practice

Assessment

- Placement Test
- Ready-made, easy-to-score Unit Tests, Midterm, and Final in .pdf and .doc formats
- Answer Key

Presentation Plus

Presentation Plus allows teachers to digitally project the contents of the Student's Books in front of the class for a livelier, interactive classroom. It is a complete solution for teachers because it includes the answer keys and audio.

Lesson Mapping Guides

Grammar and Beyond Essentials is designed to be used easily alongside academic English titles from Cambridge University Press. These include: *Academic Encounters, Final Draft, Making Connections, Prism,* and *Prism Reading.* Visit www.cambridge.org/essentials/LessonMaps to download a Lesson Mapping Guide for each title.

Academic Encounters   **FINAL** DRAFT   Making **CONNECTIONS**   PRISM   PRISM **READING**

About the Authors

Laurie Blass has more than 25 years' experience teaching and creating materials for ESL students in the United States and abroad. She is currently a full-time materials developer with a special interest in ESL for academic success and educational technology. Laurie is co-author of *Writers at Work: From Sentence to Paragraph*, published by Cambridge University Press, among many other titles.

Susan Iannuzzi has been teaching ESL for more than 20 years. She has trained English teachers on five continents and consulted on the national English curricula for countries in Africa, Asia, and the Middle East. She has authored or co-authored more than 10 English courses in use today. *Grammar and Beyond* is her first publication with Cambridge University Press.

Alice Savage is an English Language Teacher and Materials Writer. She attended the School for International Training in Vermont and is an author on the *Read This!* series, published by Cambridge University Press. She lives in Houston, Texas with her husband and two children.

 **Randi Reppen** is Professor of Applied Linguistics and TESL at Northern Arizona University (NAU) in Flagstaff, Arizona. She has over 20 years' experience teaching ESL students and training ESL teachers, including 11 years as the Director of NAU's Program in Intensive English. Randi's research interests focus on the use of corpora for language teaching and materials development. In addition to numerous academic articles and books, she is the author of *Using Corpora in the Language Classroom* and a co-author of *Basic Vocabulary in Use*, 2nd edition, both published by Cambridge University Press.

Advisory Panel

The ESL advisory panel has helped to guide the development of this series and provided invaluable information about the needs of ESL students and teachers in high schools, colleges, universities, and private language schools throughout North America.

Neta Simpkins Cahill, Skagit Valley College, Mount Vernon, WA

Shelly Hedstrom, Palm Beach State College, Lake Worth, FL

Richard Morasci, Foothill College, Los Altos Hills, CA

Stacey Russo, East Hampton High School, East Hampton, NY

Alice Savage, North Harris College, Houston, TX

Acknowledgements

The publisher and author would like to thank these reviewers and consultants for their insights and participation:

Marty Attiyeh, The College of DuPage, Glen Ellyn, IL

Shannon Bailey, Austin Community College, Austin, TX

Jamila Barton, North Seattle Community College, Seattle, WA

Kim Bayer, Hunter College IELI, New York, NY

Linda Berendsen, Oakton Community College, Skokie, IL

Anita Biber, Tarrant County College Northwest, Fort Worth, TX

Jane Breaux, Community College of Aurora, Aurora, CO

Anna Budzinski, San Antonio College, San Antonio, TX

Britta Burton, Mission College, Santa Clara, CA

Jean Carroll, Fresno City College, Fresno, CA

Chris Cashman, Oak Park High School and Elmwood Park High School, Chicago, IL

Annette M. Charron, Bakersfield College, Bakersfield, CA

Patrick Colabucci, ALI at San Diego State University, San Diego, CA

Lin Cui, Harper College, Palatine, IL

Jennifer Duclos, Boston University CELOP, Boston, MA

Joy Durighello, San Francisco City College, San Francisco, CA

Kathleen Flynn, Glendale Community College, Glendale, CA

Raquel Fundora, Miami Dade College, Miami, FL

Patricia Gillie, New Trier Township High School District, Winnetka, IL

Laurie Gluck, LaGuardia Community College, Long Island City, NY

Kathleen Golata, Galileo Academy of Science & Technology, San Francisco, CA

Ellen Goldman, Mission College, Santa Clara, CA

Ekaterina Goussakova, Seminole Community College, Sanford, FL

Marianne Grayston, Prince George's Community College, Largo, MD

Mary Greiss Shipley, Georgia Gwinnett College, Lawrenceville, GA

Sudeepa Gulati, Long Beach City College, Long Beach, CA

Nicole Hammond Carrasquel, University of Central Florida, Orlando, FL

Vicki Hendricks, Broward College, Fort Lauderdale, FL

Kelly Hernandez, Miami Dade College, Miami, FL

Ann Johnston, Tidewater Community College, Virginia Beach, VA

Julia Karet, Chaffey College, Claremont, CA

Jeanne Lachowski, English Language Institute, University of Utah, Salt Lake City, UT

Noga Laor, Rennert, New York, NY

Min Lu, Central Florida Community College, Ocala, FL

Michael Luchuk, Kaplan International Centers, New York, NY

Craig Machado, Norwalk Community College, Norwalk, CT

Denise Maduli-Williams, City College of San Francisco, San Francisco, CA

Diane Mahin, University of Miami, Coral Gables, FL

Melanie Majeski, Naugatuck Valley Community College, Waterbury, CT

Jeanne Malcolm, University of North Carolina at Charlotte, Charlotte, NC

Lourdes Marx, Palm Beach State College, Boca Raton, FL

Susan G. McFalls, Maryville College, Maryville, TN

Nancy McKay, Cuyahoga Community College, Cleveland, OH

Dominika McPartland, Long Island Business Institute, Flushing, NY

Amy Metcalf, UNR/Intensive English Language Center, University of Nevada, Reno, NV

Robert Miller, EF International Language School San Francisco – Mills, San Francisco, CA

Marcie Pachino, Jordan High School, Durham, NC

Myshie Pagel, El Paso Community College, El Paso, TX

Bernadette Pedagno, University of San Francisco, San Francisco, CA

Tam Q Pham, Dallas Theological Seminary, Fort Smith, AR

Mary Beth Pickett, Global LT, Rochester, MI

Maria Reamore, Baltimore City Public Schools, Baltimore, MD

Alison M. Rice, Hunter College IELI, New York, NY

Sydney Rice, Imperial Valley College, Imperial, CA

Kathleen Romstedt, Ohio State University, Columbus, OH

Alexandra Rowe, University of South Carolina, Columbia, SC

Irma Sanders, Baldwin Park Adult and Community Education, Baldwin Park, CA

Caren Shoup, Lone Star College – CyFair, Cypress, TX

Karen Sid, Mission College, Foothill College, De Anza College, Santa Clara, CA

Michelle Thomas, Miami Dade College, Miami, FL

Sharon Van Houte, Lorain County Community College, Elyria, OH

Margi Wald, UC Berkeley, Berkeley, CA

Walli Weitz, Riverside County Office of Ed., Indio, CA

Bart Weyand, University of Southern Maine, Portland, ME

Donna Weyrich, Columbus State Community College, Columbus, OH

Marilyn Whitehorse, Santa Barbara City College, Ojai, CA

Jessica Wilson, Rutgers University – Newark, Newark, NJ

Sue Wilson, San Jose City College, San Jose, CA

Margaret Wilster, Mid-Florida Tech, Orlando, FL

Anne York-Herjeczki, Santa Monica College, Santa Monica, CA

Hoda Zaki, Camden County College, Camden, NJ

We would also like to thank these teachers and programs for allowing us to visit:

Richard Appelbaum, Broward College, Fort Lauderdale, FL

Carmela Arnoldt, Glendale Community College, Glendale, AZ

JaNae Barrow, Desert Vista High School, Phoenix, AZ

Ted Christensen, Mesa Community College, Mesa, AZ

Richard Ciriello, Lower East Side Preparatory High School, New York, NY

Virginia Edwards, Chandler-Gilbert Community College, Chandler, AZ

Nusia Frankel, Miami Dade College, Miami, FL

Raquel Fundora, Miami Dade College, Miami, FL

Vicki Hendricks, Broward College, Fort Lauderdale, FL

Kelly Hernandez, Miami Dade College, Miami, FL

Stephen Johnson, Miami Dade College, Miami, FL

Barbara Jordan, Mesa Community College, Mesa, AZ

Nancy Kersten, GateWay Community College, Phoenix, AZ

Lewis Levine, Hostos Community College, Bronx, NY

John Liffiton, Scottsdale Community College, Scottsdale, AZ

Cheryl Lira-Layne, Gilbert Public School District, Gilbert, AZ

Mary Livingston, Arizona State University, Tempe, AZ

Elizabeth Macdonald, Thunderbird School of Global Management, Glendale, AZ

Terri Martinez, Mesa Community College, Mesa, AZ

Lourdes Marx, Palm Beach State College, Boca Raton, FL

Paul Kei Matsuda, Arizona State University, Tempe, AZ

David Miller, Glendale Community College, Glendale, AZ

Martha Polin, Lower East Side Preparatory High School, New York, NY

Patricia Pullenza, Mesa Community College, Mesa, AZ

Victoria Rasinskaya, Lower East Side Preparatory High School, New York, NY

Vanda Salls, Tempe Union High School District, Tempe, AZ

Kim Sanabria, Hostos Community College, Bronx, NY

Cynthia Schuemann, Miami Dade College, Miami, FL

Michelle Thomas, Miami Dade College, Miami, FL

Dongmei Zeng, Borough of Manhattan Community College, New York, NY

Tour of a Unit

GRAMMAR IN THE REAL WORLD

presents the unit's grammar in a realistic context using **contemporary** texts.

UNIT
4

Past Perfect and Past Perfect Progressive
Nature vs. Nurture

1 Grammar in the Real World

A Have you ever reconnected with someone from your past? Read the article about twins who lived apart for many years. What surprised the twins when they reconnected?

B Comprehension Check **Answer the questions.**

1 What was surprising about the twins' adoption?
2 What characteristics and interests did Elyse and Paula have in common?
3 What is the nature versus nurture debate?

C Notice **Underline the verbs in each sentence.**

1 Both girls knew that their parents had adopted them as infants.
2 She had been doing research on her birth mother when she made a surprising discovery.
3 Even more surprising, she learned that she had been part of a secret scientific study.

Which event happened first in each sentence? What event followed? Write the verbs. What do you notice about the form of the verbs?

1 First: _____ Then: _____

2 First: _____ Then: _____

3 First: _____ Then: _____

The SCIENCE of TWINS

[1]**identical:** exactly the same
[2]**DNA:** the abbreviation for deoxyribonucleic acid, a chemical that controls the structure and purpose of every cell
[3]**controversial:** causing or likely to cause disagreement
[4]**dominant:** more important, strong, or noticeable

Past Perfect and Past Perfect Progressive

Twins, especially identical[1] twins, have always fascinated scientists. Identical twins develop from one egg, have identical DNA,[2] and are usually very similar in appearance and behavior. There have been many studies of identical twins raised in the same family. There have also been a number of studies of identical twins separated at birth and raised in separate families. These studies have provided interesting information about the impact of *nature* (genetics) and *nurture* (the environment) on the development of the individual. However, some of the studies have been controversial.[3]

Take the case of Elyse Schein and Paula Bernstein. Elyse and Paula were identical twins separated at birth. Both girls knew that their parents **had adopted** them as infants, but neither girl knew about her twin. When Elyse grew up, she longed to meet her biological mother, so she contacted the agency that **had arranged** the adoption. She **had been doing** research on her birth mother when she made a surprising discovery. She had an identical twin. Even more surprising, she learned that she **had been** part of a secret scientific study. At the time of the adoption, the agency **had allowed** different families to adopt each twin. The agency **had told** the families that their child was part of a scientific study. However, it **had never told** the families the goal of the study: for scientists to investigate nature versus nurture.

When Elyse and Paula finally met as adults, they were amazed. They had many similarities. They looked almost identical. They **had** both **studied** film. They both loved to write. Together, the twins discovered that the researchers **had stopped** the study before the end because the public strongly disapproved of this type of research.

Although that study ended early, many scientists today make a strong case for the dominant[4] role of nature. Schein and Bernstein agree that genetics explains many of their similarities. However, recent research suggests that nurture is equally important. It is clear that the nature versus nurture debate will occupy scientists for years to come.

42

Nature vs. Nurture **43**

NOTICE ACTIVITIES

draw students' attention to the structure, guiding their own analysis of form, meaning, and use.

---

2 Past Perfect

Grammar Presentation

The past perfect is used to describe a completed event that happened before another event in the past.	Elyse finally met her sister, Paula. Paula *had been married* for several years. (First, Paula got married; Elyse met Paula at a later time.)

2.1 Forming Past Perfect

Form the past perfect with *had* + the past participle of the main verb. Form the negative by adding *not* after *had*. The form is the same for all subjects.	Elyse and Paula did not grow up together. They *had lived* with different families. They were available for adoption because their birth mother *had given* them up. "*Had* she *talked* about the study to anyone at the time?" "No, she *hadn't*." "What *had* you *heard* about this study before that time?" "I'*d heard* very little about it."

▶ Irregular Verbs: See page A1.

2.2 Using Past Perfect with Simple Past

A Use the past perfect to describe an event in a time period that leads up to another past event or time period. Use the simple past to describe the later event or time period.	LATER TIME · EARLIER TIME She learned that she *had been* part of a secret study. LATER TIME · EARLIER TIME The twins discovered that they *had* both *studied* psychology.
B The prepositions *before, by,* or *until* can introduce the later time period.	EARLIER TIME · LATER TIME Their mother *had known* about the study *before* her death. EARLIER TIME · LATER TIME Sue *hadn't met* her sister *until* last year. EARLIER TIME · LATER TIME Studies on twins *had become* common *by* the 1960s.
C The past perfect is often used to give reasons or background information for later past events.	REASON She *was* late. She *had forgotten* to set her alarm clock. BACKGROUND INFORMATION · LATER PAST EVENT He *had* never *taken* a subway before he *moved* to New York.

44 Unit 4 Past Perfect and Past Perfect Progressive

Past Perfect and Past Perfect Progressive

Data from the Real World

In writing, these verbs are commonly used in the past perfect: *come, have, leave, make,* and *take.* Had been is the most common past perfect form in speaking and writing.	The twins *had not gone* to the same school as children. The family thought that they *had made* the right decision. Psychologists praised the study because the researchers *had been* very careful in their work. The researchers *had not been* aware of each other's work on twins until they met.

Grammar Application

Exercise 2.1 Past Perfect

Complete the sentences about twins who met as adults. Use the past perfect form of the verbs in parentheses.

1 Two separate Illinois families ___*had adopted*___ (adopt) Anne Green and Annie Smith before the twins were three days old.

2 When the girls met, they were fascinated by their similarities. For example, they _____ (live) near each other before the Greens moved away.

3 As children, both Anne and Annie _____ (go) to the same summer camp.

4 Anne _____ (not/go) to college, and Annie _____ (not/attend) college, either.

5 Both _____ (marry) for the first time by the age of 22.

6 Anne _____ (get) divorced and _____ (remarry). Annie _____ (not/get) divorced and was still married.

7 Both Anne and Annie were allergic to cats and dogs and _____ never _____ (own) pets.

8 Both _____ (give) the same name – Heather – to their daughters.

9 Both _____ previously _____ (work) in the hospitality industry.

10 Anne _____ (work) as a hotel manager. However, Annie _____ (not/work) in hotels; she _____ (be) a restaurant manager.

Nature vs. Nurture 45

THEME-RELATED EXERCISES

boost fluency by providing grammar
practice in a variety of different contexts.

Exercise 2.2 Past Perfect and Simple Past

A Read the article about a famous twin study. Underline the simple past forms.
Double underline the past perfect forms.

The University of Minnesota is the birthplace of one of the most
important twin studies in the world. It started in 1979. Thomas
J. Bouchard had already been on the faculty¹ of the university
for some time when he began his study of identical twins.
Bouchard read an article about a set of twins who had been
separated at birth. The twins had recently met and had found
many similarities. They found out that they had lived near
each other for years. Bouchard was amazed by the twins'
story and decided to start the Minnesota Twins Reared Apart
Study. Bouchard began to study sets of twins that had been
separated at birth. Over the years, the Minnesota Twins Reared
Apart Study has studied around 10,000 sets of twins. The study
continues today.

¹**faculty:** the people who teach in a department in a school

B Pair Work **Compare your answers with a partner. Discuss the reason for each
of your answers.**

*In line 2, had been refers to the first event. Dr. Bouchard joined the faculty
before the twin study. The twin study began later. The study is the second event,
so started is in the simple past.*

Exercise 2.3 More Past Perfect and Simple Past

A Listen to an interview with twins who are actors. Complete the sentences
with the verbs you hear.

Claudia   Today, I'm interviewing Alex and Andrew Underhill. They appear in the *Spy Twins*
movie series based on the books of the same name. How did you get the part in
the first *Spy Twins* movie?

Alex   A friend _____*had seen*_____ the advertisement in the newspaper and later
                                         (1)
_____ us about it. We _____
                (2)   (3)
any acting before then, but we _____ to try out anyway.
                                             (4)

46 Unit 4 Past Perfect and Past Perfect Progressive

QR CODES

give easy access to audio at
point of use.

HOW TO USE A QR CODE

1 Open the camera on your smartphone.

2 Point it at the QR code.

3 The camera will automatically scan the code.
If not, press the button to take a picture.

* Not all cameras automatically scan QR codes.
You may need to download a QR code reader.
Search "QR free" and download an app.

CONTEXTUALIZED PRACTICE

moves from controlled to open-ended, teaching meaningful language for real communicative purposes.

AVOID COMMON MISTAKES

is based on a database of over 135,000 essays Students learn to avoid the most common mistakes English language learners make and develop self-editing skills to improve their speaking and writing.

C Use the time line to complete the sentences about Alex and Andrew. Use the past perfect form of the verbs in the box.

| build | decide | graduate | make | record | start |

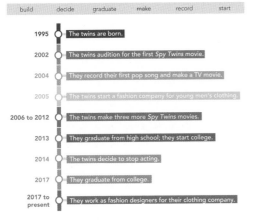

1995	The twins are born.
2002	The twins audition for the first *Spy Twins* movie.
2004	They record their first pop song and make a TV movie.
2005	The twins start a fashion company for young men's clothing.
2006 to 2012	The twins make three more *Spy Twins* movies.
2013	They graduate from high school; they start college.
2014	The twins decide to stop acting.
2017	They graduate from college.
2017 to present	They work as fashion designers for their clothing company.

1 By 2012, Alex and Andrew _had made_ four Spy Twins movies.

2 Before 2004, the twins _____ (not) a pop song.

3 By 2016, the twins _____ to stop acting.

4 The twins _____ (not) a fashion company yet in 2004.

5 The twins _____ from high school by 2015.

Past Perfect and Past Perfect Progressive

5 Avoid Common Mistakes ⚠

1 Use the past perfect or past perfect progressive to give background information for a past tense event.

   had
I ~~have~~ never seen my sister in real life, so I was nervous the first time we met.

   had been dreaming
I ~~have dreamed~~ about meeting her, and I finally did.

2 Use the past perfect or past perfect progressive to give a reason for a past event.

   had been crying
Her eyes were red and puffy because she ~~cried~~.

3 Use the past perfect (not the past perfect progressive) for a completed earlier event.

   arranged
They had ~~been arranging~~ a time to meet, but both of them forgot about it.

4 Use the past perfect (not present perfect) to describe a completed event that happened before a past event.

   had
I ~~have~~ visited her in Maine twice before she came to visit me.

Editing Task

Find and correct seven more mistakes in the paragraphs about sibling differences.

       had
    I ~~have~~ never really thought about sibling differences until my own children were born. When we had our first child, my husband and I have lived in Chicago for just a few months. We have not made many friends yet, so we spent all our time with our child. Baby Gilbert was happy to be the center of attention. He depended on us
5 for everything.
    By the time our second son, Chase, was born, we have developed a community of friends and a busier social life. We frequently visited friends and left the children at home with a babysitter. As a result of our busy schedules, Chase was more independent. One day I had just been hanging up the phone when Chase came into
10 the room. Chase picked up the phone and started talking into it. I thought he was pretending, but I was wrong. He had been figuring out how to use the phone!
    When my husband came home, he was tired because he worked all day. When I told him about Chase's phone conversation, though, he became very excited. Gilbert has never used the phone as a child. At first, we were surprised that Chase was so
15 different from Gilbert. Then we realized that because of our busy lifestyles, Chase had learned to be independent.

EDITING TASK

gives learners an opportunity to identify and correct commonly made errors and develop self-editing skills needed in their university studies.

Simple Present and Present Progressive

First Impressions

1 Grammar in the Real World

A When you meet someone for the first time, what do you notice about the person? Read the article about first impressions. What influences your first impressions?

B Comprehension Check **Answer the questions.**

1 How long does it take to form a first impression? 30 seconds

2 What is the collection of tests known as the IAT helping to reveal?

3 What is one stereotype that young and old people share?

*conscious
and
subconscious

tend to associate
the word good with
pictures of young people.*

C Notice **Find the sentences in the article and complete them. Circle the correct verbs. Then check (✓) the box that best describes the function of each verb.**

1 The average person **forms / is forming** a first impression of someone in less than 30 seconds.

☑ general fact or habit ☐ temporary action

2 Handshakes, facial expressions, and general appearance **help / are helping** to create first impressions.

☑ general fact or habit ☐ temporary action

3 Some psychologists today **research / are researching** the factors that influence how people react to others.

☐ general fact or habit ☑ temporary action

4 Specifically, Nosek **investigates / is investigating** our use of stereotypes and attitudes about others in forming first impressions.

☐ general fact or habit ☑ temporary action

What do the verbs in the simple present describe? What do the verbs in the present progressive describe?

FIRST IMPRESSIONS

Here is an interesting fact: The average person **forms** a first impression of someone in less than 30 seconds. *First impressions* **are** the opinions someone **has** about you when you **meet** for the
5 first time. What **is** your smile **telling** the other person? What **is** the way you dress **saying** about you? These factors can make a difference in the way the person **thinks** about you.

Handshakes, facial expressions, and general
10 appearance **help** to create first impressions. People are constantly **forming** these impressions of others. We do not make these impressions consciously.[1] They **are** largely subconscious.[2] However, they **tend**[3] to be extremely difficult to change.

15 Some psychologists today **are researching** the factors that influence how people react to others. For example, psychologist Brian Nosek **is** currently **using** a collection of tests known as the IAT, or Implicit Association Test, for his research. These
20 tests **are helping** to reveal our thinking processes, both conscious and subconscious, as we form our impressions of others. **Specifically**, Nosek is **investigating** our use of stereotypes and attitudes about others in forming first impressions.

25 Each test **measures** what happens while people **are making** judgments. The results **demonstrate** that people have stereotypes, and that these stereotypes **influence** their first impressions. For example, both young and old people **tend**
30 to associate the word *good* with pictures of young people.

Since first impressions **influence** what a person **thinks** about you to a great degree, it **is** important to always do your best to make a good
35 first impression.

---

[1]**consciously:** aware of what is happening
[2]**subconscious:** existing in the mind but not in one's awareness
[3]**tend:** be likely

2 Simple Present vs. Present Progressive

Grammar Presentation

The simple present and the present progressive both describe present time. The simple present describes things that are more permanent, such as general facts or habits.	*The average person **forms** a first impression in less than 30 seconds.*
The present progressive describes things that are temporary, such as things in progress now or around now.	*Psychologists **are researching** the factors that influence how people react.*

2.1 Simple Present

A Use the simple present for general facts and permanent situations.	*People **form** a first impression within 30 seconds.* *First impressions **influence** what a person thinks about you.* *I **dress** conservatively at work.*
B Use the simple present to describe routines and habits.	*The manager **asks** a lot of questions.* *We **work** for eight hours every day.*
You can use time expressions such as *always, usually, often, sometimes, never, on Mondays, once a week, two days a week,* and *twice a month.*	*The hiring manager <u>always</u> **writes** a report after an interview.* *We <u>usually</u> **follow** her recommendations.* *She **doesn't interview** candidates <u>on Mondays</u>.* *We **discuss** the manager's reports <u>once a week</u>.*
C Use the simple present for routines, scheduled events, and timetables.	*The office **opens** at 9:00 a.m.* *The train to Boston **departs** from platform 11 at 2:00 p.m.* *"**Does** the meeting always **begin** at noon?"* *"Yes, it **does**."*

▶▶ Irregular Verbs : See page A1.

📊 Data from the Real World

Research shows that we use some adverbs with the simple present more often in academic writing than in speaking.

More common in writing: *typically, frequently, traditionally*	*The interview **typically** takes three hours.*
Common in both speaking and writing: *generally, usually, normally*	*The team **generally** meets on Tuesdays.* *How do you **normally** handle complaints?*

2.2 Present Progressive

A Use the present progressive to describe what is in progress now or around the present time.

Mr. Rask is interviewing a candidate at the moment.
(The interview is happening now.)

We are interviewing candidates all month.
(Interviews may not be in progress now, but they are in progress during this month.)

B Use the present progressive to describe temporary events or changing situations.

I am studying stereotypes in the workplace.
(My studies will end in the future.)

📊 Data from the Real World

Research shows that we often use the present progressive for habits that are noteworthy or unusual. This is sometimes, but not always, because these habits are not desirable. You can use *always* or *constantly* for emphasis. *Constantly* is more formal than *always*.

She is always disturbing me when I am trying to study.

My boss is constantly asking me to stay late at work.

The present progressive form is also common with verbs that describe changing or temporary situations.

The workers at that store are constantly changing. Every week there is someone new.

We are always looking for new ideas and people with special talents.

🖱 Grammar Application

Exercise 2.1 Simple Present

Complete the sentences with the simple present of the verbs in the box.

| give | have | have | help | ~~make~~ | meet | show | start | teach | videotape |

1 According to many studies, most people _____*make*_____ judgments about others in only a few seconds.

2 Communication trainer Mary Hernandez _____ job seekers make a good first impression.

3 Ms. Hernandez _____ a course called *Making a Good First Impression* at the community college.

4 The class _____ on Mondays and Wednesdays.

5 At the first class meeting, Ms. Hernandez typically _____gives_____ students a self-assessment test.

6 The self-assessment test ___shows___ how the students judge themselves.

7 Students almost always ___have___ a positive impression of themselves.

8 After the self-assessment, Ms. Hernandez usually ___~~meet~~ video tape___ the students in mock interviews.

9 On the last day of class, students ___have___ real interviews with a representative from a local company.

10 Ms. Hernandez's class ___~~video tape~~ starts___ at 6:30 p.m. and ends at 9:00 p.m.

Exercise 2.2 Simple Present or Present Progressive?

Complete the questions about Josh and Rachel with the simple present or present progressive form of the words in parentheses. Then write answers using the information in the picture.

1 Where ___are Josh and Rachel working___ (Josh and Rachel / work) this summer?

___Josh and Rachel are working at the Bursar's Office this summer.___

2 How often ___~~does~~ do Josh and Rachel work___ (Josh and Rachel / work)?
___Josh and Rachel ~~by~~ work ~~for~~ tree ~~times~~ days per week.___

3 When ___~~does~~ does Josh ~~is~~ start~~ing~~ his job___ (Josh / start his job) in the mornings?
___Josh ~~by~~ start~~ing~~s his job at 9:00 AM.___

4 ___Is Rachel talking to a student right now?___ (Rachel / talk) to a student right now?
___Yes, Rachel is.___

5 How many ___students ~~is~~ are waiting___ (students / wait) in Josh's line?
___there they are . . .___

6 _who is making ing_ (who / make) a better first impression on the students who need help?

Rachel's making ing a better First impression.

7 When _Does Rachel Finishing_ (Rachel / finish) work in the afternoons?

Rachel Finishing es her work at 5.00PM.

8 Who _is not helping_ (who / not help) students at the moment?

Josh is not helping students at the moment.

Exercise 2.3 More Simple Present or Present Progressive?

A Complete the sentences from a brochure that participants received at a job fair. Use the simple present or present progressive form of the verbs in parentheses.

Feira de
Jemp[r]egos

Welcome to the State Employment Agency

JOB FAIR!

Representatives from over 30 big regional corporations _are participating_ (participate) in
(1)
today's state job fair. The job fair _takes_ (take) place every year. Every year, interviews
(2)
begin (begin) at 9:00 a.m. and _continue_ and (continue)
(3)   (4)
throughout the day until 6:00 p.m. The long list of participating companies is on the back of this
brochure. This year, companies A–G _are interviewing_ (interview) candidates in room 245 on the
(5)
second floor. Companies H–Z _are meeting_ (meet) candidates in room 252.
(6)

Tips for Job Seekers

Interviews generally _take_ (take) about 30 minutes. An interviewer
(7)
usually _spends_ (spend) a few minutes reading your résumé. He or
(8)
she sometimes _asks_ (ask) you to fill out an application. An interview
(9)
typically _ends_ (end) with a question-and-answer period. The average
(10)
employer _expects_ (expect) you to know a lot about the company – this is an
(11)
opportunity to demonstrate your knowledge. Also, employers _are_ always
(12)
looking (look) for new ideas, and these ideas may come from you!
(13)

B Pair Work Compare your answers with a partner. Discuss the reason for each of your answers.

A *I used the present progressive in number 1 because the phrase* today's job fair *tells me that the sentence is about something that is happening now.*

B *I agree with you. For number 2, I used . . .*

3 Stative Verbs

belong
beyond

Grammar Presentation

Stative verbs describe states and conditions. Generally, they do not describe actions.	That *sounds* like a great project. We *don't have* two chances to make a first impression.

3.1 Non-action or Stative Verbs

Use the simple present with stative verbs. Here are some common stative verb categories:

Description: *appear, be, exist, look, seem, sound*

Measurement: *cost, weigh*

Knowledge: *believe, forget, know, remember, think*

Emotions: *feel, hate, like, love, prefer*

Possession/Relationship: *belong, contain, have, need, own, want*

Senses: *hear, see, smell, taste*

Perception: *notice, see, understand*

She *seems* like a hard worker.

It *doesn't cost* anything to send your application.

He *doesn't believe* that first impressions are true. I *know* stereotypes aren't true.

Employers *prefer* motivated workers.

I *don't have* a good impression of him. I *need* a challenging career.

Can you *see* the water from your office?

When you explain the problem in that way, I *see* your point. I *understand* your viewpoint.

▶▶◀ Stative (Non-Action) Verbs: See page A2.

3.2 Verbs with Stative and Action Meanings

Some verbs have both stative and action meanings. You can use the present progressive with the action meanings of these verbs. Examples of verbs with stative and action meanings include *be*, *have*, *see*, *taste*, *think*, and *weigh*.

SIMPLE PRESENT (STATIVE MEANING)	PRESENT PROGRESSIVE (ACTION MEANING)
I *think* first impressions are important. (*think* = believe)	I *am thinking* about how to make a good first impression. (*think* = use the mind)
Do you *have* an interesting career? (*have* = own)	*Are* you *having* trouble at work? (*have* = experience)
She *is* the new manager. (*be* = description)	She *is being* difficult. (*be* = act)
He noticed that he doesn't *see* very well anymore. (*see* = view with the eyes)	He *is seeing* the eye doctor for an exam next week. (*see* = meet with)

Grammar Application

A Complete the article from a college newspaper. Circle the correct form of the verbs.

A STUDY ON STEREOTYPES

Lisa James is majoring in psychology here at Carlson College. (This semester,) she **thinks** / **is thinking** about participating in a study
(1)
on stereotypes in Professor Green's Psychology 101 class. According to Dr. Green, many people **have** / **are having** fixed ideas about members of
(2)
their own and other cultures. This is true even when they **know** / **are knowing** that the stereotypes they
(3)
have / **are having** are false.
(4)

Dr. Green **believes** / **is believing** that when
(5)
most people make generalizations about other cultures, they **don't seem** / **are not seeming** to
(6)
make these judgments on observation. Instead, they **appear** / **are appearing** to base their judgments on
(7)
ideas that they grew up with in their own cultures.

This semester, Dr. Green **has** / **is having** an
(8)
interesting time giving his students two tests: a self-assessment test and a personality test. In the self-assessment test, students describe the traits they

think / **are thinking** members of their own culture
(9)
have. The personality test gives basic information about what a person is really like. Dr. Green **believes** / **is believing** the results of the personality
(10)
test will conflict with the results of the cultural self-assessment test. Here's an example: People from one culture in the study **believe** / **are believing** that
(11)
they are hostile and argumentative. However, when these people take the personality test, they usually **get** / **are getting** very high scores for kindness
(12)
and helpfulness.

The results of studies such as Dr. Green's **appear** / **are appearing** to show that cultural
(13)
stereotypes are almost always mistaken. Lisa is looking forward to discovering what the tests say about her. Although she believes that she does not have stereotypes about people, she knows that Dr. Green **believes** / **is believing** that almost
(14)
everyone has stereotypes of some people.

B Pair Work Compare your answers with a partner. Discuss the reason for each of your answers.

I used the present progressive with the verb think *in number 1 because the action is happening now.*

Complete the conversation about stereotypes at work. Use the simple present or present progressive form of the verbs in parentheses. Use contractions when possible.

Alan Claudia, how are your interview follow-up reports going? Are you still working on them?

Claudia I ___think___ (think) they're going well. I'm almost finished.
(1)

Alan That's wonderful news. How many reports ___do___ you
(2)
___have___ (have)?
(2)

Claudia Eight. I have three more to do.

Alan Oh, I see. So you're just a little more than half finished. Our meeting ___is___ (be) always at 4:30 on Wednesdays. Why are you still
(3)
working on them?

Claudia I don't usually take this long, but this time I'm spending a lot of time on the reports because I ___'m being___ (be) very careful. I interviewed a lot of
(4)
people from many different cultures, both young and old, and from cities as well as from the countryside.

Alan So?

Claudia Some of the reports ___are___ (be) finished, but I don't want to base
(5)
my judgments on only partial information. I ___don't think___ (not think) that
(6)
the information would be useful if it's not complete.

Alan I ___know___ (know) what you mean.
(7)

Claudia This time, I ___am having___ (have) a hard time separating things like culture
(8)
and appearance from people's actual abilities.

Alan Well, it's good that you ___are___ . (be) aware of it. Let's discuss
(9)
it later.

Exercise 3.3 More Stative or Action Meaning?

A Listen to the interview about first impressions. Write the missing words.

Reporter When you ___meet___ (1) someone for the first time, how does the person's appearance affect your judgment? Today, we __are asking__ (2) people to describe how they make judgments about others.

Marta I know I __use__ (3) *injusta* unfair stereotypes when I meet someone new. To me, older people always __seem__ (4) like they need help. When I meet an older person, I __'m always thing__ (5) about my grandparents. I speak slowly and clearly, in case the person can't hear. I __know__ (6) it's wrong to think all older people are like that, but I can't help it.

Marc I feel that I __am__ (7) always very fair when I meet a new person. I __knew__ (8) people's appearances don't always say who they really are. For example, if I meet a person who __looks__ (9) sloppy,[1] *des leixada.* I __don't thing__ (10) that he or she is a lazy person.

Pessoa Preguiçosa

Bin For me, it depends on the situation. When I am interviewing people at work, I take their appearance very seriously. For example, I always notice how a person dresses for an interview. If a person's appearance __seems__ (11) sloppy or careless in an interview, I __think__ (12) he or she will be a sloppy and careless worker.

[1]**sloppy:** messy, not tidy

B Pair Work Discuss these questions with a partner: Which person in A are you most like? How much do stereotypes affect the judgments you make about people when you first meet them? Give an example.

I think I'm like Marc. I don't like to judge someone right away. For example, my landlord seems somewhat reserved when you meet him, but he's actually a really nice guy.

4 Special Meanings and Uses of Simple Present

Grammar Presentation

The simple present is frequently used for summarizing and reviewing as well as for explaining procedures or giving instructions.	Malcolm Gladwell's book Blink **persuades** the reader to believe in first impressions. Participants **follow** strict procedures for the Implicit Association Test.

4.1 Special Meanings and Uses of Simple Present

A Use the simple present to summarize scientific writing or review artistic works such as books, plays, and movies.	*The Implicit Association Test **measures** people's responses.* *Malcolm Gladwell's book Blink **discusses** the importance of first impressions. He **argues** that first impressions **are** often accurate, even if the mind **doesn't realize** it.*
B Use the simple present to explain procedures or instructions.	*To administer the test, we always **follow** the same procedures. First, we **seat** participants in every other chair. We **don't** usually **put** them next to each other.*
Commonly used expressions that show sequencing include *first, then, next, after that,* and *finally.*	*When you arrive at the job fair, first you **go** to the desk and sign in. Then you **take** a look at the list of companies and plan which companies you **want** to see.*

Grammar Application

Read the sentences. Then label each sentence R (book reviews), P (procedures and instructions), or O (other uses – facts, routines, schedules) according to where the text comes from.

1 First, students write their names at the top of the paper.   P

2 The authors end with a set of tips for always creating good first impressions.   R

3 The class meets on Tuesdays and Thursdays from 11:30 a.m. to 1:00 p.m.   O

4 This book helps readers understand the difference between how they see
  themselves and how other people see them.   R

5 The required reading for this course is *Making a Good Impression* by Dr. Al Stone.   O

6 *Making a Good Impression* includes summaries of many of the latest studies on
  how people make first impressions.   R

7 To complete the online test, students select their answers and click "Submit."   R

Use the words to write sentences that describe the main points from an article on the problems with personality tests.

1 personality tests / always / not be / accurate

   Personality tests are not always accurate.

2 job candidates / sometimes / not tell / the truth   Job candidates sometimes do not tell
   Sometimes job candidates don tell the truth

3 a job candidate's score / always / not reflect / the candidate's personality
                                               does not
   Always a job candidate's don't reflect the candidate's.

4 candidates who take some personality tests twice / sometimes / get / different scores
   Candidates who take some personality tests twice
   sentences get different score.

5 these tests / not match / people to jobs well
   these teste are match People to Jobs well
   does not always reflect

Pair Work **Choose a situation with a partner in which it is important to make a good first impression, such as a job interview or a first meeting with an important person. Describe the scene and how the person makes a good first impression. Remember to use sequencing words such as** *First, . . . ; Then . . . ; After that, . . . ;* **and** *Finally, . . .*

On the first day of work: First, the new employee shakes hands and makes eye contact with the people he or she meets.

5 Avoid Common Mistakes ⚠

1 Use the simple present with stative verbs.

        matter
First impressions ~~*are mattering*~~ *when you want to establish a relationship.*

2 Use the simple present to express facts, routines, or habits unlikely to change.

      require
Sessions ~~*are requiring*~~ *10 to 15 minutes to complete.*

3 Use the present progressive to show that something is in progress or temporary.

   isn't interviewing   *is still studying*
He ~~*doesn't interview*~~ *for jobs this year because he* ~~*still studies*~~.

4 Use the *-ing* form, not the base form of the verb, when using the present progressive.

   working
He is ~~*work*~~ *as a store clerk.*

Editing Task

Find and correct eight more mistakes in the paragraphs about first impressions.

Without a doubt, first impressions are important. Current research ~~is showing~~ *shows* that a first impression can last a long time. These days it seems that everyone talks about the significance of the first 30 seconds of a job interview or a meeting with a client. However, I ~~am believing~~ there is another side to this story.

5   Some people ~~are having~~ the ability to make a good first impression, but the impression may be false. I believe that time and experience ~~are~~ telling the truth about a person's character. Whenever I talk with someone who smiles at me and seems completely charming, I ~~am getting~~ suspicious. I think that the person is not sincere, and that he or she wants something from me. On the other hand, I often find that

10   quieter, more reserved people are more willing to help me when I ask. My colleague Jim is a good example. This fall he is work on a special project, so he is very busy, and sometimes he appears unfriendly. However, he usually stops and helps me when I ask. My friendlier colleagues usually smile, but when I ask them for help, they are making excuses.

15   In short, I ~~am not believing~~ *do not believe* that everyone who makes a good first impression deserves my trust. Maybe I am too suspicious with friendly people, but I will always give awkward or shy people a second chance. After all, I think that I may be one of them.

2 Simple Past and Past Progressive; *Used To, Would*

Global Marketing

1 Grammar in the Real World

A What is a *global market*? Read the article about global marketing. What makes global marketing campaigns successful?

B Comprehension Check **Answer the questions.**

1 What are some reasons customers in China did not buy the dolls at first?
2 Why was the campaign in Malaysia successful?
3 How are advertising campaigns different today from in the past?

C Notice **Read the sentences from the article. Check (✓) the sentence that describes an action that continued for a period of time in the past. Does the verb end in *-ing* or *-ed*?**

_____ 1 Around the same time, another American company **was showing** a series of advertisements in the United States for a shampoo product.

_____ 2 As a result, the company **adapted** its advertising to fit the local culture.

GLOBAL Marketing

In 2017, an American toy company **opened** a huge store on the main shopping street in a major city in China. The store **featured** the company's famous doll. At that
5 time, the sales of the doll **were falling** slightly in the United States, so the company **was working** on developing new markets in other countries. At the store, there **were not** many sales. Customers **would come** in and look,
10 but few **were buying** the dolls. The company **did** some research and **found out** why. The doll's image **did not appeal**[1] to young Chinese women. They **had** a preference for dolls that looked cute and **adorable**.[2] They
15 also **wanted** more affordable prices. The toy company eventually **closed** the store.

Around the same time, another American company **was showing** a series of advertisements in the United States for a
20 shampoo product. In one ad, "real women" **showed** their hair and **talked** about how much they liked the shampoo. These women **looked** like your friends and neighbors, not like models. The advertisements **were** a great
25 success. The company **decided** to create similar advertisements in Malaysia. While it **was working on** these advertisements, it **was** also **doing** research on Malaysian culture. The company **discovered** that
30 some Malaysian women **thought** that it was inappropriate[3] to show their hair in public, so it **realized** that its approach[4] **would not be** successful. As a result, the company **adapted** its advertising to fit the local culture. In the
35 new Malaysian advertisements, the women **did not show** their hair. They only **talked** about it. The ads **were** a tremendous success.

In the past, companies **would create** one advertisement and one product for all
40 markets. Today's markets include places all over the world, and the success of global marketing campaigns depends on two simple rules: understand the local culture and adapt the marketing and product to that culture.

---

[1]**appeal:** interest or attract someone

[2]**adorable:** attractive and easy to love

[3]**inappropriate:** unsuitable, especially for the particular time, place, or situation

[4]**approach:** a method or way of doing something

2 Simple Past vs. Past Progressive

Grammar Presentation

The simple past and the past progressive describe actions in the past.	American consumers **wanted** affordable prices. While the company **was working** on these advertisements, it **was** also **doing** research on Malaysian culture.

2.1 Simple Past

Use the simple past to describe actions, situations, or events that are completed. Use the simple past for actions that happened once or repeatedly in the past.	Company executives **decided** to market the dolls in China in 2017. The dolls **weren't** popular in China a few years ago. What **did** the company **market** in Malaysia? The company executives **visited** Malaysia a few times.
Past time markers, such as *yesterday, last week, two months ago,* and *in 2018* can be used with the simple past.	A company **studied** Malaysian culture <u>last year</u>. **Did** it **get** good local advice <u>last time</u>? Who **gave** the company advice <u>last week</u>?

▶▶ Irregular Verbs: See page A1.

2.2 Past Progressive

Use the past progressive to describe an activity or event in progress over a period of time in the past.	The company **wasn't selling** dolls in China at that time. Why **weren't** many people **buying** them? What **was happening** during that period?

2.3 Simple Past and Past Progressive Contrasted

A Use the past progressive to describe background activities. These activities were in progress at the same time as the main event in the sentence. Use the simple past for the main event.	BACKGROUND ACTIVITY They **were planning** a new advertising campaign MAIN EVENT in the country, so they **did** some research on the culture.
B Use the simple past, not the past progressive, with stative verbs.	The company **understood** the culture. NOT The company ~~was understanding~~ the culture.

Grammar Application

Exercise 2.1 Simple Past and Past Progressive

A Underline the past forms of the verbs in this paragraph about early American advertising.

Benjamin Franklin is one of the fathers of American advertising. He <u>was</u> an early American politician and inventor. In the early 1700s, Franklin was working in Philadelphia, Pennsylvania, as a publisher and inventor. He published a variety of books, and he was also the publisher of the newspaper *The Pennsylvania Gazette*. He used *The Pennsylvania Gazette* to advertise his inventions. Franklin filled the newspaper with ads. He also advertised books, both his own and other people's. Because of the ads in his newspaper, Franklin was making a lot of money and was selling a lot of books. These were among the first advertisements in America.

B Pair Work Compare your answers with a partner. Discuss which verbs are simple past and which are past progressive.

Exercise 2.2 Simple Past or Past Progressive?

A Read the paragraphs about a successful advertising campaign.[1] Circle the simple past or past progressive form of the verbs. Sometimes more than one answer is possible.

In the years after World War II, the U.S. government **promoted/(was promoting)** milk as a health product. In the 1960s, however, soft-drink[2] companies began to market their products very aggressively. As a result, people **soon drank/(were soon drinking)** more soft drinks and less milk. The California Milk Advisory Board (CMAB) realized that the old health-focused advertising **didn't work/(wasn't working)**.

Beginning in the mid-1970s, milk sales **went/(were going)** down in the United States, and the CMAB **(decided)/was deciding** to do something to increase sales. The CMAB members **(learned)/were learning** that the majority of people believed that milk was good for them, but they weren't drinking it.

In 1993, a new board was formed, the California Milk Processor Board (MilkPEP). This new board **(hired)/were hiring** an advertising agency to design a

new advertisement for milk. The agency **designed / were designing** a very original
ad. The ad showed a person eating something sweet or sticky (like cake or peanut
butter). The ad was funny because the person really needed milk to drink, but he or
she didn't have it. This **became / was becoming** the very successful "Got milk?"[3]
campaign. In 1994, milk sales **increased / were increasing** by over 10 million gallons a
year. This was a clear indication that the new campaign was a success.

[1]**campaign:** series of advertisements
[2]**soft drink:** a carbonated, nonalcoholic drink, also known as "pop," "soda," or "cola"
[3]**Got milk?:** an informal way of saying "Do you have milk?"

B Pair Work **Compare your answers with a partner. Then ask and answer questions about
the information in A. Use the simple past and the past progressive.**

A *What was happening in the United States beginning in the mid-1970s?*

B *Milk sales were going down.*

3 Time Clauses with Simple Past and Past Progressive

Grammar Presentation

The simple past and past progressive are used with time clauses to show the order of two past events.	*We changed our minds about the product after we saw the ads for it.* *While he was presenting the product, the audience listened attentively.*

3.1 Using Time Clauses with Simple Past

A Use time clauses beginning with the time words and phrases *after, as soon as, before, once, until,* and *when* to show the order in which two events happened. When the time clause comes first in the sentence, use a comma.	*We found out that the ad wasn't appropriate for consumers ~~when~~ while we were doing research on the market.* ~~while~~ *While we were doing research on the market, we found out that the ad wasn't appropriate for consumers.*
B Use *after* to introduce the first event.	FIRST EVENT SECOND EVENT *After the store opened, people didn't buy the dolls.*

3.1 Using Time Clauses with Simple Past *(continued)*

C Use *before* to introduce the *second* event.	FIRST EVENT *The company worked with an advertising team* SECOND EVENT *before it marketed the shampoo.*
D Use *as soon as* or *once* to introduce the first event when the second event happens immediately after.	FIRST EVENT *As soon as the company made prices* SECOND EVENT *affordable, sales improved.* SECOND EVENT *Women bought the shampoo* FIRST EVENT *once the ad fit the local culture.*
E *Until* means "up to that time." Use *until* to indicate the second event.	FIRST EVENT SECOND EVENT *There were not many sales until the company changed its advertising.*
F Use *when* to introduce the first event. *When* means "at almost the same time."	FIRST EVENT SECOND EVENT *When we thought about the low sales, we got a little worried.*

3.2 Using Time Clauses with Simple Past and Past Progressive

A Use the past progressive to describe an ongoing action. Use *while* or *when* to introduce the ongoing action.	ONGOING EVENT *While we were developing an advertising campaign,* INTERRUPTION *I got sick.*
Use the simple past to describe an action that interrupts the ongoing action. Use *when* to introduce the interruption.	ONGOING EVENT *We were discussing the new ad campaign* INTERRUPTION *when we heard about the low sales.*
B Use the past progressive in both clauses to talk about two actions in progress at the same time.	*While they were studying Malaysian culture, they were developing an advertising campaign.*

📊 Data from the Real World

In formal writing, *when* is more common than *while*.

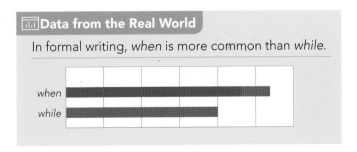

⬛ Grammar Application

Read the sentences about marketing milk. Circle the time words. Underline the time clauses. Label the earlier event with *1* and the later event with *2*.

1. After World War II ended, the milk companies in the United States wanted people to drink milk. They marketed milk as a health drink.

2. People drank more milk than soft drinks before soft-drink companies started marketing their drinks as "fun."

3. When soft-drink companies began marketing their drinks as "fun," the California Milk Advisory Board (CMAB) realized it needed to market milk differently.

4. The CMAB learned that people thought milk was boring after the board completed its market research.

5. When the CMAB discovered that 70 percent of Californians already drank milk, it decided to create a campaign to persuade them to drink more milk.

6. Before it started a new ad campaign, the new California Milk Processor Board, MilkPEP, learned that most people drink milk at home with foods like cookies and cake.

7. When the new milk ads appeared, they immediately became famous.

8. MilkPEP created a successful Spanish-language milk ad once it had success with the "Got milk?" campaign.

Read the facts about the history of advertising. Combine the sentences with the time words in parentheses. Sometimes more than one answer is possible.

1. First event: Advertising already existed in Europe.
   Second event: Europeans came to the Americas in the 1400s.

   (before) *Before Europeans came to the Americas in the 1400s, advertising already existed in Europe./Advertising already existed in Europe before Europeans came to the Americas in the 1400s.*

2. First event: Europeans were exploring the world from the fifteenth to the seventeenth centuries.
   Second event: They found new and interesting kinds of food and spices.

   (while) While Europeans ... , they

3. First event: European explorers came home.
   Second event: They introduced the items to the people from their countries.

   (as soon as) as soon as the Europeans came home they introduced the items to the people from their countries.

4 First event: Europeans didn't know anything about coffee.
Second event: They read the ads that explained what it was.

(before) Europeans didn't know anything about coffee before they read the ads that explained what it was.

5 First event: Early advertisements had no words because most people couldn't read.
Second event: Literacy became widespread in the eighteenth century.

(until) Early ... until literacy ... .

6 First event: Newspapers were the most common form of advertising.
Second event: Radio was invented in the 1920s.

(before) Newspapers ... before Radio was invented in the 1920s.

Exercise 3.3 Using Time Clauses with *When* and *While*

Complete the sentences from a report on a global marketing lecture. Use the simple past and past progressive forms of the verbs in parentheses.

1 The head of marketing of a restaurant chain __was speaking__ (speak) when
I __arrived__ (arrive).

2 When his company __was considering__ (consider) opening new restaurants, they
__realized__ (realize) that they needed some vegetarian food items.

3 The market researchers __were doing__ (do) research on the vegetarian consumer
when the managers __decided__ (decide) they needed a new, healthy menu.

4 The managers __learned__ (learn) that they had to eliminate many ingredients
with eggs and dairy products when the market researchers __were interviewing__
(interview) vegan[1] customers.

5 While they __were listening__ (listen) to customers explain how busy they were, the
market researchers __got__ (get) the idea that the company should offer
delivery service.

6 The head of marketing __was thinking__ (think) about opening up restaurants in
Chicago when he __learned__ (learn) that more people ordered take-out food
in New York City than in Chicago.

7 While the managers __were contemplating__ (contemplate) the idea of
opening up a place in New York City, a restaurant in a busy location
__became__ (become) available, and the company bought the
place immediately.

[1]**vegan:** a vegetarian who eats no animal or dairy products

A Over to You Think about important decisions you have made in your life. Write an answer to one of these questions. Use *when* and *while*.

■ What were you doing when you decided to study here?

■ What were you doing when you made an important decision about your life?

I was working in two different jobs when I decided to take classes here.

B Pair Work Discuss your sentences with a partner.

4 Used To and Would

Grammar Presentation

Used to and *would* describe past routines or repeated actions. *Used to* expresses states or habits that existed in the past, but do not exist now. *Would* can only express repeated actions.	*Our company used to sell shampoo around the world. We would study the local customs. Then we would create local marketing campaigns.*

4.1 Used To

A *Used to* is followed by the base form of the verb. It can be used for actions or states.	*Some companies used to ignore local customs.* (But they don't do that now.) *This building used to be a TV studio.* *I used to know the manager's name, but I've forgotten it.*
Use *use to* not *used to* in questions with *did*.	*Where did you use to go to school when you were young?*
The negative is *didn't use to* + the base form.	*Our company didn't use to ask for advice from the local markets.* (But our company does now.)
B Use the simple past, not *used to*, to talk about completed actions in the past.	*The company made its sales goals last year.* NOT *The company ~~used to make~~ its sales goals last year.* *The company made its sales goals for a decade.* NOT *The company ~~used to make~~ its sales goals for a decade.* *The company made its sales goals three times.* NOT *The company ~~used to make~~ its sales goals three times.*

4.2 *Would*

A *Would* is followed by the base form of the verb.	In the past, companies **would create** one advertisement for all markets.
A time expression, such as *in the past*, shows the context for the action.	*In the past*, we **would meet** for an hour every Friday to talk about marketing techniques. (But we don't do that now.)
B *Would* is only used for actions, not states.	Twenty years ago, many smaller companies **wouldn't do** a lot of marketing in other countries.
	Usually, the president of our company **would not attend** our weekly meetings.
	In the past, companies **were not** sensitive to local customs.
	NOT In the past, companies ~~wouldn't be~~ sensitive to local customs.
C Use the simple past, not *would*, to talk about completed actions in the past.	The sales team **attended** a conference last week.
	NOT The sales team ~~would attend~~ a conference last week.

Grammar Application

Exercise 4.1 *Would*

Complete part of a lecture on the history of radio and TV advertising. Use *would* and the correct verbs in the boxes.

appear	not use	~~produce~~	read

    TV commercials developed from radio commercials. In the early days of radio, radio stations sold advertising time to support themselves. Many companies **would produce** entire radio programs in order to advertise their products.
(1)
Famous Hollywood stars of the day *would appear* on these
(2)
programs. In the early days of radio, radio stations *wouldn't use*
(3)
ads that were on tape.[1] Instead, people performed the ads live. That is, an announcer
would read an advertisement on the air.[2] Today, some radio ads
(4)
are still live, but many ads are also prerecorded.

[1] **on tape:** prerecorded
[2] **on the air:** while broadcasting

advertise	buy	create	match

When television appeared, advertisers _would buy_ (5) time during a TV program for their commercials. They _would create_ (6) short, 10-second advertisements to show during these programs. They _would match_ (7) a program with viewers who were likely to buy their product. For example, they _would advertise_ (8) laundry soap to housewives who stayed home and watched serial dramas ("soap operas") during the day.

Exercise 4.2 *Used To, Would,* or *Simple Past?*

A Listen to an interview about how TV advertising has changed. Write the correct form of the verbs that you hear.

⌂   💬 ↻ ☰ ✉

Zach How has TV advertising changed over the years?

Dave In the past, we _used to create_ (1) commercials with very direct messages. Commercials _used to tell_ (2) the consumer exactly what to do. We never _used to be_ (3) vague[1] about the message at all. In addition, commercials _didn't use to try_ (4) to entertain the viewer.

Zach So, how _would_ (5) you _create_ (5) an advertising message in the old days?

Dave A commercial for our product _would say_ (6) : "Drink Fruity Juice." We _would show_ (7) the product several times in a commercial. We _didn't use to hide_ (8) the product.

Zach What changed?

Dave We _saw_ (9) some research a few years ago. It _showed_ (10) that people no longer pay attention to commercials like those. As a result, we _decided_ (11) to change our style. Now we are producing "mystery ads." Mystery ads don't show the product until the very end of the commercial. They entertain the viewer because the viewer has to figure out what the product is.

[1]**vague:** unclear

B Listen again and check your answers.

5 Avoid Common Mistakes ⚠

1 Use the base form of the verb after *would* and *used to*.

live
He used to ~~living~~ in Bangladesh, where he studied economics.

2 Use *was* or *were* with the verb + *-ing* to describe actions in progress in the past, including in sentences with two clauses.

was
The new dolls were selling well, and the company making a lot of money.

3 Use the simple past when describing specific events in the past.

had
She knew that she ~~has~~ a problem in one of her markets.

4 Use the past progressive to provide background information for an event.

was studying
I ~~studied~~ business administration in Malaysia when I got my first job.

Editing Task

Find and correct eight more mistakes in the transcript from a meeting.

Hello, everyone! Welcome to the meeting.

As many of you know, this past year *was* disappointing for many

companies. However, we ended up doing quite well here at ABC Tech.

At the beginning of the year, things *were* looking bad. In fact, our sales ~~fell~~ *were falling*

5   when I started here. However, our excellent marketing team did their

research, and they *created* new and extremely successful advertisements

after they *discovered* two shifts in consumer spending.

The first shift they saw was a shift to green marketing. Last year we

noticed that consumers would *pay* more for environmentally friendly

10   products. Therefore, our first advertisement of last year showed how

good our smartphone batteries are for the environment.

The second shift was in who advertised our products. While we ~~wrote~~ *were writing* our most

recent advertisement, research arrived that showed that celebrities sell products

better. In October we began showing famous actors and actresses using our phones,

15   and last month alone, our sales ~~rise~~ *rose* by 25 percent.

In short, while some businesses were struggling, we *were* increasing our profits.

3

Present Perfect and Present Perfect Progressive

Success

1 Grammar in the Real World

A What are the characteristics of a successful person? Read the article about Mahatma Gandhi and Bill Gates. What qualities do they have in common?

B Comprehension Check **Answer the questions.**

1 What principle did Mahatma Gandhi support? *nonviolence*
2 What does the Bill and Melinda Gates Foundation do? *Line 34*
3 What is the secret of successful people? *Line 38 - 39*

C Notice **Find the sentences in the article and complete them. Circle the correct verb forms.**

1 Although he died in 1948, his life and principles _____ people all over the world since then.
   a inspired   b have inspired   **c** have been inspiring

2 His example _____ movements for civil rights and freedom around the world ever since.
   a guided   b has guided   **c** has been guiding

3 Gates _____ the Microsoft Corporation in 1975.
   a founded   b has founded   c has been founding

Which verbs describe actions that are still happening now?

have been inspiring
believed

has been guiding

The MAKING of SUCCESS

Some people **have said** that a successful person is like a sore thumb: The person sticks out[1] wherever he or she goes. People always seem to notice something special about the person. **Have** you ever
5 **wondered** why? What makes someone successful?

For some time, researchers **have been trying** to answer this question. They have **been looking** closely at people who **have achieved** success in their lives, and they **have discovered** some very
10 interesting traits.[2]

Mahatma Gandhi is one person the researchers **have studied**. Gandhi was born in India in 1869. Although he **died** in 1948, his life and principles **have been inspiring**[3] people all over the world since then.

15 Gandhi **believed** in nonviolence, and he used this principle to help India gain independence from the British. His example **has been guiding** movements for civil rights[4] and freedom around the world ever since. In spite of great personal
20 risk, he never **gave up** on his goals to help the poor and the underprivileged, such as ethnic minorities. Additionally, he always **aimed** to live a simple life. At the time of Gandhi's death, the prime minister of India **announced** on the radio: "The light
25 **has gone out**[5] of our lives, and there is darkness everywhere."

Many people consider Bill Gates one of the most successful people in the world, and certainly one of the richest. Gates **founded** the Microsoft Corporation
30 in 1975. In 1994, he **formed** the Bill and Melinda Gates Foundation. Through this foundation, he **has contributed** billions of dollars to organizations and programs working in global health, including public-health organizations, and he continues to work for
35 world health and education.

The secret of the success of Gandhi, Gates, and other successful people is strikingly similar. They **have found** a purpose in life and are not afraid to take action, to take risks, or to work hard. Sometimes
40 they **have failed**, but they **have** always **gone on** to reach their goal.

---

[1]**stick out:** be easily noticed
[2]**trait:** a characteristic, especially of a personality
[3]**inspire:** fill someone with confidence and the desire to do something

[4]**civil rights:** the rights of every person in a society, including equality under law
[5]**light goes out:** an idiom meaning joy and hope disappear

2 Present Perfect

Grammar Presentation

The present perfect is used to describe an event that happened at an <u>unspecified time in the past</u>. This event may be completed, or it may not be completed and <u>may continue into the future</u>.	*Winners of the Gandhi Peace Prize* **have contributed** *to world peace.* *Sociologists* **have studied** *the definition of success for a long time.*

2.1 Using Present Perfect

A Use the present perfect to describe an action or event that happened at an unspecified time in the past.	*Researchers* **have discovered** *similar traits in successful people.*
The adverbs *already, ever, never,* and *(not) yet* can be used with the present perfect. *Ever* means "at any time in the past."	"**Has** *she* **received** *an award* <u>yet</u>?" "*Yes, she* **has** <u>already</u> **received** *two awards.*" "*No, she* **hasn't received** *one* <u>yet</u>." "**Have** *you* <u>ever</u> **thought** *about the meaning of success?*" "*I've* <u>never</u> **thought** *about it.*"
B Use the present perfect for actions or events that <u>started in the past and continue into the present</u>.	*How long* **has** *she* **been** *a successful businessperson?*
For, since, so far, and *still* help link between the past and the present. Other common expressions are *all day, all my life,* and *all year.*	*She's owned a successful business* <u>for</u> *15 years.* *They've worked here* <u>since</u> *May.* <u>So far</u>, *he* **hasn't changed** *jobs.* *I* <u>still</u> **haven't learned** *to relax on weekends.* *They've been in the lab* <u>all day</u>. *He* **has lived** *here* <u>all his life</u>.
C Use the present perfect to describe a recent action.	*Breaking news: The judges* **have awarded** *the Nobel Peace Prize.*
The adverbs *just* and *recently* emphasize the recent past time.	*I* **have** <u>just</u> **discovered** *the answer.* *He* **has** <u>recently</u> **given** *money to the foundation.*

2.2 Present Perfect with *For* and *Since*

A Use *for* to show the duration of time of an event that continues into the present moment.	She *hasn't worked* here <u>for</u> several years.
B In negative sentences, the preposition *in* may replace *for*.	She *hasn't seen* her <u>in</u> several years.
C Use *since* with specific dates or times to show the start of an event that continues into the present moment.	He *has lived* here <u>since</u> last year. She *hasn't worked* here <u>since</u> 2016.

Grammar Application

Exercise 2.1 Uses of Present Perfect

Read about Blake Mycoskie, a businessperson and a humanitarian. Label the bold and underlined verbs *U* (unspecified time in the past), *C* (time that continues to the present), or *R* (recent action) according to the use of the present perfect.

Blake Mycoskie is an American businessperson. He started a shoe company called TOMS in 2006. He sells a special type of shoe, the alpargata. He discovered the shoe in Argentina. Argentinean

5 farmers **have worn** alpargatas for over 100 years.

Recently, experts **have discovered** a link between children going barefoot and getting certain diseases. Mycoskie **has** always **wanted** to help children stay healthy. Therefore, every time someone buys a pair of TOMS shoes, his company gives a free pair of

10 new shoes to a child who needs shoes. Since he started TOMS, Mycoskie **has given** over a 60 million pairs of alpargatas to children in South Africa, Ethiopia, Rwanda, Argentina, Guatemala, Haiti, and the United States.

More recently, Mycoskie **started** a coffee company. It **has donated** a week of water to people in coffee-producing countries for every bag of coffee that they've

15 sold. Mycoskie's favorite quote comes from Gandhi: "Be the change you wish to see in the world."

A Complete the interview about success. Use the present perfect form of the verbs in parentheses. Use contractions when possible.

Reporter	Today, we are asking a few people about success. Are you successful? Do you know anyone who is successful? What makes someone successful?
Carlos	My friend Marta is successful. She **'s wanted** (want) to own a restaurant for years, and now she has achieved (achieve) her goal. Three years ago, she bought a restaurant. She 's/ has had (have) a successful business ever since.
Reporter	How long have you known (know) Marta?
Carlos	I 've known (know) her for 10 years.
Reporter	Has she always been (be) interested in food?
Carlos	So far, that has been (be) her only interest!
Annie	Well, I think my parents are very successful people. They haven't / have not had (not/have) any problems in years. They 've raised (raise) five happy, successful children. In fact, my youngest brother has just graduated (graduate) from college, and my older sister has recently gotten (get) married.
Ian	You know, I 've never thought (think) about it. I guess I haven't achieved (not/achieve) anything yet. I'm very happy, though! That's my idea of success!

B Group Work Read the definitions of success. Choose one definition and give examples of it using your experiences or those of someone you know. Use the present perfect and *already, never, yet, for, since, so far, still, just,* and *recently*.

Definitions

Success is having a goal and then achieving it.
Success is doing work that you love.
Success is having a lot of money.
Success is having good relationships with family and friends.

I think that success is having a goal and achieving it. My brother has always wanted to climb Mount Everest. He hasn't done it yet, but he has climbed several other mountains.

Exercise 2.3 *For* or *Since?*

Complete the sentences about successful people. Circle *for* or *since*.

1 Blake Mycoskie has started several businesses (since)/ for he graduated from college.

2 Bill Gates has worked part-time for Microsoft and part-time for the Bill and Melinda Gates Foundation **since /(for)** the past several years.

3 Bill Gates has given over $32 billion to charity (since)/ for 2007.

4 Oprah Winfrey has helped poor people **since /(for)** many years.

5 **Since /(For)** several years, actors and pop stars have spent a great deal of their time and money on charity events.

Exercise 2.4 More *For* or *Since?*

Use the words to write sentences about successful people. Use the present perfect and *for* or *since*.

1 Joe and Ling have a successful marriage. They / be married / more than 30 years
   They have been married for more than 30 years.

2 They / have / only / one fight / they first met
   They've only had one fight since they first met.

3 They / not spend / a night apart / 1988
   They have not spent a night apart since 1988.

4 Mark and Amy have a successful friendship. They / be friends / high school
   They have been friends since high school

5 They / speak / on the phone every day / the past 10 years
   They've spoken on the phone every day for the past 10 years.

6 Verónica / be / a successful single parent / many years
   Verónica has been a successful single parent for many years

7 She / raise / her three children by herself / her divorce
   She has raised her three children by herself since her divorce.

3 Present Perfect vs. Simple Past

Grammar Presentation

The present perfect <u>can refer to</u> events that <u>began in the past</u>, continue until now, and may continue in the future. The simple past expresses completed events.

"*Have you read* any books about successful people?"

"Yes. I *read* one about Ricky Sánchez last week."

3.1 Present Perfect and Simple Past Contrasted

A Use the present perfect to refer to events or repeated actions that continue into the present moment.	*Gandhi has inspired people all over the world.* (Gandhi inspired people for many years, and his ideas still inspire people now.)
Use the simple past to refer to completed actions.	*Gandhi promoted nonviolence against British rule.* (Gandhi did this while he was alive.)
B Use the present perfect to refer to an action completed at an unspecified time in the past that has an effect in the present.	*The Gates Foundation has supported health care in poor countries.* (Poor countries are benefiting from this care now.)
Use the simple past to refer to a completed action in the past that doesn't have an effect in the present.	*Bill Gates founded the Microsoft Corporation in 1975.* (This is a fact about Bill Gates's past.)

📊 Data from the Real World

In informal speaking, people sometimes use the simple past with *already* and *yet* instead of the present perfect.	*We haven't finished <u>yet</u>.* *We didn't finish <u>yet</u>.* (informal speaking)
In academic writing, always use the present perfect with *already* and *yet*.	*The foundation has <u>already</u> given millions of dollars to charities this year.*

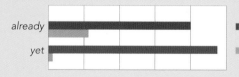

- ■ with present perfect
- ■ with simple past

Grammar Application

Exercise 3.1 Present Perfect or Simple Past?

A Complete the online interview about the actress Marlee Matlin. Circle the correct form of the verbs.

Marlee Matlin is a successful actress, writer, and producer. She is also hearing impaired. She cannot hear, but she is able to communicate in spoken English. She won an Oscar for Best Actress and has received other acting awards as well.

Kate I really admire Marlee Matlin. She didn't let her disability stop her from achieving her dreams.

Alex I don't know that much about her.

Kate Well, she began acting at a very young age. She **(played)** / **'s played**
(1)
Dorothy in The Wizard of Oz when she was seven years old.
→ ness Rapel

Alex Wow. **Did she use** / **Has she used** sign language in that role?
(2)

Kate Yes, she **did** / **has**. That play was produced by a hearing-impaired children's
(3)
organization. In 1986, she **(played)** / **'s played** a hearing-impaired woman in
(4)
Children of a Lesser God, and she won an Oscar.

Alex Has she ever played a hearing person?

Kate So far, she **performed** / **'s performed** mostly hearing-impaired roles,
(5)
but in 1994, she **played** / **'ve played** a hearing woman in the television movie
(6)
Against Her Will.

Alex What else **did she do** / **has she done** besides acting?
(7)

Kate In 1999, she **(produced)** / **'s produced** a television movie. In addition, she
(8)
was / **'s been** very busy raising four children! Her oldest child **was** / **has been**
(9)   (10)
born in 1996. She **had** / **has had** her last child in 2003.
(11)

B Pair Work Compare your answers with a partner. Discuss the reason for each of your answers.

I chose the past for number 1 because the action happened at a specific time in the past – when she was seven years old.

Exercise 3.2 More Present Perfect or Simple Past?

A Read the time line about Diane, a successful clothing designer. Complete the sentences with the present perfect or simple past.

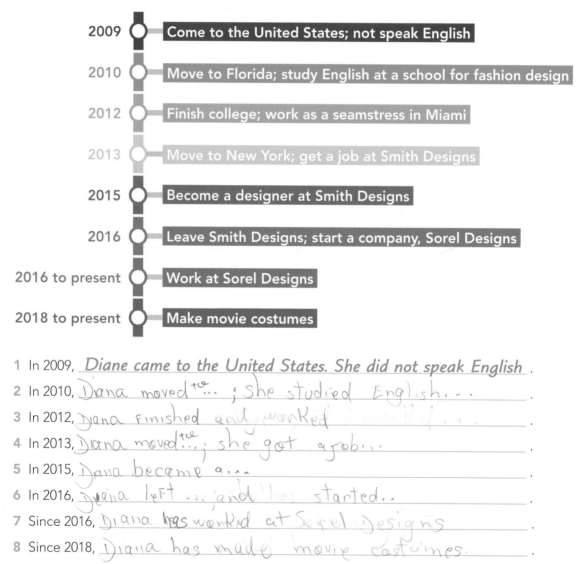

2009	Come to the United States; not speak English
2010	Move to Florida; study English at a school for fashion design
2012	Finish college; work as a seamstress in Miami
2013	Move to New York; get a job at Smith Designs
2015	Become a designer at Smith Designs
2016	Leave Smith Designs; start a company, Sorel Designs
2016 to present	Work at Sorel Designs
2018 to present	Make movie costumes

1 In 2009, *Diane came to the United States. She did not speak English* .
2 In 2010, Dana moved to... ; She studied English... .
3 In 2012, Dana finished and worked ... .
4 In 2013, Dana moved to... ; she got a job... .
5 In 2015, Dana became a... .
6 In 2016, Dana left ... and has started... .
7 Since 2016, Diana has worked at Sorel Designs .
8 Since 2018, Diana has made movie costumes.

B Over to You Think about a successful person you know: a friend, a relative, or a famous person. On a separate piece of paper, write five facts about that person's life and accomplishments. Use the simple past and present perfect. Then share your sentences with a partner.

4 Present Perfect vs. Present Perfect Progressive

[handwritten: CODA adults / F eaf / children / ongoing em progresso.]

Grammar Presentation

The present perfect and present perfect progressive can sometimes have similar meanings. However, the present perfect progressive focuses on the ongoing nature of the activity. The present perfect often suggests that the action is finished.	*I've worn / I've been wearing glasses all my life.* *I've been writing an article about the meaning of success. (I haven't finished it yet.)* *I've written an article about the meaning of success. (I've already finished it.)*

4.1 Similar Meaning: Habitual and Ongoing Actions

A Use either the present perfect or present perfect progressive for habitual actions that began in the past and continue up to the present. Some verbs that show habitual action are *live*, *study*, *teach*, *wear*, and *work*.	*Bill Gates has worked hard all his life.* *Bill Gates has been working hard all his life.*
B Use *how long* to ask about the duration of habitual actions.	*"How long have you lived / have you been living here?"* *"I've lived / I've been living here for four years."*

4.2 Different Meanings: Completed vs. Ongoing Actions

A Use the present perfect for an event that was completed at an unspecified time in the past.	*She has read a biography of Gandhi. (She finished it. She is no longer reading it.)*
Use the present perfect progressive for an event that began in the past and is still ongoing. It emphasizes the duration of the activity.	*She has been reading a biography of Gandhi. (She is still reading it.)*
Stative verbs are usually in the present perfect (not the present perfect progressive). Stative verbs include *be*, *have*, *like*, and *see*.	*They've been good friends for ages.* *He's had a lot of experience in this business.* *I've always liked learning about successful people.*
B Use the present perfect to express *how much / how many*.	*A friend of mine has painted at least 100 paintings. (at least 100 paintings = how many)*
Use the present perfect progressive to express *how long*.	*She has been painting for more than 10 years. (more than 10 years = how long)*

Grammar Application

Read the sentences. Check (✓) whether the action is completed or ongoing.

		Completed	Ongoing
1	Lara has learned Spanish very well.	☑	☐
2	Michelle has also been studying French and Japanese this semester.	☐	☑
3	Enrico has been learning a lot of languages.	☐	☑
4	Tony has been working as a chef for the past eight years.	☐	☑
5	Alex has been running his own business since he was 19.	☐	☑
6	Joe has lived in Madrid.	☑	☐
7	Ron has been living in California since 2016.	☐	☑
8	We've already eaten dinner.	☑	☐
9	Sasha and Janet have been working there since 2017.	☐	☑
10	Raymond has won three prizes for his poetry.	☑	☐
11	I've been traveling for four weeks.	☐	☑
12	Bryn has been dancing since she was a child.	☐	☑
13	My mother has been cooking since she was 12.	☐	☑
14	Luisa has written four letters to her senator.	☑	☐

A Complete the following podcast transcript with the correct forms of the verbs in parentheses. Sometimes more than one answer is possible.

Zaha Hadid was an architect. She ___designed___ (1) (design) many famous buildings around the world, including the Rosenthal Center for Contemporary Art in Cincinnati. Hadid ___studied___ (2) (study) architecture in London in the late 1970s and formed her own architecture company in 1979. Since her death in 2016, her company ___has continued___ (3) (continue) to build original and imaginative buildings and structures and ___has won___ (4) (win) many international awards.

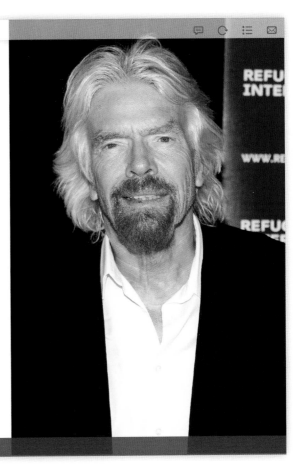

Richard Branson is one of the world's most successful businesspeople. He was born in England. He __had__ (5) (have) a hard time in school because he had a learning disability.[1] Reading was difficult for him. As a result, he __leFt__ (6) (leave) school at age 16. After that, he __started__ (7) (start) his first business. Later, he __opened__ (8) (open) a record shop called Virgin Records. Since then, he __has started__ (9) (start) new businesses in many different industries, including transportation, entertainment, and communications.

[1]**learning disability:** a condition that affects a person's ability to learn

B Pair Work Compare your answers with a partner. Discuss the reason for each of your answers.

In number 1, I wrote designed *because the action is complete and it is in the past. So, I didn't choose* has designed.

C Listen to the podcast and check your answers.

I have been eating dinner.

D Over to You Think about your life story. Write answers to these questions on a separate piece of paper. Use the simple past, the present perfect, and the present perfect progressive. Share your answers with a partner.

- Have you accomplished something important (for example, learned a language, graduated from high school, saved money for an important purchase)? How did you do it?

- What are some things that you have done recently that make you feel happy? How long have you been doing them?

- What have you been doing recently that makes you feel successful?

5 Avoid Common Mistakes ⚠

1 Use correct subject-verb agreement when forming the present perfect.

        have
Young people ~~has~~ always gone to college with high expectations.

2 Use the present perfect (not the present perfect progressive) for a time period that starts in the past and is completed.

        finished
He has ~~been finishing~~ two books since last week.

3 Remember to include *been* for the present perfect progressive.

            been
The definition of success has ˄ changing over the years.

4 Use the present perfect progressive (not the present progressive) for actions that began in the past and are still continuing.

has been
He ~~is~~ studying for six hours, and he refuses to stop.

Editing Task

Find and correct eight more mistakes in the paragraphs about a student's success in his job.

I am a college student by day and a sous-chef[1] by night. My studies are important,
but my restaurant job ~~have~~ *has* taught me what I really need to know about success. I ~~am~~ 've been
working in the kitchen of Da Lat, a French-Vietnamese bistro, for three years, and the
job has been a wonderful experience for me because I have learned many new skills.

5   First, I have ~~been~~ becoming a much better planner since I started working at
Da Lat. Planning and preparation are very important in a kitchen. If the chef ~~have~~ *has* not
prepared the ingredients well beforehand, it will take too long to make each dish,
and customers will complain. We start our preparation early each day, and by the
time the first customer comes, we have been working for 6 hours.

10   Second, I have been developing better interpersonal skills. For example, I have
~~been~~ *received* ~~receiving~~ two promotions in the last two years. Last year, I became a line cook
because I had learned to pay attention to what others might need before they ask.
I think that for the past few months, I ~~am~~ *have been* paying better attention in other areas of my
life as well.

15   My college education is important, but I will always be grateful for my job at
Da Lat. This job ~~have~~ *has* given me mental and social skills for my future.

[1]**sous-chef:** the head chef's assistant

Past Perfect and Past Perfect Progressive

Nature vs. Nurture

1 Grammar in the Real World

A Have you ever reconnected with someone from your past? Read the article about twins who lived apart for many years. What surprised the twins when they reconnected?

B Comprehension Check **Answer the questions.**

1 What was surprising about the twins' adoption?
2 What characteristics and interests did Elyse and Paula have in common?
3 What is the nature versus nurture debate?

C Notice **Underline the verbs in each sentence.**

1 Both girls knew that their parents had adopted them as infants.
2 She had been doing research on her birth mother when she made a surprising discovery.
3 Even more surprising, she learned that she had been part of a secret scientific study.

Which event happened first in each sentence? What event followed? Write the verbs. What do you notice about the form of the verbs?

1 First: _____   Then: _____

2 First: _____   Then: _____

3 First: _____   Then: _____

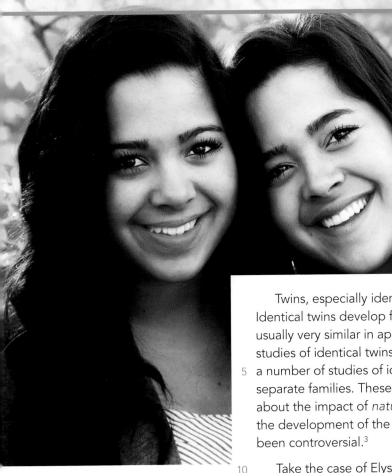

The SCIENCE of TWINS

[1]**identical:** exactly the same

[2]**DNA:** the abbreviation for deoxyribonucleic acid, a chemical that controls the structure and purpose of every cell

[3]**controversial:** causing or likely to cause disagreement

[4]**dominant:** more important, strong, or noticeable

Twins, especially identical[1] twins, have always fascinated scientists. Identical twins develop from one egg, have identical DNA,[2] and are usually very similar in appearance and behavior. There have been many studies of identical twins raised in the same family. There have also been
5 a number of studies of identical twins separated at birth and raised in separate families. These studies have provided interesting information about the impact of *nature* (genetics) and *nurture* (the environment) on the development of the individual. However, some of the studies have been controversial.[3]

10 Take the case of Elyse Schein and Paula Bernstein. Elyse and Paula were identical twins separated at birth. Both girls knew that their parents **had adopted** them as infants, but neither girl knew about her twin. When Elyse grew up, she longed to meet her biological mother, so she contacted the agency that **had arranged** the adoption. She **had**
15 **been doing** research on her birth mother when she made a surprising discovery. She had an identical twin. Even more surprising, she learned that she **had been** part of a secret scientific study. At the time of the adoption, the agency **had allowed** different families to adopt each twin. The agency **had told** the families that their child was part of a scientific
20 study. However, it **had** never **told** the families the goal of the study: for scientists to investigate nature versus nurture.

When Elyse and Paula finally met as adults, they were amazed. They had many similarities. They looked almost identical. They **had** both **studied** film. They both loved to write. Together, the twins discovered
25 that the researchers **had stopped** the study before the end because the public strongly disapproved of this type of research.

Although that study ended early, many scientists today make a strong case for the dominant[4] role of nature. Schein and Bernstein agree that genetics explains many of their similarities. However, recent research
30 suggests that nurture is equally important. It is clear that the nature versus nurture debate will occupy scientists for years to come.

2 Past Perfect

Grammar Presentation

The past perfect is used to describe a completed event that happened before another event in the past.	*Elyse finally met her sister, Paula. Paula **had been** married for several years. (First, Paula got married; Elyse met Paula at a later time.)*

2.1 Forming Past Perfect

Form the past perfect with *had* + the past participle of the main verb. Form the negative by adding *not* after *had*. The form is the same for all subjects.	*Elyse and Paula did not grow up together. They **had lived** with different families.* *They were available for adoption because their birth mother **had given** them up.* *"**Had** she **talked** about the study to anyone at the time?"* *"No, she **hadn't**."* *"What **had** you **heard** about this study before that time?"* *"**I'd heard** very little about it."*

▶▶ Irregular Verbs: See page A1.

2.2 Using Past Perfect with Simple Past

A Use the past perfect to describe an event in a time period that leads up to another past event or time period. Use the simple past to describe the later event or time period.	<small>LATER TIME</small> <small>EARLIER TIME</small> *She **learned** that she **had been** part of a secret study.* <small>LATER TIME</small> <small>EARLIER TIME</small> *The twins **discovered** that they **had** both **studied** psychology.*
B The prepositions *before, by,* or *until* can introduce the later time period.	<small>EARLIER TIME</small> <small>LATER TIME</small> *Their mother **had known** about the study <u>before</u> her death.* <small>EARLIER TIME</small> <small>LATER TIME</small> *Sue **hadn't met** her sister <u>until</u> last year.* <small>EARLIER TIME</small> <small>LATER TIME</small> *Studies on twins **had become** common <u>by</u> the 1960s.*
C The past perfect is often used to give reasons or background information for later past events.	<small>REASON</small> *She <u>was</u> late. She **had forgotten** to set her alarm clock.* <small>BACKGROUND INFORMATION</small> <small>LATER PAST EVENT</small> *He **had** never **taken** a subway before he <u>moved</u> to New York.*

📊 Data from the Real World

In writing, these verbs are commonly used in the past perfect: *come, have, leave, make,* and *take.*

Had been is the most common past perfect form in speaking and writing.

The twins **had not gone** to the same school as children.

The family thought that they **had made** the right decision.

Psychologists praised the study because the researchers **had been** very careful in their work.

The researchers **had not been** aware of each other's work on twins until they met.

Grammar Application

Exercise 2.1 Past Perfect

Complete the sentences about twins who met as adults. Use the past perfect form of the verbs in parentheses.

1 Two separate Illinois families ___*had adopted*___ (adopt) Anne Green and Annie Smith before the twins were three days old.

2 When the girls met, they were fascinated by their similarities. For example, they _____ (live) near each other before the Greens moved away.

3 As children, both Anne and Annie _____ (go) to the same summer camp.

4 Anne _____ (not / go) to college, and Annie _____ (not / attend) college, either.

5 Both _____ (marry) for the first time by the age of 22.

6 Anne _____ (get) divorced and _____ (remarry). Annie _____ (not / get) divorced and was still married.

7 Both Anne and Annie were allergic to cats and dogs and _____ never _____ (own) pets.

8 Both _____ (give) the same name – Heather – to their daughters.

9 Both _____ previously _____ (work) in the hospitality industry.

10 Anne _____ (work) as a hotel manager. However, Annie _____ (not / work) in hotels; she _____ (be) a restaurant manager.

A Read the article about a famous twin study. Underline the simple past forms. Double underline the past perfect forms.

The University of Minnesota is the birthplace of one of the most important twin studies in the world. It started in 1979. Thomas J. Bouchard had already been on the faculty[1] of the university for some time when he began his study of identical twins. Bouchard read an article about a set of twins who had been separated at birth. The twins had recently met and had found many similarities. They found out that they had lived near each other for years. Bouchard was amazed by the twins' story and decided to start the Minnesota Twins Reared Apart Study. Bouchard began to study sets of twins that had been separated at birth. Over the years, the Minnesota Twins Reared Apart Study has studied around 10,000 sets of twins. The study continues today.

[1]**faculty:** the people who teach in a department in a school

B Pair Work Compare your answers with a partner. Discuss the reason for each of your answers.

In line 3, had been *refers to the first event. Dr. Bouchard joined the faculty before the twin study. The twin study began later. The study is the second event, so* started *is in the simple past.*

A Listen to an interview with twins who are actors. Complete the sentences with the verbs you hear.

Claudia Today, I'm interviewing Alex and Andrew Underhill. They appear in the *Spy Twins* movie series based on the books of the same name. How did you get the part in the first *Spy Twins* movie?

Alex A friend ___*had seen*___ the advertisement in the newspaper and later
                        (1)
_____ us about it. We _____
            (2)   (3)
any acting before then, but we _____ to try out anyway.
                                                    (4)

Claudia   How many twins were at the audition?

Andrew   When we got there, we _____ (5) that about five other sets

of twins _____ (6) for the audition.

Alex   We also noticed that all the twins were wearing matching outfits. Until that

audition, we _____ (7) never _____ (7) the

same clothes in our whole lives. We decided to run out to the nearest shopping

mall to buy some matching clothes. The audition _____ (8) just

_____ (8) when we _____ (9) .

Claudia   _____ (10) you _____ (10) the *Spy Twins* novels

before your audition?

Andrew   Yes. The third book _____ (11) when we

_____ (12) to the first audition.

Claudia   What's it like being twins? Are you two close? Do you do the same things?

Alex   Yes, in lots of ways.

Andrew   We definitely think the same way.

Alex   Right! Once, we took the same test
in school. Of course, we were in the
same grade, but we had different
teachers. We had exactly the same
answers correct, even though we

_____ (13)

in the same classroom!

Claudia   Wow! I guess you're a lot alike in many
ways! Well, thanks, Alex and Andrew.
It's been great talking with you.

B Listen again and check your answers.

C Use the time line to complete the sentences about Alex and Andrew. Use the past perfect form of the verbs in the box.

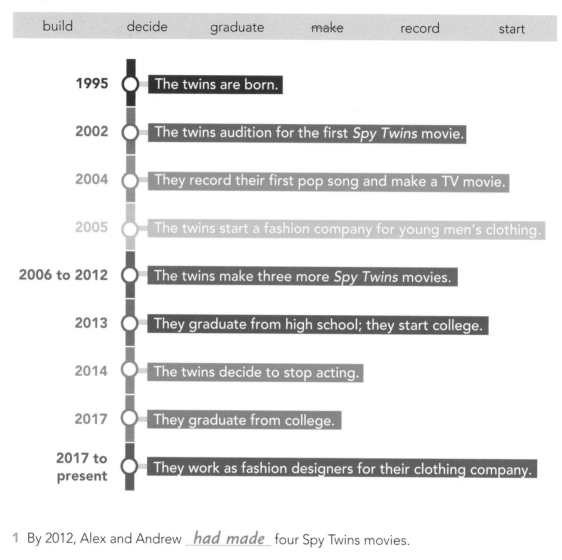

| build | decide | graduate | ~~make~~ | record | start |

1995 ○ The twins are born.

2002 ○ The twins audition for the first *Spy Twins* movie.

2004 ○ They record their first pop song and make a TV movie.

2005 ○ The twins start a fashion company for young men's clothing.

2006 to 2012 ○ The twins make three more *Spy Twins* movies.

2013 ○ They graduate from high school; they start college.

2014 ○ The twins decide to stop acting.

2017 ○ They graduate from college.

2017 to present ○ They work as fashion designers for their clothing company.

1 By 2012, Alex and Andrew _**had made**_ four Spy Twins movies.

2 Before 2004, the twins _____ (not) a pop song.

3 By 2016, the twins _____ to stop acting.

4 The twins _____ (not) a fashion company yet in 2004.

5 The twins _____ from high school by 2015.

3 Past Perfect with Time Clauses

Grammar Presentation

The past perfect is often used with time clauses for events that occurred in an earlier time period leading up to a later event or time period.	*By the time Elyse discovered her sister, people* **had forgotten** *about the twin study.*

3.1 Order of Events

A Use time clauses to show two separate past time periods. Use the past perfect to signal an event that occurred in an earlier time period.	*Elyse* **had moved** <u>*by the time*</u> *the researchers called her.*
The time words *after*, *as soon as*, *before*, *by the time*, *until*, and *when* can introduce the time clauses.	<u>*After*</u> *they* **had met**, *they noticed their many similarities.* <u>*Until*</u> *Elyse started her research, she* **hadn't known** *about the twin study.*
B With *before* and *after*, the past perfect is not always necessary because the order is clear. In this case, the past perfect emphasizes the earlier time period.	*Elyse* **moved** <u>*before*</u> *she met her twin.* OR *Elyse* **had moved** <u>*before*</u> *she met her twin.*
C In time clauses with *when*, the use of the past perfect in the main clause usually shows a good amount of time between events.	<u>*When*</u> *Paula met Elyse, she* **had** *already* **learned** *about the research.* (She learned about the research. She met Elyse some time later.)
D The use of *as soon as* with the past perfect shows that one event happened very soon after the other.	<u>*As soon as*</u> *the researchers* **had learned** *about the public's reaction to the study, they* **stopped** *it.* (The scientists learned about the public's reaction to the study. They stopped the study very soon after that.)
The use of the simple past in both clauses shows that one event happened very soon after the other.	<u>*When*</u> *Paula met Elyse, she* **learned** *about the research.* (She learned about the research very soon after she met Elyse.)

⌨ Grammar Application

Exercise 3.1 Order of Events

A Read the blog entry about twin studies. Underline the past perfect form of the verbs.

B Pair Work Discuss why the past perfect is used in each case in A. Then find a sentence with a time clause that describes two events that happened at the same time or almost the same time. What is the form of the verbs in this sentence?

⌂   ☰ ✉

TWIN WORLD by Cory Daniels

Before her twins were born, Kim Lee <u>had read</u> a lot about twin studies. After she had done a little research, Kim found an early reading study for twins. She contacted the researchers and learned that she had to wait until the twins were four years old. When she enrolled the twins in the study, she hadn't known that the twins needed to give a DNA sample. As soon as Kim learned this, she took the twins out of the study. Kim thought that taking a DNA sample was an invasion of her children's privacy.

Exercise 3.2 Time Clauses

Complete the article about siblings[1] who were separated as children. Circle the correct time word. Write the simple past or past perfect form of the verbs in parentheses. Sometimes more than one answer is possible.

⌂   💬 ↻ ☰ ✉

[1]**sibling:** a brother or sister

[2]**family tree:** a drawing that shows all the members of a family, usually over a long period of time, and how they are related to each other

There are many stories of non-twin brothers and sisters who are separated for one reason or another and meet again as adults. Here are a couple.

Glenn Mint and Bruce Mathews are brothers. They had never met (until)/after
(1)
Glenn __*started*__ (start) working at the same company as Bruce. Bruce was surprised
(2)
because the new employee looked just like him. They started asking each other questions.

Before/After they met, each man _____ (know) that he had a sibling.
(3)   (4)

Before/As soon as Glenn _____ (discover) Bruce's birth date,
(5)   (6)
he knew Bruce was his long-lost brother.

Quin Mara, 82, knew that she was adopted and that she had siblings, but she had never

met them. After/Until a relative _____ (find) a family tree,[2] Quin
(7)   (8)
learned the names of her siblings and started looking for them. Until/By the time she saw
(9)
the family tree, she _____ (not/know) that she was the youngest
(10)
of nine children. As soon as/Before she _____ (discover) that,
(11)   (12)
she began to look for her brothers and sisters. She was very happy because five of her
siblings were still alive. Before/After she _____ (meet) them, she
(13)   (14)
didn't know that they had spent the last several decades looking for each other.

Exercise 3.3 Combining Sentences

Read the story about how environment affects personality. Combine the sentences with the time words in parentheses. Use the past perfect for the earlier event and the simple past for the later event.

1 Diego and Shannon were married for a few years.
Then they decided to have a baby.

(when) _When Diego and Shannon had been married_

for a few years, they decided to have a baby.

2 Diego and Shannon did not think much about the nature versus nurture debate. Then their first child, Mario, was born.
(until) _____

_____

3 Diego and Shannon didn't have much experience with music. Then they became parents.

(before)_____

_____

4 Three-year-old Mario saw an electronic keyboard in a shop. Then he asked his parents to buy

him one.

(after) _____

_____

5 Diego and Shannon heard Mario playing the keyboard. Then they realized their son's musical talent.

(as soon as) _____

_____

6 Diego and Shannon realized Mario's talent. Then they enrolled him in piano classes.

(as soon as) _____

_____

7 Diego and Shannon enrolled Mario in piano classes. Then Mario became an excellent musician.

(after)_____

_____

8 Mario took a few years of piano classes. He started composing music.

(by the time) _____

_____

4 Past Perfect Progressive

Grammar Presentation

The past perfect progressive emphasizes the ongoing nature of a past activity or situation leading up to a more recent past time.	*Living with a roommate was hard for me in the beginning. I **had been living** alone for years.*

4.1 Forming Past Perfect Progressive

Form the past perfect progressive with *had + been + -ing* form of the verb. Form the negative by putting *not* between *had* and *been* or using the contraction *hadn't*.	*She knew Boston well when I visited her. She**'d been living** there for years.* *When my brother visited me, I **had not / hadn't been living** there long.*

4.2 Using Past Perfect Progressive

A Use the past perfect progressive for an action or situation that continued up to an event or situation in past time. This can show a reason or give background information.	*He looked tired because he **had been working** all night.* *My eyes were sore because I **hadn't been wearing** my contacts.*
B With some verbs such as *live, play, teach, wear,* and *work,* use either the past perfect or past perfect progressive. The meaning is similar.	*The twins **had lived** in different cities before they **discovered** each other.* or *The twins **had been living** in different cities before they **discovered** each other.*

Grammar Application

Exercise 4.1 Past Perfect Progressive

Complete the story about brothers who reconnected after many years. Use the past perfect progressive form of the verbs in parentheses.

Mark and Peter were brothers. Their parents could not take care of them. One family adopted Mark, and another family adopted Peter. Mark and Peter __had been dreaming__ (dream) of
(1)
finding each other since 2015. When they finally met, they were surprised by how much they had in common. For most of their adult lives, their jobs had been related, even though they _____ (not/work) in
(2)
the same business. Mark _____ (make) furniture, and Peter
(3)
_____ (sell) furniture. Mark _____
(4)   (5)
(interview) for jobs in furniture stores and decided to take a new position at Mark's store. Peter _____ (talk) to a friendly customer when he
(6)
saw a man who looked like him walk into the store. Peter quickly stopped what he
_____ (do) and introduced himself. That first day, Peter
(7)
and Mark talked for hours. They found out that they _____
(8)
(not/live) in the same city, but they had attended schools in the same district for most of their childhood. They _____ (cross) paths for many years
(9)
without ever meeting. They had never expected to have so much in common.

A Complete the interview with a woman who found her three siblings after many years. Use the past perfect progressive, the past perfect, or the simple past form of the verbs in parentheses. Use contractions when possible. Sometimes more than one answer is possible.

Vijay Tell us how you found your family.

Paula I _'d been looking_ (look) for my sister all my life. I _____
(1)
(not / have) much luck, though. Then one day, I turned on the TV. A talk show was
(2)
on. The host of the show was interviewing three siblings – two brothers and a half
sister.[1] Different families _____ (adopt) the siblings many
(3)
years before.

Vijay And?

Paula They _____ (talk) about me before I turned on the program.
(4)
The siblings had recently reunited, and they _____ (search) for
(5)
a fourth sibling for the past several months. I called the TV station, and we all finally
_____ (meet).
(6)

Vijay So, you _____ (look) for a sister all your life, and you found
(7)
three siblings!

Paula Yes, it was wonderful! We all met at one of the network offices the following week.
After we _____ (speak) for a while, it was obvious to me that
(8)
they _____ (look) for me all their lives, too.
(9)

[1]**half sister:** a sister who is biologically related by one parent only

B Pair Work **Discuss these questions with a partner.**

■ Choose a sentence in A in which you can use either the past perfect or the past perfect progressive. Why are both possible here?

■ In which sentence in A is only the past perfect correct?

C Over to You **Do an online search for twins, siblings, or other family members who reunited after many years. Write five sentences about their experiences. Use the past perfect and the past perfect progressive.**

5 Avoid Common Mistakes ⚠

1 Use the past perfect or past perfect progressive to give background information for a past tense event.

    had
I ~~have~~ never seen my sister in real life, so I was nervous the first time we met.

    had been dreaming
I ~~have dreamed~~ about meeting her, and I finally did.

2 Use the past perfect or past perfect progressive to give a reason for a past event.

                        had been crying
Her eyes were red and puffy because she ~~cried~~.

3 Use the past perfect (not the past perfect progressive) for a completed earlier event.

          arranged
They had ~~been arranging~~ a time to meet, but both of them forgot about it.

4 Use the past perfect (not present perfect) to describe a completed event that happened before a past event.

    had
I ~~have~~ visited her in Maine twice before she came to visit me.

Editing Task

Find and correct seven more mistakes in the paragraphs about sibling differences.

        had
    I ~~have~~ never really thought about sibling differences until my own children were born. When we had our first child, my husband and I have lived in Chicago for just a few months. We have not made many friends yet, so we spent all our time with our child. Baby Gilbert was happy to be the center of attention. He depended on us
5 for everything.

    By the time our second son, Chase, was born, we have developed a community of friends and a busier social life. We frequently visited friends and left the children at home with a babysitter. As a result of our busy schedules, Chase was more independent. One day I had just been hanging up the phone when Chase came into
10 the room. Chase picked up the phone and started talking into it. I thought he was pretending, but I was wrong. He had been figuring out how to use the phone!

    When my husband came home, he was tired because he worked all day. When I told him about Chase's phone conversation, though, he became very excited. Gilbert has never used the phone as a child. At first, we were surprised that Chase was so
15 different from Gilbert. Then we realized that because of our busy lifestyles, Chase had learned to be independent.

Be Going To, Present Progressive, and Future Progressive

Looking Ahead at Technology

1 Grammar in the Real World

A How is technology used today? Read the article about technology use in the future. What is one way that technology use will develop?

B Comprehension Check **Answer the questions.**

1 What are some ways technology will change in the future?

2 How will people in the future access the Internet?

3 What is "wearable tech"?

C Notice **Find the sentences in the article and complete them.**

1 Market research suggests that in the future we _____ on the Internet even more than we are now.

2 Scientists predict that ingestibles _____ the way we treat all sorts of diseases.

3 As technology changes, devices such as wearable tech

_____ more and more popular.

How many different verb forms in items 1–3 did the author of the reading use to talk about the future?

Looking AHEAD at Technology

Technology has become an essential part of everyday life for many people. We depend on the Internet, for example, for easy access to information and communication. Computers, cell

5 phones, and other handheld gadgets provide constant entertainment. No one knows for sure what technology **is going to bring** us in the future. However, there is no doubt that it **will continue** to drastically affect how we live and work.

10 Market research[1] suggests that in the future we **will be depending** on the Internet even more than we are now. Wearable tech is already here, with many people using bracelets and watches to track their health, activity, sleep, and fitness.

15 Smartglasses are popular too, connecting us to the Internet as we go about our day. The prediction, though, is that smartglasses **will** soon **include** "bone induction audio," allowing us to talk to our digital assistants or listen to music without needing

20 earbuds. Sound **will** simply **travel** through the bones in our heads instead.

Some people **will not want** their technology to be wearable, so what **is going to be** new and exciting for them? The answer is "ingestibles."

25 Ingestibles are smart tablets filled with sensors that you **will swallow** just like you swallow an aspirin. They **will allow** doctors to track what is happening inside your body. The sensors **will send** data about your body back to an external monitor. This way, doctors

30 **will** also **be able to check** that your medication is working correctly. Scientists predict that ingestibles **are going to change** the way we treat all kinds of diseases, from the common cold to cancer.

In the future, there **will be** many advances

35 in technology and many changes in the ways technology affects our lives. As technology changes, devices such as smart clothing **will become** more and more popular. In short, it is clear that almost everything we do **will happen**

40 with the help of technology.

Pill cam

[1]**market research:** the study of consumer behavior

2 Be Going To, Present Progressive, and Simple Present for Future

Grammar Presentation

Be going to and the present progressive are used to describe future plans. The simple present is used to describe a scheduled future event.	I'm going to buy some smartglasses someday. My parents probably aren't going to buy smartwatches. I'm buying a smartwatch tomorrow.

2.1 Be Going To vs. Present Progressive for Future Plans

A Use be going to + base form of the verb to express general intentions and plans for the future.	I'm going to buy a 3D TV someday.
You can use expressions like probably, most likely, I think, and I believe with this form.	My parents probably aren't going to buy one. I think they are going to save their money for a trip instead.
B Use the present progressive to express definite plans and arrangements for the future, especially when a time or place is mentioned.	I'm buying a 3D TV tomorrow. The class is taking a trip to the science museum next week.
C In many cases, both forms can be used to express the same idea.	I'm watching a movie this evening. I'm going to watch a movie this evening.

2.2 Simple Present for Scheduled Events

Use the simple present for scheduled events in the future and for timetables. Some common verbs for this use include arrive, be, begin, finish, leave, and start.	The conference begins on Monday and ends on Friday. Beginning June 10, all trains to New England leave from platform 14.

Grammar Application

A Complete the conversation about e-readers. Use *be going to* or the present progressive and the verbs in parentheses. Sometimes more than one answer is possible.

Mei I _'m going to buy_ (buy) some smartglasses one of these days. Any suggestions?
(1)

Kyle Look at this ad. Big Buy _____ (have) a sale on the iSights next week.
(2)

Mei How much are they?

Kyle They _____ (lower) the price to $69.
(3)

Mei That's great. I _____ (visit) a friend near that area next week.
(4)
I'll stop by.

Kyle That's a great price.

Mei Yes, it's quite a deal. You know, I think companies _____ (give)
(5)
smartglasses away someday. They're getting less and less expensive. Soon they'll
be free!

Kyle I've got to go. I _____ (meet) some friends for dinner. What _____
(6)   (7)
you _____ (do) tonight?
(7)

Mei I _____ (go) straight home. I'm tired.
(8)

B Pair Work Compare your answers with a partner. Discuss the reason for each
of your answers.

In the first sentence, one of these days *made the plan seem like an intention
because he wasn't really sure, so* be going to *is correct.*

Look at the clues. Then complete the sentences about a new phone. Use *be going to*, the
present progressive, or the simple present form of the verbs in parentheses.

1 Clue: definite plan
Best Product _is launching_ (launch) a new YouPhone next week.

2 Clue: scheduled event
The new YouPhone _____ (become) available in stores on Friday, January 15.

3 Clue: definite plan
All employees _____ (prepare) for a busy first day of sales.

4 Clue: definite plan

All stores _____ (open) at 8:00 a.m. that day.

5 Clue: definite plan

The stores _____ (give) away water and free coffee to customers in line.

6 Clue: scheduled event

School _____ (close) early that day because of a holiday.

7 Clue: future intention

The newspaper _____ (interview) Anne Green, a representative from BestProduct.

8 Clue: future intention

Ms. Green _____ probably _____ (speak) for a few minutes and then answer some questions.

Exercise 2.3 More *Be Going To*, Present Progressive, or Simple Present?

A Complete the article about a social networking site. Use *be going to,* the present progressive, or the simple present form of the verbs in parentheses. Sometimes more than one answer is possible.

CHANGES AHEAD for Youth Network

Youth Network, Inc., announced today that it ___*is buying*___ (buy) FacePlace, the
(1)
popular social networking website. FacePlace has already accepted Youth Network's offer
of $3.1 billion. The company has not made any definite plans, but it _____ probably
(2)
_____ (start) asking people to pay for the site. It won't be free anymore.
(2)
In addition, some people think that the network _____ (put) ads on
(3)
the site. Another possibility is that Youth Network _____ (show) its TV
(4)
programs on FacePlace. Next week, FacePlace technicians _____ (meet)
(5)
with Youth Network technicians to help with the changes. They _____
(6)
(plan) to shut down the old FacePlace website at 1:00 a.m. on Saturday, August 10. The new Youth
Network site _____ (go) live at 6:00 a.m. the next day.
(7)

B Pair Work Compare your answers with a partner. Discuss the reason for each of your answers.

In item 1, the plan seems definite because the company made an announcement to the press, so the company arranged the action. The present progressive is correct.

3 *Will* and *Be Going To*

Grammar Presentation

Will and *be going to* can both express future plans and predictions. They can also be used in other ways, for example, to make a promise or to express an expectation.	Smartglasses **will allow** us to connect to the Internet almost anywhere. Technology **is going to become** easier to use. I'**ll help** you with your computer.

3.1 *Will* and *Be Going To* for Predictions and Expectations

A Use *will* and *be going to* for predictions, expectations, or guesses about the future.	People **will connect** to the Internet from almost anywhere. I'**m not going to** have Internet access while I'm on vacation.
B You can use *certainly, definitely, likely, maybe, perhaps,* and *probably* to show degrees of certainty.	Technology will <u>certainly</u> be more sophisticated in the future.
Use *certainly, definitely, likely,* and *probably* after *will* or after *be*.	There will <u>probably</u> be many people at the concert next week. Doctors are <u>definitely</u> **going to use** ingestibles in the future.
Use *maybe* and *perhaps* at the beginning of sentences.	<u>Maybe</u> I'**ll get** a smartwatch this year.
C Use *be going to* to predict the future when there is present evidence.	My computer is behaving strangely. I think it'**s going to crash**.
D Generally, in speaking, *be going to* is used for intentions and plans. However, in academic writing, *will* is used much more frequently.	By 2030, people throughout the world **will use** many types of wearable tech.

3.2 Will for Requests, Offers, and Promises

Use *will* for requests, offers, and promises.	*Will you **help** me buy a computer?* *I'll **research** the best buys for you.*

3.3 Will for Quick Decisions

Use *will* for decisions made at the time of speaking.	*"We need someone to take notes for our group."* *"I'll **do** it."* (quick decision)
The same verb with *be going to* expresses a previous decision.	*"Bob **is going to do** it."* (previous decision)

Grammar Application

Exercise 3.1 *Will or Be Going To?*

A Complete the phone conversation between an employee and a technician in the tech department. Circle *will* or *be going to*. If both are possible, circle both.

Bill Tech Department, Bill speaking.

Kate Hi, Bill. This is Kate in Business Development. My laptop is behaving very strangely this morning. It **will / 's going to** crash at any minute. **Will you / Are you going to** (1) (2) send someone to look at it?

Bill Of course, I **will / am going to** . (3)

Kate Soon?

Bill I promise. I**'ll / 'm going to** send Dave in five minutes. (4)

Kate Bill, **will you / are you going to** send Silvia instead, please? She's fixed this same (5) problem before.

Bill Oh, OK. Then Silvia **will / is going to** be there in about five minutes. (6)

Kate Thanks, Bill. Bye.

A few minutes later:

Silvia Hi, Kate. Are you having problems with your laptop again?

Kate Uh-huh. This is the fourth time! I think I**'ll / 'm going to** ask for a new computer. (7)

Silvia I**'ll / 'm going to** look at it for you. (8)

Kate Thanks, Silvia.

B Pair Work Compare your answers with a partner. Discuss the reason for each of your answers.

I chose be going to *for item 1 because the speaker is making a prediction based on evidence. She said her computer was behaving strangely. That's evidence that it might be crashing.*

Exercise 3.2 More *Will* or *Be Going To*?

A Listen to a discussion about education and technology. Complete the sentences with the form of the verbs you hear.

Ms. Ng _____Will_____ everyone please _____be_____ quiet? The noise
                      (1)   (1)
_____ it hard to hear our speaker. And _____
                      (2)   (3)
someone please _____ the windows? The air
                              (3)
conditioner isn't working well.

Alex I _____ it.
                      (4)

Ms. Ng Thanks. And _____ you all please _____
                              (5)   (5)
your smartphones? I promise I _____ you
                                              (6)
to do anything else except enjoy today's presentation. OK, today,
we _____ from an expert on education, Dr. Paul Bell.
              (7)
I'm sure you _____ all _____ him very interesting.
                    (8)   (8)

Dr. Bell Thank you. Well, it's clear that the world of the college student
_____ very different in a matter of a few years.
              (9)
For example, we already know that colleges _____
                                                              (10)
more courses online. This _____ money for schools and
                                      (11)
for students. Students _____ money on transportation
                                  (12)
costs because they can learn anywhere. Online learning also means that
schools and individuals _____ fewer resources such
                                      (13)
as paper and fuel. But what _____ the consequences of online education
                                  (14)
_____ ?
              (14)

B Find an example of each meaning, and write the number of the item next to it.
   __1__ a request   _____ a promise
   _____ a prediction based on evidence   _____ an offer

C Group Work Make predictions or share expectations about the future of phones, TVs, movies, schools, cars, or something else. As a group, write five sentences. Use *will* and *be going to*. Share your sentences with the class.

4 Future Progressive

Grammar Presentation

The future progressive emphasizes an action that will be in progress at a specific time in the future.	We **will be treating** many diseases with technology in 10 years. Everyone **is going to be using** wearable tech in 2025.

4.1 Forming Future Progressive

A Form the future progressive with *will* or *be going to* + *be* + verb + -*ing*.	People **will be working** on mobile devices instead of laptops in five years. Consumers **are not going to be using** coins and paper money by the year 2025.
B Use the future progressive to describe or ask about an action in progress at a time in the future.	**Will** you **be working** tomorrow at noon?
Use *certainly*, *definitely*, *likely*, and *probably* after *will* or *be going to* to show degrees of certainty. Use them before *won't*.	I definitely **won't be watching** TV tonight. **I'll probably be working** on my project all afternoon.
C Sometimes *will* + base form and future progressive are very similar in meaning, especially when the future event will occur at an indefinite time.	I think the computer specialist **will arrive** later. I don't see her. I think the computer specialist **will be arriving** later. I don't see her.

4.2 Future Progressive and *Be Going To* Contrasted

The future progressive and *be going to* can both express plans and intentions.	
Use the future progressive for a more formal tone.	Mr. Lee, **will** you **be coming** with me to the lecture on technology tomorrow? (more formal)
Use *be going to* for a less formal tone.	Marie, **are** you **going to come** with me to the lecture tomorrow? (less formal)

Grammar Application

Exercise 4.1 Future Progressive

Complete the interview about the future of TV. Use the future progressive form of the verbs in parentheses.

Claire Mr. Reyes, you've been involved in the television industry for well over 30 years. We know that the TV industry is changing rapidly. Tell us about its future.

Mr. Reyes Certainly. The television industry _will be creating_ (create) all of its own
(1)
shows in the future. It _____ (save) a lot of money this
(2)
way because it _____ (not/buy) the shows from other
(3)
producers. In addition, people _____ (watch) TV using
(4)
many different types of media.

Claire What do you mean?

Mr. Reyes I mean that we _____ (use) mobile devices instead
(5)
of televisions to watch TV shows. People _____
(6)
(not/watch) by themselves, either. They _____
(7)
(socialize) through social networks as they watch TV.

Claire How will that work?

Mr. Reyes Viewers _____ (send) messages, and they
(8)
_____ (chat) with others while they watch. In fact, they
(9)
are already doing so. This will affect marketing, too.

Claire In what way?

Mr. Reyes Advertisers _____ (ask) viewers to share their opinions
(10)
of the things they are viewing, such as products in ads or clothes worn
by actors.

Claire It sounds as though advertising will become even more interactive.

Mr. Reyes Exactly.

Claire Thank you very much, Mr. Reyes, for taking the time to talk to us.

A Complete the formal announcement of a lecture on the future of movies. Use the future progressive form of the verbs in parentheses. Sometimes more than one answer is possible.

The Future of Movies

Presented by Dr. Maria Sanderson
Michaels Hall
8:00 p.m., Friday, January 7

What __will__ people __be seeing__ (see) at the movies 10 years from
(1)   (1)
now? _____ we _____ (watch) only 3D movies? _____
(2)   (2)   (3)
people _____ (watch) movies in theaters, or will theaters disappear?
(3)
Dr. Sanderson _____ (discuss) the future of the movie industry and
(4)
the movie-going experience in general. She _____ (give) examples
(5)
of past, present, and future film technology, and she _____ (take)
(6)
questions from the audience.

B Complete the conversation between two students about the lecture in A. Use *be going to* or the future progressive and the verbs in parentheses. Sometimes more than one answer is possible.

| Chao | __Are__ you __going to go__ (go) to the lecture? |
| | (1)   (1) |

Verónica Yes, I _____ definitely _____ (attend). What about you?
(2)   (2)

Chao No, I _____ (not / go). I'm not interested. Why _____ you
(3)   (4)
_____ (go)?
(4)

Verónica I'm taking film history, so it will help me with my class. I _____ (take)
(5)
notes. I _____ also _____ (ask) questions.
(6)   (6)

Over to You What will you be doing 20 years in the future? Where will you be living? What will you be doing for entertainment? Write five sentences about the way you imagine the future. Use the future progressive. Share your sentences with a partner.

5 Avoid Common Mistakes ⚠

1   **Use the future progressive to talk about actions that will be in progress at a future time.**

be working
You won't see me next week because I will ~~work~~ in Seoul.

2   **Use the simple present for scheduled events.**

starts
The video conference ~~will~~ always ~~start~~ at 4:00 p.m.

3   **Remember to use *be* with *be going to*.**

am
I ˄ going to give a presentation on the twenty-fifth of next month.

4   **Use the present progressive (not *will*) when talking about definite plans.**

are traveling
We ~~will travel~~ to the home office at the end of the month.

Editing Task

Find and correct the mistakes in the email about travel plans.

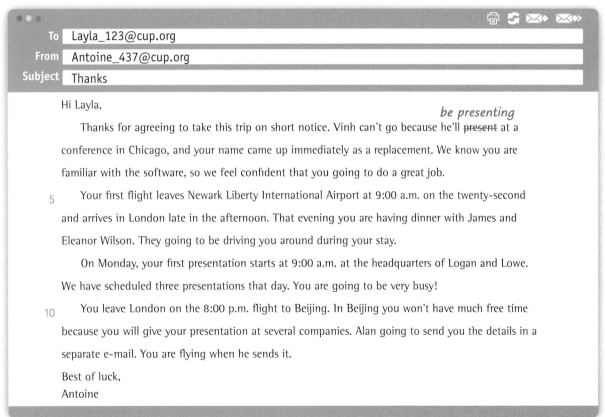

To   Layla_123@cup.org
From   Antoine_437@cup.org
Subject   Thanks

Hi Layla,
                                                                                                       be presenting
    Thanks for agreeing to take this trip on short notice. Vinh can't go because he'll ~~present~~ at a
conference in Chicago, and your name came up immediately as a replacement. We know you are
familiar with the software, so we feel confident that you going to do a great job.

5   Your first flight leaves Newark Liberty International Airport at 9:00 a.m. on the twenty-second
and arrives in London late in the afternoon. That evening you are having dinner with James and
Eleanor Wilson. They going to be driving you around during your stay.

    On Monday, your first presentation starts at 9:00 a.m. at the headquarters of Logan and Lowe.
We have scheduled three presentations that day. You are going to be very busy!

10   You leave London on the 8:00 p.m. flight to Beijing. In Beijing you won't have much free time
because you will give your presentation at several companies. Alan going to send you the details in a
separate e-mail. You are flying when he sends it.

Best of luck,
Antoine

Future Time Clauses, Future Perfect, and Future Perfect Progressive

Business Practices of the Future

1 Grammar in the Real World

A What automatic technology do you use? Read the article about automation. What are the pros and cons?

B Comprehension Check **Answer the questions.**

1 What will many companies do in the future? Why?

2 What are some risks of automation?

C Notice **Complete these sentences from the article.**

1 By 2020, many companies _____ at least some of their employees' jobs and **saved** large sums of money because they _____ automation.

2 That figure _____ change **until** **people are confident that their jobs will be secure.**

Look at the verbs that you wrote. There are three different forms for describing the future. Which form describes completed future events?

SMART businesses have their eye on AUTOMATION

For a long time, the world's businesses have been using mechanization. Mechanization is the term for using machines instead of animals or your own hands to do work. More and more
5 businesses are now thinking about automation. *Automation* is the term people use to describe the way information technology works automatically – without direction from a human, in other words. Instead of employing hundreds of people to
10 make, pack, send, deliver, or store things, you use technology and, sometimes, robots and other machines to do all of that for you.

By 2020, many companies **will have eliminated**[1] at least some of their employees' jobs and **saved**
15 large sums of money because they **will have been using** automation. **When these businesses move to automation**, we will see increasing numbers of drones delivering goods, robots serving coffee and pizza, bots organizing our calendars for us, and
20 refrigerators reminding us to buy fresh milk.

It sounds great at first. We will not need to do as much work because machines will do it for us. Automation has risks, however. Some people say that automation will lead to boredom
25 and unhappiness. Psychologists warn that the satisfaction humans get from making an effort to achieve a task will be lost, and that will make us unhappy. Seventy percent of Americans are already expressing concerns about automation
30 and the effect it will have on their lives. That figure probably will not change **until people are confident that their jobs will be secure**.

Although companies will save a lot of money by using the new technologies, one study
35 suggests that by the 2030s, about one job in five **will have been put** at risk from automation. However, estimates are not always reliable, so we watch and wait to find out.

---

[1]**eliminate:** remove or take away

2 Future Time Clauses

Grammar Presentation

Future time clauses show the order of future events.	*After people* **buy** *our phones, we'll* **use** *drones to deliver them.* *We're going to* **research** *robots before we* **choose** *one.*

2.1 Using Time Clauses for Future Events

A Use the simple present in the time clause. Use the future with *will* or *be going to* in the main clause.	*After I* **buy** *my new phone, I'll* **use** *the cloud to store my data.* *We're going to* **research** *cloud services before we* **choose** *one.*
You can also use the present perfect in the time clause to emphasize the completion of the event.	*Until business* **has improved***, the company won't hire new employees.*
B Use time clauses with *after, as soon as, once,* and *when* when the event in the time clause happens first.	FIRST EVENT *As soon as / Once they use automation, their* SECOND EVENT *business will improve.* SECOND EVENT FIRST EVENT *I'll find a good job after I graduate.*
C Use time clauses with *before* and *until* when the event in the time clause happens second.	FIRST EVENT SECOND EVENT *I'll finish the report before I leave.*
Use *until* to show when the event in the main clause will stop or change.	 *continue working* *call* *I'll continue working on the report until she calls.*
In time clauses with *not … until,* the action in the time clause happens first.	SECOND EVENT *We won't start using the software until all* FIRST EVENT *employees are trained.*
D The time clause can come first or last in the sentence. Use a comma when the time clause comes first.	*Once we start using automation, we'll save money.* *She is going to move as soon as she finds a better job.*

2.2 Using Time Clauses with *When* and *While* for Ongoing Events

A Use *when* or *while* with the simple present in the time clause and *will* or *be going to* in the main clause to show two events that are happening at the same time.	*I'll be taking* my vacation *while* the company *moves* to its new office.
You can also use the present progressive in the time clause to express an ongoing event.	*The staff is going to wait* outside *while / when* we're *discussing* our budget.
B Use the simple present in the *when* clause to interrupt an ongoing event in the main clause.	*We'll be meeting when he arrives.* (The meeting will be happening. He will arrive during the meeting.)

Grammar Application

Exercise 2.1 Using Future Time Clauses

A Read the sentences about automation. Underline the time clauses, and circle the conjunctions in each clause. Double underline the main clauses.

1 (Once) a company starts using automation, <u>it will serve more customers</u>.

2 Companies will start saving a great deal of money as soon as they move to automation.

3 Companies are going to have difficulty competing until they begin to use bots and robots.

4 After companies have moved to automation, they will receive technological support and updates on new technology.

5 Once people believe that their jobs are secure, they are going to feel less anxious about automation.

B Complete the sentences from a meeting about automation. Circle the correct form of the verbs.

1 I think we **are going to attract** / **attract** more international customers once we **are going to start** / **start** using automation.

2 I'm concerned that our jobs **will not be / is** safe once we **begin / will begin** to use automation.

3 As soon as our company **will start / starts** using automation, we **are going to save / save** a lot of money. We will be able to eliminate our production department.

4 We **are going to save / have saved** up to $50,000 annually after we **will change / have changed** to using robots.

5 I'm pretty worried that the company **isn't going to save / hasn't saved** money until automation **will become / becomes** more reliable.

6 As soon as the company marketing department **will develop / has developed** faster drones, we **have / will have** better delivery services.

7 We **won't approve / approve** using drones until the manager **has approved / will approve** the budget.

Complete the conversation about social networking in advertising. Use the correct form of the verbs in parentheses. Sometimes more than one answer is possible.

Erin OK, everyone. We're going to have to find cheaper ways to market our products.

Bo I'm sure that while we *'re discussing* (discuss) the new budget next week, we'll
(1)
think of some inexpensive ways to market our products.

Erin We need to use social networking sites more than we do now.

Bo I agree. Let's prepare a presentation. Lisa can write some descriptions of our new

products. I'll do research on the most popular social networking sites while you

_____ (find) the budget figures.
(2)

Erin Sounds good. While we _____ (do) that, the art department will work
(3)
on some drawings for our profile page.

Bo OK. I'll investigate how other food companies market themselves on social

networking sites while the art department _____ (work) on
(4)
the drawings.

Erin Look for Dan's Imported Food. That's our biggest competitor.

Bo Right. I'm sure that when I _____ (study) Dan's page, I'll get some
(5)
good ideas. I'll take notes while I _____ (look) at it.
(6)

Erin While you _____ (analyze) Dan's page, I'll think about how we can use
(7)
apps for marketing as well.

Bo Great idea. While you _____ (think) about apps, I'll get some
(8)
information on the impact promotions can have.

Erin Good plan! Let's get moving!

Exercise 2.3 Time Clauses with *When*

Look at Jared's meeting agenda. Then complete the sentences about what is going to happen. Pay close attention to the sequence of events. Use *will* or the future progressive of the verbs in parentheses. Sometimes there is more than one correct answer.

August 23

8:00–8:20	Introduce new employees
8:15	Sara arrives; introduce Sara
8:20–10:00	Brainstorm for new budget
10:00–10:20	Take break
10:00	Print worksheets
10:20	Return from break; hand out worksheets; put everyone into small groups
10:20–11:30	Small-group discussions; walk around and take notes
11:30	Vice president arrives; reassemble group

1 I *will be introducing* (introduce) the new employees when Sara arrives.

2 When Sara arrives, I _____ (introduce) her.

3 I _____ (print) the worksheets when the group takes a break.

4 I _____ (hand out) the worksheets when the group returns from the break.

5 When people return from the break, I _____ (put) them into small groups.

6 When people work in small groups, I _____ (walk) around and _____ (take) notes.

7 When the vice president arrives, the groups _____ (finish) their discussions.

8 I _____ (reassemble) the group when the vice president arrives.

A Combine the sentences from Marta and Aaron's "to-do" list. Note that *M* is Marta and *A* is Aaron. Use *after, until,* or *when* with the present perfect in the time clauses. Sometimes more than one answer is possible.

1 Jan.–Feb. (M & A): Research and plan the business
 Mar. (M): Get a loan

 After Marta and Aaron have researched and planned the business, Marta
 will get a loan./Marta will get a loan after Marta and Aaron have
 researched and planned the business.

2 Mar.–Apr. (M & A): Get business training
 May–Jun. (M & A): Get management training

3 Apr. (A): Think of a name for the business
 May (M): Find a location for the business

4 Sept. (M): Get a tax identification number
 Oct. (M & A): Buy equipment for the business

5 Nov. (M & A): Promote the business
 Dec. (M & A): Open the business

6 First week of Dec. (M & A): Have a sale
 Dec. 25–31: Close for one week

B Pair Work Compare your sentences with a partner. What are some different ways to express the same ideas?

 A *I wrote "After Marta and Aaron have done some research, they will get a loan."*
 B *I wrote "Marta and Aaron won't get a loan until they have done some research."*

3 Future Perfect vs. Future Perfect Progressive

Grammar Presentation

The future perfect is used to describe events that will be completed at a time in the future. The future perfect progressive describes events that will be in progress at a time in the future. These forms are much more common in speaking than in academic writing.

By 2025, many companies *will have eliminated* some of their employees' jobs.

By 2025, our company *will have been using* bots for ten years.

3.1 Forming Future Perfect

Form the future perfect with *will + have* + the past participle of the main verb. Form the negative by putting *not* between *will* and *have*, or use *won't have*.

By May, we *will have opened* the new office.

Will the team *have finished* the project by next week?

By next week, the team *won't have finished* the project.

3.2 Forming Future Perfect Progressive

Form the future perfect progressive with *will + have + been* + the *-ing* form of the main verb. Form the negative by putting *not* between *will* and *have*, or use *won't have*.

By May, I *will have been working* here for a year.

How long *will you have been working* here by next month?

We *won't have been working* here for very long.

3.3 Future Perfect and Future Perfect Progressive Contrasted

A Use the future perfect for an event that will be completed by a time in the future.

I will have made my decision before tomorrow.

Will she *have told* you her decision by noon?

B Use the future perfect progressive for an event that will be in progress at a time in the future.

How long *will he have been working* in the computer industry on his fortieth birthday?

C You can introduce a particular future time with a preposition such as *before* and *by* (*by that time, by then*) or a time clause in the simple present.	*He'll have been working* for us for 10 years <u>by next June</u>. *They just moved to Dallas, so they won't have been living there long <u>when you visit next month</u>.*
You can use *already* to express certainty about future situations.	*We can't change the plan. The managers will <u>already</u> have had their meeting by Monday.* *They'll have <u>already</u> made a decision by the time we get there.*
D Use the future perfect, not the future perfect progressive, with stative verbs such as *have, hear,* and *know*.	*She will have known about it by then.* NOT *She ~~will have been knowing~~ about it by then.*

Grammar Application

Exercise 3.1 Future Perfect

Look at the schedules. Then complete the sentences with the future perfect. Use the negative when necessary.

> 10:45 a.m.: Katie will finish the report.
> 11:00 a.m.: The meeting will start.
> 11:15 a.m.: Kyle will arrive.

1 Katie __*will have finished the report*__ by the time Kyle arrives.

2 The meeting _____ by the time Kyle arrives.

3 By 11:00, Kyle _____ .

> 12:30 p.m.: The meeting will end.
> 1:30 p.m.: Kyle and Katie will go out to eat lunch.
> 2:30 p.m.: Kyle and Katie will return from lunch.

4 By 12:40, the meeting _____ .

5 By 1:40, Kyle and Katie _____ .

6 By 2:15, Kyle and Katie _____ .

> 5:30 p.m.: Kyle's wife arrives home.
> 6:00 p.m.: Kyle leaves work.
> 7:30 p.m.: Kyle and his family will eat dinner.

7 Kyle's wife _____ before Kyle leaves work.

8 Kyle _____ by 6:15.

9 At 6:45, Kyle and his family _____ .

Future Perfect Progressive

Read Eric's work schedule. Then complete the sentences with the information in the schedule. Use the future perfect progressive and *for*.

Tuesday	Wednesday	Thursday–Friday
8:30: Be at work 12:00: Lunch meeting with Mark at restaurant 1:00–4:00: Discuss new project 5:00: Meet with Japanese tutor; cancel tutoring sessions for Wed.– Fri. 6:15–7:15: Call from Japan	8:00: Pick up laptop from IT 9:00–5:00: Attend software training; bring lunch from home	9:00–5:00: Attend software training; bring lunch from home 6:00–8:00: Work out at the gym

1 By 4:30 on Tuesday, Eric / work / hours

By 4:30 on Tuesday, Eric will have been working for eight hours.

2 By 4:00 on Tuesday, Eric / discuss the new project / hours

_____

3 By 6:45 on Tuesday, Eric / talk on the phone / hour

_____

4 By 4:00 on Wednesday, Eric / attend a software training / hours

_____

5 By 5:00 on Friday, Eric / attend a software training / days

_____

6 By 7:15 on Friday, Eric / work out at the gym / minutes

_____

A A company is making its building energy-efficient and healthier for its employees. Read the time line. Then listen to questions about the time line. Circle *Yes* or *No*.

February 2015 ○ Approve the building plans

March 2015 ○ Find a temporary site for workers

April 2015 ○ Move into the temporary site

May 2015 ○ Construction firm starts construction; installs solar heating system

October 2015 ○ Finish all construction; "green" interior designer arrives; install new workstations

February 2016 ○ Move back into the building

June 2016 ○ Water department inspects water quality

August 2016 ○ Send report on building improvements to finance department

March 2017 ○ New law starts that requires all buildings to have energy-saving features

August 2017 ○ OSHA[1] (Occupational Safety and Health Administration) visit

[1]**OSHA:** a U.S. government agency that inspects companies' workplaces to make sure that the companies follow health and safety laws

1	Yes	(No)	3	Yes	No	5	Yes	No	7	Yes	No
2	Yes	No	4	Yes	No	6	Yes	No	8	Yes	No

B Listen again and check your answers.

C Over to You Answer the questions. Then share your answers with a partner.

- What year will it be in two years?
- What will you have accomplished by that time?
- What will you have been doing until then?

4 Avoid Common Mistakes ⚠

1 **Use future forms in the main clause and present forms for the time clause.**

We will buy it after we ~~will~~ get back from our trip.

2 **Remember to use the future perfect when describing a future event that occurs before another future event.**

will have
They left by the time we get there, so we won't see them.
 ^

have moved
By that time, you will ~~move~~.

3 **Make sure you do not confuse the future perfect progressive with other forms.**

living
In June, we will have been ~~lived~~ in Texas for two years.

4 **Remember to use *will* when forming the future perfect.**

will
By this time next year, she have gotten a better job.
 ^

Editing Task

Find and correct seven more mistakes in the paragraph about the future of health care.

have changed
　　Experts say that in the next few years, the health-care industry will ~~change~~ in many ways because of technology and the Internet. I plan on working in this industry, so it is fascinating for me to know that by the time I graduate, the job market has changed dramatically. One change that interests me is in the doctor-

5　patient relationship. By that time, technology will empower patients because they will have been used the Internet to gather information and discuss information with others. Also, doctors will have been used smart medication for a few years, so the results of a patient's treatment will already be available to both the patient and the doctor. By the time a patient arrives for an appointment, the doctor and patient will

10　have been discussed many options. Also, when a patient will arrive at the office for his appointment, he will not have to fill out forms. The doctor have already seen the patient's information on screen. The whole health-care system will have improved, so more people will live in a state of good health.

1 Grammar in the Real World

A Have you ever forgotten something important? Read the article about memory improvement. Which memory-improvement technique do you think works best?

B Comprehension Check **Answer the questions.**

1 What must you do to remember something, according to Gini Graham Scott?
2 What is visualization?
3 What are some ways to exercise your brain?

C Notice **Find the sentences in the article and complete them.**

1 You _____ **give** a class presentation, and you are terrified.

2 You _____ **brought** your notes with you, but where are they?

3 Scott says that you _____ first **take in** information in order to save it in your memory.

Which sentences tell you it is necessary to do something?

How to Improve Your Memory

Some people have excellent memories, but most of us struggle to remember at times. You know the feeling: You **have to give** a class presentation, and you are terrified. As you wait your turn, you repeat the information over and over in your mind, but you keep forgetting a
5 key point. You **should have brought** your notes with you, but where are they? You **can't remember**. If you are more forgetful than you would like to be, you **might want to follow** the advice of memory-improvement experts. Whether you want to memorize a speech or simply remember where you left your cell phone, these experts offer
10 tips to jumpstart[1] your brain.

Gini Graham Scott, PhD, is the author of *30 Days to a More Powerful Memory*. She points out that if you want to remember something, it is necessary that you pay attention. You **must observe** what you want to learn. People often forget things simply because
15 they weren't concentrating. Scott says that you **have to** first **take in** information in order to save it in your memory. Other experts agree that visualization is an effective technique forgetful people **should try**. Create a mental picture – a picture in your mind – of what you want to remember. The more unusual the image, the easier it will be to recall.
20 For example, if you want to remember the due date for a final project, you **could visualize** that date flashing in bold colors on a giant television screen. The scene **has to be** unusual and animated for the memory to stick. Memory specialists agree that the more you exercise your brain, the better you will be able to remember information. How
25 can you give your brain a workout?[2] You **might want to tackle** the daily crossword puzzle. Changing a daily routine **is** also **supposed to work**. In addition, you **could challenge** your brain by writing with your nondominant[3] hand or by taking a different route to school or work.

In today's multitasking[4] world, a good memory is crucial. Without
30 it, you **cannot maintain** order and priorities in your life. Fortunately, there are remedies[5] for forgetfulness. Practice careful observance, creative visualization, and mental exercise to improve your memory.

---

[1]**jumpstart:** start something more quickly by giving it extra help

[2]**workout:** a period of exercise

[3]**nondominant:** not as important, strong, or noticeable

[4]**multitask:** work on several tasks at the same time

[5]**remedy:** a substance or method for curing an illness, or a way of dealing with a problem or difficulty

2 Modals and Modal-like Expressions of Advice and Regret

Grammar Presentation

The modals and modal-like expressions *could*, *had better*, *might*, *might want to*, *ought to*, and *should* can be used to express advice and regret.

You **should try** to improve your memory.
I **should have** followed your advice.

2.1 Modals and Modal-like Expressions of Present and Future Advice

A Use *could* and *might* to offer advice and suggestions or to give choices.	He **could do** some puzzles to improve his memory. You **might try** some tips for improving your memory.
Might (*not*) is often used with *want to* to give suggestions.	You **might not want to** start with the most difficult math problem. Try this one – it's easier.
B Use *should* to say something is a good idea. Use *shouldn't* to say something is a bad idea.	Greg **should improve** his memory. Kate **shouldn't spend** so much time doing crossword puzzles.
Ought to is also possible, but less common. *Ought not* (*to*) is rare.	We **ought to take** a memory class together.
C Use *had better* (*not*) only in informal conversation to give strong advice, especially as a warning.	You**'d better pay** attention now. (Or you will be in trouble.)
There is often a negative consequence if the advice or warning is not followed.	She **had better not forget** my book again tomorrow. (Or I will never lend her anything again.)
Had is almost always contracted, and often omitted, in informal conversation.	He**'d better** remember to bring his ID next time.

▶▶ Modals and Modal-like Expressions: See page A3.

2.2 Modals and Modal-like Expressions of Past Advice and Regret

A Use *ought to have* or *should have* + the past participle for past events or situations that were advisable but did not happen.	*She **ought to have been** at the lecture, but she was sick.* (Being at the lecture was a good idea, but she wasn't there.) *You **should have made** an effort to improve your memory.* (Improving your memory was a good idea, but you didn't do it.)
B Use *shouldn't have* + the past participle for past situations in which bad decisions were made. It is often used to express regret.	*He **shouldn't have taken** that difficult class.* (But he did, and now he's frustrated.) *We **shouldn't have listened** to him.* (But we did, and now we're sorry.)
C *Should (not) have* may be used to criticize.	*You **should have followed** his advice.* (But you didn't, and now look at the trouble you're in.)

Grammar Application

Exercise 2.1 Present and Future Advice

A Complete the class discussion about improving memory. Circle the correct words or expressions.

Ms. Yost So, let's review our discussion about improving memory. What advice do experts give students? Sara?

Sara You (should) /'d better not pay attention to what you're learning.
(1)

Ms. Yost Right. So, for example, what's one good way to pay attention?

Sara Um, you **'d better / could** take notes while you're reading.
(2)

Manuel Or you **might / 'd better** take notes during lectures.
(3)

Ms. Yost Right. Do you have any other advice?

Manuel I think students **'d better / shouldn't** use a computer to take notes.
(4)
They **might not / should** use a pen and a piece of paper.
(5)

Ms. Yost Good idea. In fact, studies show that writing information by hand – instead of using a keyboard – helps you remember it better.

B Pair work Compare your answers with a partner. Discuss the reason for each of your answers.

I use had better not *for warnings. This isn't a warning. It's advice. So I chose* should *in number 1.*

A Read the study tips from an article. Then complete the email to a friend. Use the tips and the modals in parentheses.

Study Tips

1 Try visualizing to remember dates and names.

2 Read your textbook two or three times.

3 Try teaching someone else the material.

4 Don't wait until the last minute to study.

5 Get plenty of sleep before a test.

Hi _____ ,

    I know you're having trouble studying for tests. I just read some study tips online. Here's some advice:

1 (could) *You could try visualizing to remember dates and names.*

2 (ought to) _____

3 (might) _____

4 (should not) _____

5 (had better) _____

I hope this helps! Talk to you soon.

Best,

_____

B Pair Work Tell a partner which tips you use. Then think of two more study tips and share them with another pair.

A Complete the conversation about Phoebe, a student who plagiarized. Use the correct form of the words in parentheses.

Jake   What happened to Phoebe? I heard she left college.

Sofia   She committed plagiarism. She really ___*shouldn't have copied*___ those articles
                                                (1 not / should / copy)
    from the Internet.

Jake   I know. She _____
(2 should / take)
notes on the web articles. Then she

_____
(3 ought to / summarize)
her notes.

Sofia   You're right. She

_____ credit
(4 should / give)
to the sources of the ideas, too. Why do you

think she did that, anyway?

Jake   Maybe she was under pressure or waited too

long to start her paper. She _____ earlier.
(5 ought to / start)

Sofia   I agree. She _____ until the last minute.
(6 should / not / wait)

Jake   Or she _____ to the teacher if she was having
(7 should / talk)
problems. Maybe we _____ her.
(8 should / help)

Sofia   Yes, let's try to be more helpful the next time a classmate is stressed!

B Pair Work   Compare your answers with a partner. Do you agree with the students' advice about Phoebe? What other advice would you give Phoebe?

C Group Work   Think about a time when you made a decision you regret, or a time when a friend made a bad decision. What should you (or your friend) have done to make the situation better? Write five sentences with *should not have* + the past participle.

3 Modals and Modal-like Expressions of Permission, Necessity, and Obligation

Grammar Presentation

The modals and modal-like expressions *be allowed to, be required to, be supposed to, can, have to,* and *may* are used to express permission, necessity, and obligation in the present, past, and future.	We **weren't supposed to see** the answers for the memory test. They **will have to take** the test again. Students **may not take** the memory improvement class more than once.

3.1 Modals and Modal-like Expressions of Permission

A Use *can (not)* and *may (not)* to talk about permission in the present and future.	Students **can register** for the class now.
	You **may wait** until next week to register.
	I **can't miss** more than two classes.
	You **may not join** after the first class.
Use *could (not)* as the past form of *can (not)*.	We **could ask** questions at the end of the lecture, but we **couldn't interrupt** the lecture.
B You can also use *be (not) allowed to* for permission in the present, past, and future. For the future, add *will* before *be (not) allowed to*.	We **aren't allowed to talk** during the test. He **was allowed to talk** during the test, but he **was not allowed to use** his books. They **will be allowed to use** their notes tomorrow. She **won't be allowed to use** her notes.
You can use *permitted* instead of *allowed* in formal speech and writing.	Students **are not permitted to refer** to notes during examinations.

3.2 Modals and Modal-like Expressions of Necessity and Obligation

A Use *be required to*, *be supposed to*, *have to*, *must*, and *need to* to express necessity or obligation in the present and future. *Must* and *be required to* are more formal and are not often used in speaking.	You **are required to take** the class. Teachers **are supposed to hand out** the syllabus on the first day of class. Everyone **is required to work** hard. Applicants **must have** experience for this job.
Use *will be required to*, *will have to*, and *will need to* for future time.	You **will need to write** an essay for this course.
B Use *be not supposed to* or *must not* for the present and future to say that something is inappropriate or to express prohibition.	Students **are not supposed to take** their books into the exam room. (It is inappropriate.) You **must not talk** during the exam. (There is no choice.)
C Use *were required to*, *were supposed to*, or *had to* to describe necessity and obligation in the past.	The applicant **was required to take** a test. I **was supposed to stay** after class last week. We **had to arrive** at 7:00 a.m. for the exam.
There is no past form of *must*. Use *had to* instead.	He **had to reschedule** his exam yesterday. NOT He ~~must~~ reschedule his exam yesterday.

3.2 Modals and Modal-like Expressions of Necessity and Obligation *(continued)*

D The negative forms of *be required to, have to,* and *need to* describe choices or options.	*You **are not required to show** your ID.* (It is optional.) *You **didn't have to remain** in the exam room after you finished.* (It was your choice.) *Students **won't need to bring** their own pencils next time.* (It will be your choice.)

Grammar Application

Exercise 3.1 Present and Future Permission

A Complete the rules for a college Spanish class. Use the present or future form of the words in parentheses. Sometimes more than one answer is possible.

SPANISH 101 *CLASSROOM RULES*

DICTIONARIES

Students ___*can bring*___ monolingual dictionaries along to class, but they _____
        (1 can / bring)   (2 not / may / use)

any bilingual dictionaries at all. Students _____ print dictionaries during tests.
                                               (3 can / use)

However, they _____ online dictionaries during tests.
                      (4 not / be allowed to / access)

LAPTOPS

You _____ laptop computers to class for note taking only.
                (5 be allowed to / bring)

You _____ laptops for Internet searches during class.
           (6 not / must / use)

COMPUTER LAB

Students _____ the lab until they have purchased the book.
              (7 not / may / use)

B Rewrite the sentences about the students in the Spanish class. Use the rules in A and the correct form of the words in parentheses.

1 Emily wants to bring a bilingual dictionary to class. (be permitted to)

   She isn't permitted to bring a bilingual dictionary to class.

2 Eric wants to use an online dictionary during a test. (be allowed to)

   _____

3 Ann wants to use a print dictionary during tests. (may)

   _____

4 Maria wants to bring a laptop to class. (can)

_____

5 James wants to check his email on his laptop during class. (be permitted to)

_____

6 David hasn't bought the textbook yet. He wants to go to the lab. (can)

_____

Exercise 3.2 Past Permission

A Complete the conversation about classroom rules. Use the correct past form of the words in parentheses.

Ming   Last semester, I ___*could bring*___ a monolingual dictionary to class.
                             (1 can / bring)

Danielle   Yes, but you _____ it during tests.
                            (2 not / can / use)

Ming   That's right. And we _____ laptops to class,
                            (3 be permitted to / bring)
   but we _____ the Internet during class.
                 (4 not / be allowed to / search)

Danielle   No, but we _____ on the Internet in the
                      (5 be allowed to / go)
   computer lab after we finished our work.

Ming   _____ we _____ our own language at all during
     (6)   (6 be allowed to / speak)
   English class? I can't remember.

Danielle   No. We _____ that. We even had to ask
                 (7 not / be allowed to / do)
   our classmates questions in English.

B Over to You   Think about a test or exam you took in the past. What could or couldn't you do? Write five sentences with *could (not)*, *(not) be allowed to*, or *(not) be permitted to*. Then share your sentences with a partner.

Exercise 3.3 Present and Future Necessity and Obligation

Read the teacher's classroom rules and suggestions. Then rewrite the rules with the words in parentheses. Use the negative when necessary.

1 Read articles in English every day. It is an option. (have to)

   You don't have to read articles in English every day.

2 Don't be afraid to ask questions in class. (must)

_____

3 Turn in all your homework. I expect this. (be supposed to)

_____

4 Bring a flash drive next week. (must)

_____

5 Write an essay at the end of the semester. (be required to)

_____

6 Don't text during class. I expect this. (be supposed to)

_____

7 Send your writing assignments by email. It is an option. (need to)

_____

Exercise 3.4 More Present and Future Necessity and Obligation

A Listen to the psychology department announcement about a memory study. Circle *S* if the meaning of the sentence you read is the same as the one you hear. Circle *D* if the meaning of the sentence you read is different from the one you hear.

1 Ⓢ D   Participants must attend two sessions.

2 S D   Sessions are not supposed to take more than one hour.

3 S D   Participants are not supposed to be younger than 18 years of age.

4 S D   Each participant must not have poor vision.

5 S D   Each participant is supposed to have normal hearing.

6 S D   Participants do not have to speak Mandarin.

7 S D   Participants are required to be students at the university.

8 S D   Participants must email the researcher by July 31.

B Listen again and check your answers.

Exercise 3.5 Past Necessity and Obligation

A Complete the story about an older person's learning experience. Use the correct forms of the words in parentheses.

When my grandmother was in high school, she ___*had to follow*___ a lot of rules
                                              (1 have to / follow)
and regulations, and she _____ very hard. There
                                (2 have to / work)
were no computers, so she _____ notes by hand. She
                                    (3 have to / take)
_____ hundreds of textbook pages a week and write
        (4 be required to / read)
several papers each semester. She _____ any classes.
                                        (5 not / be supposed to / miss)
She _____ class every day in order to pass. Of course,
        (6 have to / attend)
there was no Internet then, so she _____ to the library
                                            (7 have to / go)
to do research. High school in her time was very different from how it is today!

B Over to You Write five sentences about some rules and regulations that you remember in a learning environment in the past, for example, in another school you attended. Share your sentences with a partner and discuss this question: How did the rules and regulations help you to learn?

4 Modals and Modal-like Expressions of Ability

Grammar Presentation

The modals *be able to* and *can* are used to express ability in the present, past, and future.	*I couldn't remember anything the professor said.* *I won't be able to pass the test.* *She can remember dates well.*

4.1 Modals and Modal-like Expressions of Present and Future Ability

A Use *be able to* and *can* to describe ability in the present.	*I am able to remember faces well, and I can usually remember names as well.*
Use *be not able to* and *can't / cannot* for negative statements in the present. *Be not able to* is more formal than *can't*.	*He isn't able to meet us today.*
B Use *can* and *will be able to* to describe ability in the future.	*We can meet the professor at noon tomorrow.* *He will be able to see us then.*
Use *can't* and *will not / won't be able to* for negative statements in the future. Notice that *not* comes before *be* in the future form.	*I can't go to the lecture on Friday.* *We won't be able to take the memory test until next month.*

4.2 Modals and Modal-like Expressions of Past Ability

A Use *could (not)* to describe general ability in the past. *Was / were (not) able to* is also possible, especially to talk about a particular ability or talent.	*When I was younger, I could be very persuasive.* *I could understand the lecture, but I couldn't remember all of the information.* *She was able to read by the time she was four.*

4.2 Modals and Modal-like Expressions of Past Ability (continued)

Use *was/were able to*, not *could*, to describe ability on a particular occasion in the past.	*Once, I was able to convince my friend to memorize 100 new words in a week.* NOT *Once, I ~~could~~ convince my friend to memorize 100 new words in a week.*
B Use *could have* + the past participle to describe situations in which a person had the ability to do something but did not do it.	*I could have taken the memory test last Saturday, but I didn't sign up for it.*
Use *couldn't have* + the past participle to describe situations in which a person didn't have the ability to do something.	*Eric couldn't have known the answer to that question. He didn't study at all.*

Grammar Application

Exercise 4.1 Past, Present, and Future Ability

Complete the story about memory loss. Use the past, present, or future form of the words in parentheses.

A few years ago, Alicia was a successful physician. She was very popular with her

patients because she ___could diagnose___ their problems quickly and accurately.
(1 can / diagnose)

Alicia's favorite pastime was riding her bike. She _____
(2 can / ride)

her mountain bike for hours in the hills around her town. Then one day last year, a

car came up behind Alicia while she was riding on a narrow road, and it hit her. The

accident caused a serious brain injury, even though she was wearing a helmet.

Alicia is in full-time therapy now. Today, she _____
(3 be able to / do)

many things. However, when she finishes therapy, she _____
(4 not / be able to / return)

to her old job because of her memory loss. Therefore, Alicia is planning to help other

people with her condition. Once Alicia is ready, she _____ of
(5 be able to / take care)

other patients.

Complete the sentences about Diana. Use *could have* and the correct form of the verbs in parentheses.

1 Diana had an accident like Alicia's. She was riding a bike in the hills when a car hit her. The driver ___*could have avoided*___ (avoid) hitting her, but he was driving too fast.

2 She went to a doctor, but he didn't think her injuries were serious. Diana didn't think the doctor _____ (make) a mistake about her diagnosis.[1]

3 Diana went to work after the accident, and her behavior seemed normal. Her co-workers _____ (not/imagine) that she had a brain injury.

4 The first clue that Diana was not well was when she went to a nearby store. She forgot how to get home. A neighbor had to help her. She _____ (not/remember) the way without help.

5 Finally, Diana found a specialist, Dr. Lee, who diagnosed her correctly and helped her get a service dog. Diana probably _____ (manage) fine by herself, but she was very thankful for the service dog because it made her life easier. Now she is in a memory rehabilitation program and doing well.

[1]**diagnosis:** when a doctor says what is wrong with someone who is ill

5 Avoid Common Mistakes ⚠

1 **When talking about advice and regret in the past, remember to use *have* + the past participle after a modal, not the simple past form of the verb.**

have
I should ⌃ remembered her name, but I didn't expect her to be at the party, and I got confused.

2 **Remember to use a form of *be* in *be allowed to* and *be supposed to*.**

was
The president ⌃ supposed to attend the 2 o'clock meeting, but he didn't show up.

3 **Use *did not have to* when talking about a choice in the past.**

did not have to email
I ~~must not have emailed~~ the office manager, but I wanted to be sure he was aware of the problem.

Editing Task

Find and correct six more mistakes in the paragraphs about multitasking.

is
Technology ⌃ supposed to simplify life; however, in reality, it has led to people trying to do too many things at once. One example is driving while texting or talking on a phone. After an accident, drivers who are caught by the police admit that they should turned off their phones when they got in the car, but they did not. They must

5 not have called someone while driving, but they did.

Another issue is multitasking in the classroom. Many of my teachers have had a difficult time dealing with students who search the Internet while listening to lectures. One of my instructors said he ought to required a password last semester to log onto the Internet during class. Students must not have gone online, but they sometimes

10 checked email or visited websites instead of listening to the lecture. As a result, students were often distracted.

In contrast, my friend had an instructor who had the opposite view. My friend did not worry about taking notes because students not allowed to – even on paper! The professor thought all note taking was a form of multitasking; instead, he handed

15 out worksheets with highlights of his lecture. At the end of the semester, some students complained. They argued that the professor should not banned computers in class because students today are used to multitasking.

Modals of Probability: Present, Future, and Past

Computers and Crime

1 Grammar in the Real World

A How do you protect personal information like computer passwords? Read the article about hacking. What are some ways to prevent hackers from stealing personal information?

B Comprehension Check **Answer the questions.**

1 What age are many hackers?

2 What information do some hackers steal?

3 Is anyone's computer completely safe from hackers?

C Notice **Read the sentences. Check (✓) the box next to each sentence to show if the action or situation is possible or very certain.**

	Possible	Very Certain
1 Cyber hacking **can** happen to anyone.	☐	☐
2 In fact, it **might be** too easy.	☐	☐
3 There are other hackers who **must have** more malicious intentions because they steal credit card numbers and other personal information.	☐	☐
4 In short, if you act safely and responsibly, hackers **will** likely **have** a hard time breaking into your computer.	☐	☐

Which bold words in the sentences tell you that an action or situation is possible?

HACKING:
A Computer Crime on the RISE

Cyber[1] hacking **may be** the most common computer crime today. Cyber hacking occurs when a person accesses someone else's computer without permission and steals information. It **can happen** to anyone. It **might** even **have happened** to someone you know.

5   The truth is that hacking is not difficult to learn. In fact, it **might be** too easy. Young adults tend to be skilled at using computers, so it **may not be** surprising to learn that a large number of computer hackers are teenagers. They **might hack** into other computers for the challenge – to see if they can do it and get away with it.

10 There are other hackers, however, who **must have** more malicious[2] intentions because they steal credit card numbers and other personal information.

     Severe[3] penalties for these cyber crimes **should have stopped** hacking by now, but they have had little effect. It does not look like

15 cyber hacking **will go** away anytime soon. For protection against hacking, anyone who uses a computer or other technological device **should be** aware of hackers and **should be using** antivirus software. Another safety measure is to use complex[4] passwords, which **could prevent** attacks from being successful.

20   In short, if you act safely and responsibly, hackers **will** likely **have** a hard time breaking into your computer. However, even these safety measures cannot guarantee that your information is safe.

[1]**cyber:** related to computers

[2]**malicious:** intended to harm or upset other people

[3]**severe:** extreme

[4]**complex:** having many connected parts, making it difficult to understand

2 Modals of Present Probability

Grammar Presentation

Modals of present probability are used to express how likely it is that something is happening now.	Your computer **may be** at risk of being hacked. He **must not be** worried about data security.

2.1 Modals of Present Probability

A Choose a modal depending on how certain you feel about something.

most certain	*can't, couldn't, have to, must (not)*
certain	*ought to, should (not)*
least certain	*could, may (not), might (not)*

Hackers **can't be** interested in my data.

Your password **must not be** secure.

Antivirus software **should protect** you.

It **shouldn't be** difficult to find good software.

Good antivirus software **could cost** a lot.

That software **might not be** good enough.

B Use *can't* and *couldn't* when you are almost certain something is not likely or not possible.

He **can't be** online now. His computer is broken.

Meg **couldn't be shopping** for a new laptop. Her old computer works perfectly.

You can also use *can't* and *couldn't* to express disbelief or surprise.

Your brand-new computer is broken? You **can't be** serious!

C Use *have to* and *must (not)* when you are mostly certain or when you think there is only one logical conclusion.

As a lawyer, he **has to know** that hacking into computers is illegal!

Large companies **must worry** about the security of their data.

In formal speaking and writing, *must* is much more common than *have to*.

People without antivirus software **must believe** they are not at risk.

D Use *ought to* and *should* (not) when you have an expectation based on experience or evidence. *Should* is more common than *ought to*. *Ought not to* is rare.

That computer **should be** available in the store because I saw it on the store's website.

You **shouldn't have** trouble figuring out my password because it's an easy one.

E Use *could, may (not)*, and *might (not)* when you are unsure or when you don't have much evidence.

I **could have** a virus on my computer because it isn't working normally.

I **might not buy** a new computer this year because my old one still works fine.

▸▸ Modals and Modal-like Expressions: See page A3.

Grammar Application

A Complete the interview about hacking. Use the correct modals and the information in parentheses to help you. Sometimes more than one answer is possible.

Jason Today we are asking people: How secure is your computer or smartphone? Could you be the victim of a hacker?

Emily It's impossible. Hackers _can't/couldn't_ (1) be interested in my computer. I don't have anything valuable on it. **(impossible)**

Jason But you _____ (2) have some valuable information on your computer. Everyone does. **(a logical conclusion)**

Emily What do you mean?

Jason I'm sure you've bought things online at some point. Your credit card information _____ (3) be on your computer. **(a logical conclusion)**

Carlos Well, I'm certain that my phone is safe. It _____ (4) be of interest to anyone, especially a hacker. **(unlikely)**

Jason Oh, you _____ (5) have GPS – global positioning software – on your phone, then. Because if you did, you'd feel differently. **(a logical conclusion)**

Carlos But I *do* have GPS on my phone . . .

Jason Well, that _____ (6) make you a little less sure, then, because GPS is one of the things that hackers are interested in. It lets them see where you go every day. **(expectation based on evidence)**

Carlos My GPS? That _____ (7) be true! **(surprise)**

Belén You know, my computer _____ (8) be of interest to a hacker for some reason, I guess. **(unsure)**

Jason I'm afraid that's true.

B Pair Work Compare your answers with a partner. Take turns saying the sentences with other modals that have the same meaning.

Hackers can't be interested in my computer.

Exercise 2.2 More Present Probability

A Over to You Read the statements. Then respond with information that is true for you. Use modals of present probability to show how certain you feel that the statements are true for you. Explain why.

1 A person can hack into your computer or smartphone at any time.

   That can't be true. I have excellent security software.

2 It is very likely that a thief will steal your identity.

   _____

3 Your credit card number is not safe.

   _____

4 Your home is very safe. It's unlikely that a burglar can enter and take valuable items from you.

   _____

5 The downtown area of your city or town is dangerous at night. It's a bad idea to walk there alone at night.

   _____

6 It's very safe for children to walk to school alone in your neighborhood.

   _____

B Pair Work Take turns asking questions about each other's statements.

You say that it can't be true that a person can hack into your computer because you have good security, but good security is sometimes not enough. For example, banks tend to have good security, but hackers get into their computers.

3 Modals of Future Probability

Grammar Presentation

Modals of future probability with *could, may, might, ought to, should,* and *will* express the probability of something happening in the future.	Your new computer **should be** here next week. I **won't buy** a new computer next year because my current one is still fairly new.

3.1 Modals of Future Probability

A Choose a modal depending on how certain you are about something.

most certain	*will (not)*
certain	*should (not), ought to*
least certain	*may (not), might (not), could*

Hackers **will be** interested in our company's financial data.

Our new website **should be** ready by next week.

The secure web page **ought to be** available soon.

She **could learn** a lot about Internet security in her course next month.

B Use *will* and *won't* to express strong certainty.

The company **will hire** very few people this year.

You can add words like *probably* and *likely* to weaken the certainty.

The company <u>probably</u> **won't hire** any students.

C Use *should (not)* and *ought to* when you have an expectation based on experience or evidence.

The software **should be** ready by Friday. (Because it is almost ready now.)

We **shouldn't expect** new passwords until Monday. (Because it usually takes a few days.)

D Use *could*, *may (not)*, and *might (not)* when you are unsure or when you don't have much evidence.

The company **could start** storing personal data as early as next month.

A manager **might join** us next week.

You can also use these modals with a progressive form of the verb.

The class **may be** <u>starting</u> soon. There are a lot of students in the room.

Grammar Application

Exercise 3.1 Future Probability

A Complete the ad with *will* and the verbs in parentheses.

I-SAFE HOME SECURITY SYSTEM

The home of the future ___*will be*___ (be) safer. Homeowners _____ (be) able to control everything in the home with the new I-safe Home Security System.
(1)
(2)

Here are just a few of I-SAFE's features:

▶ You _____ (not/need) to worry about the new nanny. I-safe
    (3)
_____ (let) parents use their computers or smartphones at work to watch
    (4)
the nanny.

▶ I-safe _____ (allow) you to control appliances and heating and cooling systems
    (5)
from wherever you are.

▶ I-safe _____ (lock) the doors to your home for you.
    (6)

▶ The I-safe Home Security System _____ (be) available this spring.
    (7)

B Complete the conversation about the I-safe. The speakers are not very certain about the claims in the ad. Circle the correct words.

| Customer | Are you going to sell the I-safe system next spring? |

| Sales clerk | It **will likely**/ will be available next spring, but the manager isn't sure. |
    (1)

| Customer | Can I use the I-safe to control the TV from my smartphone? |

| Sales clerk | You **will/should** be able to control the TV, but I'm not really sure. |
    (2)

| Customer | I have a nanny. If I install I-safe cameras to watch her from time to time, she **should/may not** be happy about being on camera. |
    (3)

| Sales clerk | You're right, there **shouldn't/could** be some concerns about privacy. |
    (4)

| Customer | I use a tablet while I commute to work on the train. I haven't read anything about using the I-safe with my tablet. I-safe probably **won't/shouldn't** work with it, right? |
    (5)

| Sales clerk | I'm not quite sure, but it **ought to/will** send images to your tablet. |
    (6)

| Customer | OK. Thanks for your help. |

C Pair Work Imagine that the I-safe company is going to give away its product for free for one month. Will you get an I-safe? Why or why not? Use modals in your answers.

A *I probably won't get an I-safe because I'm not very worried about home security.*
B *I might get one. I'm not sure because there could be some privacy issues with it.*

Exercise 3.2 More Future Probability

A Listen to the conversations about future probability. Write the missing words.

Conversation 1

Anne   Someone broke into the Lees' apartment, and now they're moving.

Martín   That's awful. Where are they going to go?

Anne   I'm not sure. ___*They'll*___ probably move to the suburbs.
               (1)

Martín   But Joe Lee has a good job here in the city. _____ be able to
                                               (2)
move very far away.

Anne   I know. And the children are in school in the city. _____ want to
                                             (3)
change schools.

Martín   Well, I wish them luck.

Conversation 2

Truong   I spoke with Andrew Martinez yesterday. Guess what? _____ buy
                                             (4)
a home security system.

Ben   I know. We went to a home security show last week. He liked the system with
the cameras that send images to your phone. _____ be the
                                         (5)
system he's going to buy.

Truong   _____ learn a lot from Andrew when he puts in his system.
               (6)

Conversation 3

Reporter   The airport commissioner announced today that Bay City Airport will start
using cameras with sensors that will detect heart rate and body temperature.
_____ be ready by next year.
               (7)

Josh   I read about the cameras online as well. In fact, I heard that _____
                                                    (8)
start using the cameras by the end of this year.

Katie   _____ be interesting to see what happens.
               (9)

B Listen again and check your answers.

4 Modals of Past Probability

Grammar Presentation

Modals of past probability with *can*, *could*, *may*, *might*, and *must* are used to make inferences or guesses about the past.	A hacker **couldn't have accessed** this computer! I have the best protection available. A hacker **might have found** a way to break into it.

4.1 Forming Modals of Past Probability

Form modals of past probability with modal + *have* + the past participle of the main verb. Form the negative by putting *not* between the modal and *have*. Only use contractions with *could* and *can*.	The company **may have been** careless with security. I **must not have turned off** my phone. She **could have changed** her password, but I'm not sure. It **couldn't have been** Joe's fault. He wasn't here.

4.2 Using Modals of Past Probability

A Choose a modal depending on how certain you are that something happened. most certain — *couldn't, can't* certain — *must (not)* least certain — *may (not), might (not), could*	You **couldn't have chosen** a strong password. Kim guessed it immediately! Someone **must have stolen** all the passwords because hackers have gotten into every computer. The computer **may not have had** strong antivirus software because it was older.
B Use *can't have* or *couldn't have* when you are absolutely certain something was impossible or unlikely.	I **can't have entered** the wrong password! I've had the same one forever. He **couldn't have hacked** our computers. He doesn't know how.
C Use *must (not) have* when you feel certain about something or when you believe there is only one logical conclusion.	I **must not have written** the password down. I can't find it anywhere. You **must have received** the security email. Ms. Liu sent it to everyone.
D Use *could have*, *may (not) have*, or *might (not) have* when there isn't much evidence or when you are guessing.	He **may not have followed** the security advice because he didn't believe it was important. He **might have changed** his password. I don't think he is still using his old one.

Data from the Real World

May (not) have, could (not) have, and might (not) have are the most common modals used for speculating about the past in speaking and writing. Must (not) have is less common. Cannot/can't have is relatively rare.

may (not) have	████████████████
could (not) have	███████████████
might (not) have	██████████
must (not) have	████
cannot/can't have	█

Grammar Application

Exercise 4.1 Past Probability

Complete the article about credit card fraud. Use the correct form of the words in parentheses.

CREDIT CARD FRAUD: How Does It Happen?

There was a $10,000 charge from a jewelry store on Claudia's credit card statement.

She didn't buy any jewelry, so someone ___*must have stolen*___ her credit card number.
(1 must / steal)

Claudia said, "I _____ the victim of credit card theft."
(2 not / could / be)

However, someone obviously _____ her card information.
(3 must / obtain)

How _____ that _____ ? There are many ways a
(4)   (4 could / happen)

person _____ Claudia's credit card information. Someone
(5 might / steal)

_____ Claudia's credit card number when she used her card
(6 may / steal)

in a store or a restaurant. In addition, a thief _____ a credit card
(7 could / take)

account statement or a bill from her mailbox or her trash.

Exercise 4.2 More Past Probability

Write a response for each situation. Use the words in parentheses with modals of past probability to write guesses or logical conclusions. Sometimes more than one answer is possible.

1 Isabela can't find her wallet.

___*She may / might / could have lost it.*___
(**guess:** she / lose / it)

2 There was a charge on Bo's bill that he didn't recognize.

_____
(**logical conclusion:** someone / steal / his credit card number)

3 Bo paid his credit card bill, even though he didn't recognize some of the charges.

_____

(**logical conclusion:** he/not/call/the credit card company)

4 The waiter took a long time to bring Hong's credit card back.

_____

(**guess:** he/copy/the card number)

5 Terry threw an unopened letter from her credit card company into the trash.

_____

(**logical conclusion:** she/not/think/it was important)

Exercise 4.3 Using Modals of Past Probability

Read the article about tips for avoiding identity theft. Then complete the sentences about examples of identity theft. Use the tips to write logical conclusions or guesses about what has happened. Sometimes more than one answer is possible.

HOW TO AVOID Identity Theft

 Write to credit card companies. Tell them to remove your name from their mailing lists.

 Check your credit card bill carefully each month. Make sure there are no incorrect charges on it.

 Don't carry all of your credit cards with you.

 Make scans of important documents, such as your passport, and keep the copies in a safe place in your home.

 Check that emails from your bank and other businesses are authentic. Never give personal information in an email.

1 Fred gets a lot of credit card offers in the mail. He never opens them.

He must not have called the companies and asked them to remove his
name from their mailing lists.

2 Sarah paid her credit card bill, but there were charges on it for things she did not buy.

_____

3 A pickpocket stole Luis's wallet while he was riding the bus. Now Luis has to cancel all of his credit cards.

_____

4 Wei went to Canada on a business trip and lost his passport. It took longer than usual for him to leave the country because he didn't know his passport number.

5 Nicole responded to an email that she thought was from her bank, and now she is missing money from her account.

5 Avoid Common Mistakes ⚠

1 **Do not use *must* to talk about future probabilities.**

   will/may
It ~~must~~ be even more difficult to catch cyber criminals in the future.

2 **Remember to use *be* + verb + *-ing* when using the progressive with modals.**

    be
He might∧working.

3 **Use the correct word order when using modals of probability to talk about the past.**

   not
He must∧have ~~not~~ locked the computer because the thief was able to get his information.

Editing Task

Find and correct four mistakes in the paragraph about computer hackers.

What happens to computer hackers who decide to stop hacking? They might find that cyber crime can lead to interesting careers. For example, some companies hire a

                                                          will

computer hacker with the hope that the former cyber criminal ~~must~~ become a brilliant security consultant in the future. Although some say that these companies might

5 taking a risk by hiring these former criminals, the companies seem to believe that the risk is worth it. Adrian Lamo was breaking into computer systems for fun in high school. However, when he hacked into the *New York Times* in 2002, the newspaper must have not thought it was funny, because he was arrested. He now uses his skills for a different purpose and works as a consultant. Robert Tappan Morris might have ended his

10 chances for a good job when he created the Morris worm, a particularly bad computer virus, in 1988. However, he is now on the faculty of the famous Massachusetts Institute of Technology (MIT). Apparently, they believe that a reformed hacker must be able to stop future cyber crimes. In short, while computer hackers sometimes go to prison for their crimes, these days their career opportunities may increasing.

Nouns and Modifying Nouns

Attitudes Toward Nutrition

1 Grammar in the Real World

A What makes a person healthy? Read the article about health habits today. Are people as healthy today as they were in the past?

B Comprehension Check **Answer the questions.**

1 Why does Michael Pollan argue that many modern food products are not truly food?

2 How did people stay active in the past?

3 What are some diseases related to obesity?

C Notice Look at the nouns in bold. Write **C** next to each noun that you can count and **NC** next to each noun that you can't count. Then look at the words that modify some of the nouns. Are they all adjectives? Circle the ones that are not adjectives. What part of speech are they?

1 green and brown **food**   3 food **products**   5 **obesity**

2 heart **disease**   4 the **elderly**

A HEALTH CRISIS

Obesity has become **a major problem** in the United States. According to recent National Institutes of Health studies, less than one-third of **Americans** over the age of 20 are at a healthy
5 weight. That means that two-thirds of the **adult population** is overweight, and one-third of all **adults** are obese.[1]

Modern U.S. society is partially responsible for this **alarming health trend**. Processed,
10 prepared, and packaged **food** has very little nutritional value. Michael Pollan, author of *Food Rules*, argues that **many modern food products** are not truly **food** at all. They contain a great deal of **fat** and refined[2] **sugar** but very little – or
15 no – nutrition.

One other cause of obesity is the unhealthy choices people are making in **their lifestyles**. **Exercise** used to be part of everyday **life**. It was a necessary part of a society where work depended

20 mostly on farming and physical labor.[3] Today, people often sit at a computer all day, watch hours of TV, use personal cars, and have little daily exercise.

Health experts have been studying ways to
25 reduce obesity because there is a link between obesity and other serious **diseases**, such as **diabetes**[4] and **heart disease**. **One way** is to eat more **green and brown food**, such as green **vegetables** and brown **rice** and **grains**. These
30 foods help people use calories, and they aid digestion.[5] In contrast, people who have a **diet** of mostly fast food, white sugar, white flour, and **fat** are at greater risk of obesity. **These diets** contain calories that easily become **fat** when people do
35 not use them for **energy** and exercise.

Experts recommend fewer **servings of** unhealthy food, bigger **portions of** healthy food, and a more active lifestyle.

---

[1]**obese:** extremely fat

[2]**refined:** made more pure by removing unwanted material

[3]**physical labor:** work that involves effort from the body

[4]**diabetes:** a disease in which the body cannot control the amount of sugar in the blood

[5]**digestion:** the ability of the body to create energy from food

2 Nouns

Grammar Presentation

There are two types of common nouns in English: count and noncount.	COUNT NOUN **Vegetables** are good for you. NONCOUNT NOUN Good **nutrition** is essential for good health.

2.1 Count Nouns

Count nouns are nouns that you can count and make plural. Use a singular or plural verb with count nouns.	This **apple** tastes great. **Vegetables** are very important and keep us healthy.
Use a determiner such as *a/an*, *the*, *this*, and *his* with singular count nouns.	Is *a* **tomato** *a* **vegetable**? There's *an* **onion** in *the* **refrigerator**. *This* **banana** doesn't taste ripe. *His* **sandwich** looks delicious.
You can use a plural count noun with or without a determiner such as *a few*, *many*, *some*, *these*, and *those*.	*Some* **diets** don't work very well. **Diets** often don't work very well.

2.2 Irregular Plural Nouns

A Some plural nouns have irregular forms. These are the most common irregular plural nouns in academic writing.	man – men woman – women child – children person – people foot – feet tooth – teeth
B Some nouns have the same form for singular and plural.	one fish – two fish one sheep – two sheep
C Some nouns are only plural. They do not have a singular form.	clothes headphones pants glasses jeans scissors

2.3 Noncount Nouns

A Noncount nouns are nouns that cannot be counted. Use a singular verb with noncount nouns.

Here are some common categories of noncount nouns.

Abstract concepts: *health, nutrition*

Activities and sports: *dancing, exercise, swimming, tennis, yoga*

Diseases and health conditions: *arthritis, depression, diabetes, obesity*

Elements and gases: *gold, hydrogen, oxygen, silver*

Food: *beef, broccoli, cheese, rice*

Liquids: *coffee, gasoline, oil, tea*

Natural phenomena: *electricity, hail, lightning, rain, thunder*

Particles: *pepper, salt, sand, sugar*

Subjects: *economics, genetics, geology*

Areas of work: *construction, business, medicine, nursing*

Good **health** is very important.

Yoga has been my favorite activity for years.

Obesity has become a serious problem.

Oxygen is the most common element in the body by weight.

Broccoli isn't popular with my family.

Tea has many health benefits.

Hail consists of small balls of ice.

Too much **salt** isn't good for you.

I wasn't very good at **economics** in college.

She's studying **nursing**.

B You can use a noncount noun with or without a determiner. Use a determiner after you have already mentioned the noun and wish to give more information.

Cheese is one of my favorite foods, but I don't like <u>the</u> **cheese** on this pizza. It's too stringy.

C You can use *the* + certain adjectives to describe a group of people with the same characteristic or quality: *the dead, the disabled, the educated, the elderly, the living, the poor, the rich, the unemployed.* Use a plural verb.

The elderly sometimes <u>don't eat</u> well.

The poor <u>are</u> often <u>not able to buy</u> nutritious food.

The unemployed <u>are</u> especially <u>affected</u> by the poor economy.

▸▸ Noncount Nouns and Measurement Words to Make Noncount Nouns Countable: See page A5.

📊 Data from the Real World

Some common noncount nouns in speaking and writing are:

advice	equipment	information	music	research	stuff
bread	evidence	knowledge	news	rice	traffic
cash	fun	luck	permission	safety	water
coffee	furniture	milk	progress	security	weather
damage	health	money	publicity	software	work

Exercise 2.1 Count Nouns

A Complete the excerpt from a web article about nutrition. Circle the correct verbs.

A healthy diet **include /(includes)** a lot of fresh fruit and vegetables. Vegetables **is / are**
(1)   (2)
especially low in calories and high in nutrients such as vitamins and minerals. Therefore, it's a good

idea to add more fruit and vegetables to your diet if you want to improve your health.

Current nutrition guidelines **suggest / suggests** eating about four or five servings of fruit and
(3)
vegetables a day. One serving **is / are** about a half cup. Nutrition experts also **suggest / suggests**
(4)   (5)
choosing fruit and vegetables by color – dark green, yellow, red, and so on – and eating a variety

of colors each day. This is because fruit and vegetables with a lot of color often **contain / contains**
(6)
the highest amounts of nutrients. Half a cup of broccoli, for example, **has / have** 50 milligrams of
(7)
vitamin C and only about 15 calories.

Low-calorie fruit, such as tomatoes and berries, **is / are** also a good choice. A medium tomato
(8)
has / have only about 20 calories and 15 milligrams of vitamin C. Blueberries **has / have** 80
(9)   (10)
calories and 15 milligrams of vitamin C per cup. Intensely colored fruit and vegetables often

contain / contains antioxidants, chemicals that protect cells from disease. Antioxidants also
(11)
enhance / enhances the effects of vitamin C and protect the heart and your health!
(12)

B Over to You What else do you know about the benefits of fruit and vegetables?
Write five sentences about fruit and vegetables. Share your sentences with a partner.

Exercise 2.2 The + Adjective

Complete the statements about nutritional issues that affect different groups of people.
Rewrite the words in parentheses with *the* + adjective.

1 *The wealthy* (People who are wealthy) tend to have a better diet than poor people
   do because they can easily shop for and buy whatever they need.

2 _____ (People who are poor) often do not have convenient access to fresh
   fruit and vegetables because there are few good supermarkets in poor neighborhoods.

3 There often are free food programs for _____ (people who are homeless) in
   large urban areas.

4 _____ (People who are elderly) sometimes have poor nutrition because they
   might suffer from diseases that cause a loss of appetite.

5 _____ (People who are young) are becoming less healthy in America because of too much junk food and a lack of exercise.

6 In Minneapolis and in many other parts of the country, farmers' markets are opening in areas that are easier for _____ (people who are disabled) to access.

7 _____ (People who are unemployed) in the United States can get help buying food by applying for SNAP, the government-sponsored Supplemental Nutrition Assistance Program.

8 We usually assume that _____ (people who are educated) make wise choices when they eat, but this is not always true.

Exercise 2.3 Count or Noncount Noun?

A Complete the magazine article about health. Add plural endings to the nouns in bold where necessary. If a noun does not have a plural, write **✗** on the line.

Tips for a HEALTHY LIFE

Due to the worldwide epidemic of obesity, many people are concerned about their health **✗** . Specialist _____ who study how the body works have some **advice** _____ for
(1)   (2)   (3)
you: exercise more and eat healthier food.

The Harvard School of Public Health recommends adding more exercise to your daily life. With the exception of some people who work in very active **occupation** _____
(4)
such as **construction** _____ or landscaping, many of us simply do not move enough
(5)
throughout the day. **Exercise** _____ not only helps burn calories, it also lowers the risk
(6)
for many **illness** _____ such as **heart disease** _____ and diabetes. One way to increase
(7)   (8)
activity is through aerobic exercise such as **swimming** _____ . Aerobic exercise increases
(9)
your intake of **oxygen** _____ , which helps you burn fat faster. However, many physical
(10)
activities count as exercise, including **dancing** _____ and **gardening** _____ .
(11)   (12)

The next step is changing our diet. Some **research** _____ shows that a plant-based
(13)
diet is a good choice. People who eat less meat tend to be healthy. They do not usually eat processed food that is high in fat, sugar, and **salt** _____ . The Harvard School of Public
(14)
Health suggests that we follow a plant-based diet. They suggest eating fresh fruit and **vegetable** _____ and whole grains such as brown **rice** _____ . They also recommend
(15)   (16)
preparing your food from fresh **ingredient** _____ .
(17)

There is a lot of confusing **information** _____ about nutrition, but exercise and simple,
(18)
unprocessed food are all you really need to live a healthy life.

B Pair Work Make a list of the noncount nouns in A. Then work with a partner and identify which category the nouns in A are from: abstract concepts, activities and sports, diseases and health conditions, food, subjects, particles, or areas of work. Then think of one more noun for each category.

A *Health* is an abstract concept.

B *Right. And* kindness *is another abstract concept.*

3 Noncount Nouns as Count Nouns

Grammar Presentation

When we refer to noncount nouns as individual items, they can sometimes have a count meaning. They may also be made countable with measurement words describing specific quantities.

NONCOUNT NOUN
Light makes plants grow.

MEASUREMENT + COUNT NOUN
A bunch of lights were visible in the distance.

3.1 Making Noncount Nouns Countable

A Some noncount nouns can have a count meaning when we refer to individual items within a general category.	*I always put cheese on my pasta. (general category)* *English cheeses are very strong. (individual kinds)* *Food is essential to life. (general category)* *Some foods contain a lot of sugar. (individual food items)*
B Use measurement words to make noncount nouns countable. Here are common measurement words and expressions. Abstract concepts: *a bit of, a kind of, a piece of* Activities or sports: *a game of* Food: *a drop of, a grain of, a piece of, a serving of, a slice of* Liquids: *a cup of, a gallon / quart of, a glass of* Natural phenomena: *a bolt of, a drop of, a ray of* Particles: *a grain of, a pinch of* Subjects and occupations: *an area of, a branch of, a field of, a type of* Miscellaneous: *an article of* (clothing), *a bunch of* (people, objects), *a crowd of, a group of, a pack of* (wolves, dogs, wild animals), *a piece of* (furniture, equipment, news)	*Eight glasses of water are on the table.* *There is a piece of cake in the refrigerator.* *A bit of kindness goes a long way.* *I play five games of tennis a week.* *Would you like a piece of pie?* *The recipe calls for two cups of oil.* *A few drops of rain are enough to ruin a picnic.* *A pinch of salt makes food taste good.* *Two branches of medicine are cardiology and neurology.* *There were a bunch of people at the store.*

▶ Noncount Nouns and Measurement Words to Make Noncount Nouns Countable: See page A5.

Grammar Application

A Complete the conversation about purchasing food through the Internet. Use the correct form of the nouns in parentheses. Sometimes more than one answer is possible.

Jake   Do you have any __*experience*__ (experience) buying food online?
(1)

Emily   Yes, I've bought different kinds of imported _____ (cheese), a
(2)

variety of _____ (coffee), and different sorts of _____ (tea).
(3)   (4)

Jake   I didn't know you liked _____ (cheese) so much.
(5)

Emily   I don't. I bought all of those _____ (cheese) as gifts.
(6)

Jake   Anyway, how was the shopping?

Emily   I've had many good _____ (experience) with online shopping.
(7)
The prices were reasonable, and the items arrived in good condition.

Jake   Did it take a long _____ (time) for the items to arrive?
(8)

Emily   Not usually. Two _____ (time) they were late.
(9)

Jake   Do you ever buy _____ (fruit) online?
(10)

Emily   I don't think that's a good idea, but I have friends who buy _____
(11)
(fruit) like *cherimoya* and *durian* online without any problems.

Jake   It's probably safe to buy _____ (coffee) and _____ (tea)
(12)   (13)
online, right?

Emily   Sure. I've also bought items like _____ (sugar) and
(14)
_____ (flour) online.
(15)

Jake   Why would you do that?

Emily   I buy hard-to-get _____ (sugar) such as *demerara* and *turbinado*
(16)
online because I can't find them in my local store.

Jake   And there are special types of _____ (flour), too?
(17)

Emily   Well, I have a friend who is allergic to wheat, so I get a few different gluten-free
_____ (flour) from a special diet site.
(18)

B Pair Work Compare your answers with a partner. Discuss the reasons for each of your answers.

I chose the noncount noun experience in item 1 because the speaker is talking about an abstract concept.

Complete the sentences with the correct quantifier from the box. Add determiners and any other necessary words. Sometimes more than one answer is possible.

~~bit~~	cup	gallon	glass	piece	serving
can	drop	game	grain	pinch	slice

1 Let me give you *a bit of* advice: Stop worrying about calories, and just eat food that's good for you.

2 Should we play _____ chess after dinner?

3 Please cut a very thin

_____ bread

for me.

4 _____ fruit is

about a half a cup.

5 _____ tea has less caffeine

than a cup of coffee.

6 Doctors recommend drinking 32 ounces of water a day, but it's hard to remember to drink

four _____ water each day.

7 This sauce needs just _____ salt – not too much!

8 The cupboard is empty. There isn't even _____ rice

left there!

9 Here's a bottle of soy sauce. Just put a tiny _____ soy

sauce on the fish. We're trying to cut down on sodium.

10 The chocolate cheesecake that you baked looks absolutely delicious! Could you cut

_____ for me?

11 I've brought you _____ chicken soup to help with your

cold. It's not homemade, but I think it will help you feel better.

12 If you're going to the supermarket, could you pick up _____

milk? The children drink so much of it and we need a lot.

Exercise 3.3 More Measurement Words with Noncount Nouns

A Write the correct quantities of food in Luis's blog. Use the words in the box. Add any other necessary words.

1 / bottle / water	~~quart / olive oil~~	2 / piece / fish
1 / box / pasta	2 / loaf / bread	wedge / cheese

THE WANDERING GOURMET

by Luis Martinez

The highlight of my trip to San Francisco was the Ferry Plaza Farmers' Market. I spent a lot of money! My chef friend, Lisa, came with me. She made a delicious dinner from the ingredients. Here's what we bought:

1 *a quart of olive oil*   **2** _____   **3** _____

4 _____   **5** _____   **6** _____

B Pair Work Compare your answers with a partner. Then work together to think of more noncount nouns that you can use with each measurement word.

A *You can also say a quart of water.*

B *Or a quart of milk.*

4 Modifying Nouns

Grammar Presentation

Adjectives that modify nouns, including nouns acting as adjectives, follow a specific order.	*That was a **delicious green Washington** apple!* (opinion + color + origin) *I saw a **shocking government** report on nutrition.* (opinion + type)

4.1 Order of Modifiers

The order of modifiers is as follows:

Opinion/ Evaluation	Size	Age	Shape	Color	Origin	Material	Type
delicious traditional useful	large short small tall	antique new old two-year-old young	round square triangular	black green yellow	French imaginary scientific	cotton leather metal	dog government shoulder

▶◀ Order of Adjectives Before Nouns: See page A6.

4.2 Using Modifiers

A Do not use commas between two adjectives from different categories.	OPINION ORIGIN *That was a **delicious French** cake.* OPINION TYPE *It was a **disappointing medical** report.* SIZE MATERIAL *You'll need a **big metal** pan.*
B Use *and* or a comma between two adjectives of opinion.	OPINION OPINION *The food has an **interesting** <u>and</u> **memorable** taste.* *The food has an **interesting, memorable** taste.*
Use *and* between two colors or two materials used as adjectives.	COLOR + COLOR *She bought a **red** <u>and</u> **yellow** dress.* MATERIAL + MATERIAL *The **cotton** <u>and</u> **silk** tablecloth is new.*

Grammar Application

Exercise 4.1 Order of Adjectives

Complete the sentences with the adjectives in parentheses. Remember to use the correct order.

1 Wei got a ___*new French glass*___ (French / glass / new) coffeemaker for his 25th birthday.

2 Every other week, Mei's Kitchen will feature _____ (easy / Asian / new) recipes for you to try at home.

3 SNAP is a _____ (government / useful) food program for people who are out of work.

4 We went to the farmers' market in the city last Saturday and bought a lot of _____ (small / purple) potatoes.

5 The _____ (Thai / new) restaurant downtown has a _____ (rectangular / lovely) dining room area with _____ (red / beautiful) walls.

6 There were _____ (lovely / white) flowers in some _____ (glass / antique / tall) vases on the tables.

Exercise 4.2 More Order of Adjectives

A On a separate sheet of paper, write five sentences about things in the picture. Use two or three adjectives in each sentence. Choose adjectives from the box, or think of your own adjectives.

antique	large	silver
beautiful	long	small
clean	metal	square
cotton	oval	tall
delicious	rectangular	white
enormous	round	wooden

There are clean white napkins in the tall clear glasses.

B Over to You Think of a party or wedding that you attended. Write five sentences to describe the decorations and the food. Use two or three adjectives in each sentence.

A Listen to a restaurant review. Complete the sentences with the missing words. Pay attention to punctuation and adjective order.

Last week, we ate at Le Bambou, an ___*elegant new*___ Vietnamese
(1)
restaurant in town. We ordered several _____
(2)
dishes. We highly recommend the _____ spring
(3)
rolls. They were a _____ appetizer, and they
(4)
were perfect for the _____ evening. The main
(5)
course was a _____ chicken dish served with
(6)
_____ vegetables.
(7)
We were especially impressed with Le Bambou's atmosphere. It has a
_____ dining room. The tables were covered
(8)
with _____ tablecloths, and they were all lit by
(9)
_____ candles in _____
(10)   (11)
holders. The walls were painted a lovely shade of blue, and the color gave the
restaurant a sense of calm. The serving dishes looked like _____
(12)
antiques. There were _____ dragons on the
(13)
plates.

All in all, Le Bambou was a _____ experience.
(14)

B Listen again and check your answers.

C Over to You Choose a restaurant that you know. Write a review of the restaurant similar to the review in A. Share your sentences with a partner.

Last month we went to the lovely, popular neighborhood restaurant called Buon Appetito …

5 Avoid Common Mistakes ⚠

1 **When a noun modifies another noun and a number comes before it, use the singular form of the noun.**

An ~~eight-years-old~~ *eight-year-old* child should be able to pronounce all of the ingredients.

2 **When a noun is followed by a prepositional phrase, the verb agrees with the noun, not the object of the preposition.**

The company behind these products ~~advertise~~ *advertises* to young children.

3 **Do not make noncount nouns plural.**

The author has ~~advices~~ *advice* for shoppers.

4 **Remember to use the plural form of count nouns.**

These ~~vegetable~~ *vegetables* taste good when they are served raw with salad dressing.

Editing Task

Find and correct seven more mistakes in the paragraphs about children's eating habits.

What does a ~~ten-years-old~~ *ten-year-old* child eat in a day? Specialists in nutrition is finding out that the news is not good. As a result, they are looking for ways to improve children's eating habit. They are also involved in trying to help families make healthier choice.

5 Most experts suggest that a few key practices can help families. One of these practices are common sense: people should eat unprocessed food. When there is a choice between canned corn and fresh corn, people should choose the fresh corn. Secondly, people should read labels carefully. Because labels contain a lot of informations, people should familiarize themselves with the nutrition and calorie content of their favorite products. Finally, people can boost the health content of

10 certain kinds of food. For example, it is possible to substitute whole-grain flours for white flour in most recipes.

Parents and children live busy lives, but research shows that when a healthy child becomes a 40-years-old adult, that person can look forward to a healthy old age.

1 Grammar in the Real World

A How does color affect your mood? Read the magazine article about the effects of color on mood. What is your favorite color? How does it affect your mood?

B Comprehension Check Answer the questions.

1 Why is it important to choose colors carefully when decorating a room?

2 What advice did the decorator give to the Wangs?

3 What are some examples of color-feeling associations?

C Notice Find the words in the article. Then circle the meaning of each set of words within the context.

1 bright orange walls

    a a group of walls in general   b specific walls

2 the orange walls

    a a group of walls in general   b specific walls

3 a sensitive person

    a one example from a category or group   b something in particular that was previously mentioned in the text

4 the problem

    a one example from a category or group   b something in particular that was previously mentioned in the text

Can you make a generalization about the use of *a/an*, *the*, and no article?

The **EFFECTS** of **COLOR** on **MOOD**

Research has shown that colors have **a** direct impact on our feelings. Therefore, it makes sense for people to surround themselves with colors that make them feel good. Successful decorating depends on making **the** right
5 color choices.

It is beneficial to choose colors that make people feel comfortable, happy, relaxed, energized, or whatever mood is desired. Bright orange walls in **a** bedroom, for instance, may keep **a** sensitive person awake, whereas light blue seems to
10 have **a** relaxing effect. Maya Romero of Omaha, Nebraska, suffered from chronic insomnia. **A** friend suggested that **the** orange walls in her bedroom might be contributing to **the** problem. Maya listened to her friend's advice and painted **the** walls light blue. Since then, she has had much less
15 trouble sleeping.

Color affects moods in a variety of ways. Yellow is **a** cheerful, uplifting color for **most** people. However, strong shades of yellow can be overwhelming when used for **an** entire room. Light yellow, on the other hand, can lift **a**
20 person's mood like **a** room filled with sunshine. Similarly, green can revive **the** spirit. This may be because green reminds us of nature.

Typically, people experience **the** color blue as comforting. However, it is better to avoid using too much blue in one
25 room. **A** room with blue walls and blue furniture can seem cold and overly formal. Christopher and Marie Wang of Duvall, Washington, moved into **a** new home and painted **the** walls in their living room blue. Then they filled the room with furniture of varying shades of blue. They loved it, but they noticed that
30 conversation died when they sat in **the** room with guests. They asked advice from **a** decorator to see if **the** problem was related to **the** decor. **The** decorator suggested that they replace their icy blue carpet with **a** carpet in warm colors, such as dark red or warm beige. She also recommended replacing
35 their classic-style furniture with more comfortable pieces. **The** Wangs report that, after they made **the** changes, **the** living room quickly became their favorite room for entertaining.

Clearly, **the** colors in an environment have **a** tremendous impact on **the** people who live or work there. Certain colors
40 can improve moods dramatically, while others can actually bring on feelings of sadness or loneliness. It is crucial to carefully consider color choices when decorating **a** living space or office.

2 Indefinite Article, Definite Article, and No Article

Grammar Presentation

The indefinite articles *a* and *an* and the definite article *the* come before singular count nouns. The definite article *the* can come before plural count nouns and noncount nouns.

The color blue in *a* bedroom may relax people.
Choosing colors is *an* important part of decorating.
The orange walls contributed to her insomnia.

2.1 Indefinite Articles: *A/An*

A Use *a/an* before a singular count noun when the noun is part of a category or if it is a profession.	Blue is *a* color. The power of color is *an* issue that many researchers study. Her sister is *an* interior decorator.
B Use *a/an* to introduce a singular count noun when you first mention it.	*A* room with blue walls can seem formal. *An* orange bedroom can keep you awake.
C Use *a/an* before a singular count noun to give definitions or make generalizations.	*A* decorator is a person who chooses colors and furniture for a room. *A* yellow room is more cheerful than *a* blue room.

2.2 Definite Article: *The*

A You can use *the* before singular count nouns, plural count nouns, and noncount nouns.	Where is *the* chair? *The* salespeople are very knowledgeable. *The* furniture in her house looks new.
B Use *the* before a noun when you mention it a second time.	FIRST MENTION SECOND MENTION I took *an* interesting class. *The* class was about the effects of color on people's moods.
C Use *the* when a noun gives more information about a previously mentioned noun. The second noun is associated with the first noun.	This is *a* good study on colors. **The** research makes some good points. That is *a* very interesting article. **The** information in it explains a lot about the power of color.

2.2 Definite Article: *The (continued)*

D Use *the* when the listener or reader can physically see or visualize the noun.	*Push the button in front of you.* *Your class is in the room just below this one.*
E Use *the* when the noun is unique.	*The students are learning about the sun, the Earth, and the solar system.*
F Use *the* before a singular noun used to represent a whole class or category. This is very formal.	*The male robin is more colorful than the female.*

2.3 No Article

Use no article when a noncount noun or a plural count noun is used to make a generalization.	*Research has taught us many things about the ways that we are affected by colors.* *Colors can affect our moods.*

Grammar Application

Exercise 2.1 *A/An or The?*

Complete the textbook excerpt about color theory. Circle the correct articles. Sometimes more than one answer is possible.

CHAPTER 3: Color Theory

What is color theory? It is **a**/**the** tool and **a/the** guide for understanding colors. There are different
₍₁₎ versions of color theory, but in **a/the** basic version, there are three primary colors. **A/The** colors
₍₃₎ are blue, red, and yellow. As you can see by looking at **a/the**
₍₅₎ color wheel, mixing equal parts of two primary colors produces a secondary color. For example, if you mix blue and red, you get purple. If you mix red and yellow, you get **a/the** color orange.
₍₆₎

Tertiary colors are also created by mixing two primary colors. However, to make **a/the** tertiary color, you use unequal amounts
₍₇₎ of two colors. By doing that, you get colors like blue-green and yellow-orange.

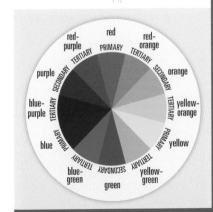

Fig. 8.1: Color Wheel

Now, look at **a/the** color wheel again. **A/The** colors that lie opposite each other on **a/the**
(8)   (9)   (10)
color wheel are called complementary colors. For example, **a/the** colors red and green are
(11)
complementary colors. So are **a/the** colors orange and blue. Look at **a/the** square below.
(12)   (13)
It contains **a/the** complementary colors red and green. Stare at it for
(14)
15 seconds, then stare at **a/the** white wall or **a/the** piece of white paper.
(15)   (16)
Did you notice that the "ghost" image (the image you see on the white
wall or paper) has the opposite colors? **A/The** green half of the square
(17)
becomes red and **a/the** red half becomes green. This is one characteristic
(18)
of complementary colors.

Exercise 2.2 *A/An, The,* or No Article?

A Listen to the web article about color harmony. Write *a/an, the,* or Ø for no article.

COLOR
Harmony

Some colors go together while some colors don't. Why?
Is there a way to understand why some colors work better
together than others? As many artists and designers know, __Ø__
(1)
color harmony is based on _____ color theory.
(2)

Let's think about _____ ways color harmony works in a room. One main rule of color
(3)
harmony is that one color must be stronger than _____ other colors in the room. In other
(4)
words, one color must be more intense than the others or cover a larger area than the others.

Another rule of color harmony is that you should not put two very intense colors next to each
other. For example, you should not have _____ bright red sofa on top of _____ bright
(5)   (6)
green rug. _____ human eye cannot focus on both colors at the same time, and _____
(7)   (8)
colors may seem to vibrate.

A third rule of color harmony is that the colors in a room should be related to each other
in some way. You can determine colors' relationships to each other by looking at _____
(9)
color wheel. Colors that are next to each other on the color wheel, such as red and red-orange,
will usually look good together. You can also put _____ complementary colors together.
(10)
These are colors that are on opposite sides of the color wheel, such as yellow and purple.
Color triads go well together, too. These are three colors that are the same distance from each
other on the color wheel. For example, _____ primary colors, red, blue, and yellow, form a
(11)
color triad. The secondary colors, green, purple, and orange, also form a color triad.

B Over to You What is your favorite color combination? Write five sentences describing why you like this color combination and describing things that you own in these colors. Use nouns with *a/an*, *the*, and no article in your sentences. Then share your sentences with a partner.

My favorite color combination is pink and orange. I like it because both colors are bright. I have a T-shirt with the colors pink and orange. The shirt was a gift from my sister. I also have a pair of pink and orange shoes.

3 Quantifiers

Grammar Presentation

Quantifiers are words such as *all (of)*, *some (of)*, and *a lot of* that describe an amount or number.	*All of the colors go well together.* *I have some information about colors.*

3.1 Quantifiers with Count Nouns and Noncount Nouns

A Quantifiers describe both large and small quantities or amounts. They are used with both count and noncount nouns.	**More** ↑↓ **Less**	*all (of)* *many/a lot of* *quite a few (of)/a great deal of* *some (of)* *a few (of)/a little (of)* *few (of)/little (of)* *not a lot of/not many (of)/not much (of)* *not any (of)/none of/no*
B Use the following quantifiers only with count nouns: *quite a few (of), few, a few (of), not many (of)*		*Quite a few painters have studied at that art school.* *A few painters shared the paint.* *Few students have time for art classes.* *Not many students have found a summer job.*
C Use the following quantifiers only with noncount nouns: *a great deal of, a little, little, not much (of)*		*We have a great deal of work to do.* *I have a little information.* *She has little patience.* *There is not much time left to complete the work.*

3.1 Quantifiers with Count Nouns and Noncount Nouns *(continued)*

D Use *a few* to say there are some but not many.

Use *few* for a very small number.

There are always *a few* <u>students</u> who want to major in art.

There are *few* <u>scholarships</u> for international students.

E Use *a little* and *little* with noncount nouns.

Use *a little* to say there is some but not much.

Use *little* for a very small amount.

I have *a little* money, so I can pay for it.

I have *little* money. I don't have enough money.

3.2 Quantifiers That Are Used with Count Nouns and Noncount Nouns

The following quantifiers can be used with both count and noncount nouns:

Count Nouns	Noncount Nouns
All of the <u>students</u> in my class work hard.	I gave him *all of* the <u>money</u>.
She used *a lot of* <u>colors</u> in her painting.	I don't have *a lot of* <u>time</u> today to study.
Most of the <u>answers</u> are clear.	I knew how to use *most of* the <u>software</u>.
Some of the <u>students</u> don't know a lot about art.	I painted *some of* the <u>time</u> while I was on vacation.
I didn't take *a lot of* <u>notes</u> in class.	He didn't have *a lot of* <u>help</u> on the project.
We don't have *any* <u>solutions</u>.	They didn't put *any* <u>effort</u> into the job.
None of the <u>students</u> is absent.	*None of* the <u>work</u> is good.
There are *no* <u>excuses</u> for poor work.	That room has *no* <u>sunshine</u>.

3.3 Quantifiers and *Of*

A Use a quantifier without *of* when a noun is used in an indefinite or general sense.

Some students are late.

I was interested in *a few* art classes.

B Use a quantifier with *of* when the noun is specific and known to both the speaker and listener. Use *of* before a determiner such as *the, my, your, his, her, our, their, these,* or *those.*

Some of <u>the</u> students at my school are very smart.

A few of <u>the</u> activities in class require artistic ability.

C The quantifiers *a great deal of, a lot of,* and *none of* always include *of.*

A lot of people are interested in art.

NOT *A lot* people are interested in art.

Grammar Application

Exercise 3.1 Quantifiers

A Complete the article about color blindness. Circle the correct quantifiers.

COLOR BLINDNESS

Color blindness is a condition in which a person cannot see the difference between certain colors. **All of /(Many)** people think that color-blind people see **no / none** colors at all and only see black and
(1)   (2)
white. However, complete color blindness is very rare. **Not much / Not many** people are completely
(3)
color blind. However, **many / much** people do have some degree of color blindness. A large number
(4)
of the men in the world are color blind. Very **few / little** women, however, are color blind.
(5)

A great deal of / Quite a few people who suffer from weak color vision have red-green color
(6)
blindness. They cannot tell the difference between red and green. Think about the color purple. It is
made up of two colors: red and blue. If you have **a little / a few** red color blindness, and you look at a
(7)
bright purple flower, you may be able to see **a little / a few** red, but the flower will look almost blue.
(8)
If you have a more serious case of red color blindness, the flower may look completely blue to you.

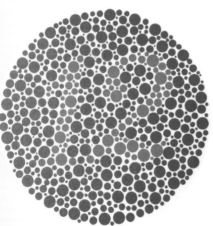

You'll see **no / none of** the red at all.
(9)

So why are some people color blind? We have red, blue, and green cones in our eyes. You need to have **all / little** of the types
(10)
in order to see colors correctly. If you don't have **all / much** of the
(11)
types of cones, or if **few / some** of them are not working right, you
(12)
may see a red flower as green or a green vegetable as brown.

Look at this image. It is an Ishihara plate. Ishihara plates are
made up of different-colored dots. Do you see a number within
the circle? If not, you may have weak red-green color vision.

B Pair Work Work with a partner. Think about some activities (getting dressed, driving, watching TV, reading, using a computer) that people with color blindness might have trouble with. Write four sentences. Use different quantifiers in each sentence.

Many people with color blindness will have difficulty matching their socks.

Exercise 3.2 More Quantifiers

A Complete the report about car sales. Use the quantifiers in the box and the chart below. Use each quantifier only once. Sometimes more than one answer is possible.

a great deal of	~~little~~	many of	no
few	many	most	quite a few

Anderson Auto Sales

Percentage of Sales by Color 2017 & 2018

	White	Silver	Black	Gray	Red	Blue	Brown	Green	Yellow	Other
% of Total Sales 2018	23	19	14	15	3	7	9	5	1	3
% of Total Sales 2017	19	32	12	9	12	9	2	0	2	3

1. In 2018, there was *little* demand for yellow cars.
2. In 2017, they had ______________ success in selling green cars.
3. When Anderson Auto Sales created sales projections for 2019, they probably did not plan to sell ______________ yellow cars.
4. ______________ the cars sold in 2017 were white, silver, or black.
5. ______________ of the cars sold in 2018 were white, silver, or black.
6. Compared to 2017, ______________ the cars sold in 2018 were gray.
7. Compared to 2017, ______________ customers favored red cars in 2018.
8. Compared to 2017, ______________ customers bought brown cars in 2018.

B Rewrite five sentences from A using different quantifiers.

In 2018, there wasn't much demand for yellow cars.

1 ______________________________

2 ______________________________

3 ______________________________

4 ______________________________

5 ______________________________

C Over to You Do Internet research to find out the most popular car colors this year or last year. Discuss your findings with a partner.

Exercise 3.3 Using Quantifiers with *Of*

Listen to the interview with the students about changes to their school. Complete the sentences with *of* or **✗** when *of* is not used.

CHANGES AT BAY CITY UNIVERSITY

Mark Recently, our university hired some __✗__ interior designers and color experts
(1)
to redesign the interior of the library at Bay City University. I asked a group of
students at the college what they thought about this. Here's what they said:

Josh Some __of__ my friends don't like it. They think the colors are too bright.
(2)
Some _____ people don't like to study at the library because the bright colors
(3)
make them uncomfortable.

Amy All _____ my friends love the new colors, but we know that some _____ people
(4)   (5)
don't like the color choices. You can never please all of the people when you
make a change, though.

Lynn A few _____ the people I know think it's great! They like being surrounded by
(6)
a lot _____ bright colors. I think a few _____ students would probably prefer to
(7)   (8)
have softer colors in the library, though.

Paulo None _____ my friends study in the library anymore. All _____ them study in
(9)   (10)
the dorms because they don't like the colors in the library. But I like the new
design. There were no _____ students studying on the first floor of the library
(11)
this morning, so I had the whole place to myself.

A Over to You Interview some of your classmates. Have each student answer this question: *If you could make your room one color, which color would you choose and why?* Write the answers in the chart. Then write sentences about your classmates using quantifiers.

Name	Male (M) or Female (F)	Color
David	M	blue
Maria	F	beige (light brown)

Few of the male students chose blue. A lot of the female students chose beige.

B Group Work Share your sentences in a small group. What are the most popular colors for the women in your class? What are the most popular colors for the men in your class?

4 Avoid Common Mistakes ⚠

1 **Do not use *much* with plural nouns.**

              many
We interviewed ~~much~~ interesting candidates, and we ended up hiring Ms. Stevens.

2 **Use an article before a singular occupation.**

    an
I am ᴧassistant researcher.

3 **Write *a lot* as two words.**

       a lot
I have ~~alot~~ of friends.

Editing Task

Find and correct six more mistakes in this paragraph about color and memory.

Color and Memory

According to recent research, natural colors can help people remember things better. Felix A. Wichmann, ^a research scientist, and two of his colleagues conducted experiments on color and memory. In the first experiment, participants looked at 48 photographs of nature scenes. None of the photographs were of people. Half of the
5 photos were in black and white, and half were in color. Afterward, they looked at the same 48 photos mixed up with alot of new photos. They had to say which ones they had already seen. They remembered the color scenes much better than the black-and-white ones. None of the participants were sure about all of the photos. Another experiment involved much artificially colored photos. When artificially colored photos
10 were included in the set of 48 photos, participants forgot much of the photos. They did not remember the artificially colored photos any better than they remembered the black-and-white photos. These findings suggest that it is not just any colors that help to create alot of our memories. Only natural colors have that power.

Why is this research important? For one thing, advertiser may find these
15 results interesting. If advertiser uses natural colors in ads, consumers may be able to remember them better.

11 Pronouns

Unusual Work Environments

1 Grammar in the Real World

A What are the characteristics of a good workplace? Read the article about a unique workplace. How is this workplace unique?

B Comprehension Check **Answer the questions.**

1 What are some of the perks that SAS gives its employees?

2 What are some reasons SAS gives its employees these perks?

3 What does the voluntary turnover rate at SAS seem to show?

C Notice **Find the sentences in the article. What nouns do the words in bold refer to?**

1 Imagine **yourself** living the good life and working at the same time.

2 **Another** is a free health care facility.

3 These innovations also encourage employees to interact with **each other**.

THE COMPANY YOU KEEP

Imagine **yourself** living the good life[1] and working at the same time. Employees of SAS do that every day. The SAS Institute is a software development firm[2] in North Carolina. For over twenty years, it has been on *Fortune* magazine's list of "Best 100 Companies to Work for in America."

In the late 1980s, SAS started giving its employees free candy. The perks[3] grew from there. There is now a long list of on-site services at SAS. These include a fitness center, massage therapy, dry cleaning, and a beauty salon. **Anyone** can walk on the nature trails outside the offices at SAS and enjoy gourmet food in the cafeteria. The perks reduce distractions so **everyone** can focus on work. These innovations[4] also encourage employees to interact with **each other**.

The company benefits[5] are impressive as well. One benefit is a company child-care center. **Another** is a free health care facility. For employees and their families, there is also counseling and support for issues such as parenting, financial planning, and stress management.

With a voluntary turnover rate[6] of only 2 percent, most employees seem satisfied with their jobs and are not considering leaving. This appears to show that the perks and benefits are a success. While not all companies go to such extremes to keep their employees happy, it is clear that this strategy works well for SAS.

---

[1]**the good life:** a happy and contented life without financial problems

[2]**firm:** a company

[3]**perk:** a special, extra service that companies offer their employees, such as free or low-cost health club memberships

[4]**innovation:** something new or different

[5]**benefit:** a helpful service given to employees in addition to pay

[6]**turnover rate:** the percent of workers who leave a company

2 Reflexive Pronouns

Grammar Presentation

Reflexive pronouns are used to talk about actions when the subject and object of a sentence are the same person or people. They are often used for emphasis to say that the action is performed by that person and nobody else.

*We should enjoy **ourselves** at work.*
*Sue **herself** determines how she is evaluated.*
(Sue determines this, not someone else.)

2.1 Forming Reflexive Pronouns

There is a reflexive pronoun for each subject pronoun.

I	**myself**	*we*	**ourselves**
you	**yourself**	*you* (plural)	**yourselves**
he	**himself**	*they*	**themselves**
she	**herself**		
it	**itself**		

2.2 Using Reflexive Pronouns as Objects

A Use a reflexive pronoun when the subject and object of a sentence are the same.

SUBJECT   OBJECT
*They can get **themselves** treats during the workday.*

SUBJECT   OBJECT
*We introduced **ourselves** to the new staff.*

B Use a reflexive pronoun after an imperative in which you are directly addressing the reader or listener. The implied subject of the sentence is *you*.

*Imagine **yourself** living the good life and working at the same time.*
*Give **yourselves** a day off!*
*Ask **yourself** if this company is right for you.*

C Reflexive pronouns are often used with the following verbs:

be hard on
be proud of
believe in
blame
enjoy
feel good about
help
hurt
look at
push
remind
see
take care of
tell

*She was always hard on **herself**.*
*He was very proud of **himself** and his grades.*
*You have to believe in **yourself**. You can do it.*
*They blamed **themselves** for what happened.*
*We really enjoyed **ourselves** at the conference.*
*Eating well helps you feel good about **yourself**.*
*Please help **yourselves** to some food.*
*I hurt **myself** carrying those heavy boxes.*
*Look at **yourself** in the mirror.*
*She should push **herself** to work harder.*
*He reminded **himself** to get to work early.*
*The company saw **itself** as an innovator.*
*Take care of **yourself**. You're working too hard.*
*I tell **myself** that I am good at what I do.*

2.2 Using Reflexive Pronouns as Objects *(continued)*

D Use an object pronoun, not a reflexive pronoun, after prepositions when the meaning is clear without a reflexive pronoun. If the meaning isn't clear, use a reflexive pronoun.

They took the candy home with them. (They couldn't take the candy home with someone else.)

I'm very proud of myself. (I could be proud of someone else.)

▸▸ Verbs That Can Be Used Reflexively: See page A6.

2.3 Other Uses of Reflexive Pronouns

A You can put the reflexive pronoun directly after a noun or pronoun for greater emphasis or at the end of the clause for less emphasis.

The manager herself gave us candy. (more emphatic)

I interviewed the candidates myself. (less emphatic)

B Use *by* + a reflexive pronoun to mean *alone* or *without help.*

I can work by myself, or I can work on a team.

John completed the whole project by himself.

🖱 Grammar Application

Exercise 2.1 Reflexive Pronouns

A Complete the statements about conditions at different companies. Circle the correct reflexive pronouns.

1 When the CEO and the head of Human Resources saw **himself /(themselves)** in the "100 Best Companies" article, they were surprised.

2 A pet cannot take care of **itself / ourselves** while its owner is on a business trip, so JM Corporation offers free pet care to its employees.

3 My company lets us take special days off, so I gave **itself / myself** a day off from work on my birthday.

4 The president helped to make the company a good place to work, so he was very proud of **herself / himself** when JM Corporation got the "100 Best Companies" award.

5 Susan and I own our company, so we can give **themselves / ourselves** a vacation anytime.

6 Before you go to your interview, you should ask **myself / yourself** why you want to work at JM Corporation.

7 Our new CEO introduced **ourselves / himself** to us at a meeting this morning.

8 Our manager said, "You and your team should congratulate **yourself / yourselves**. You all did a great job on the last project!"

B Over to You Answer the questions with information that is true for you.
Use reflexive pronouns.

- How do you take care of yourself?

- What should people tell themselves before a job interview?

- Think about a time when a friend or family member felt good about himself or herself.
  What happened?

Exercise 2.2 Reflexive Pronouns as Objects

Complete the excerpt from the Careers page of a company website. Write the correct
reflexive or object pronoun.

🏠   💬 ↻ ☰ ✉

▌▊▐ Work at **JM CORPORATION!** ▊▐▌

Imagine ___*yourself*___ working at JM Corporation! Read these comments from our
                     (1)
happy employees and their families:

Jane   Recognition makes JM a great place to work. If we challenge

          _____ and take on special projects, we get rewarded. Also, I
                  (2)

          can give _____ a day off whenever I want.
                          (3)

Manuel We love the benefits, such as child care. My wife couldn't imagine

          _____ leaving the twins all day while she worked. Now, she
                  (4)

          takes the twins to work with _____ every day.
                                                (5)

Lisa   The work-life balance is great here. At JM Corporation, I never take my

          work home with _____ . For example, I can get everything
                                  (6)

          done by Friday and enjoy _____ on the weekends. Just ask
                                          (7)

          _____ : If you could have all this and a great salary, wouldn't you
                  (8)

          want to work here, too?

Exercise 2.3 Other Uses of Reflexive Pronouns

A Complete the sentences with reflexive pronouns. Use the information in parentheses
to help you.

1 Bianca is a highly valued employee. She is able to handle difficult management crises
   ___*by herself*___ (alone).

2 Bianca _____ (emphasis) always takes responsibility for any problems
   on a project.

3 I _____ (emphasis) think she would be a good candidate for promotion.

4 Robert is on Bianca's team, but he prefers to work _____ (alone).

5 Only Robert _____ (emphasis) can learn to become a better team player.

6 Two other team members would also rather work _____ (alone).

7 Bianca recognized this issue and suggested team-building training _____ (emphasis).

8 Only the employees _____ (emphasis) can fix this problem, in my opinion.

B Group Work Ask and answer the questions with your group members. Use reflexive pronouns. Then share your group's answers with the class.

■ What kind of company do you imagine yourself working at someday?

■ What kind of job do you see yourself doing someday?

■ What kind of work tasks can you do by yourself?

Paulo imagines himself working at a big international company someday. He sees himself being the manager of a large group. He doesn't want to work by himself.

3 Pronouns with *Other/Another*

Grammar Presentation

Another, others, the other, and *the others* are pronouns that refer back to a noun. *Each other* and *one another* are reciprocal pronouns. They are used when two or more people do the same thing.	*Some employees are happy, but **others** are not.* *The fitness center is one benefit. **Another** is the dry-cleaning service.* *Employees help **each other**.*

3.1 Pronouns: *The Other, the Others, Others, Another*

A Use *the other* to describe the remaining member of a pair. Use *another* to describe an additional member of a group. It means *one more*.	*I have two favorite sports. One is swimming. The other is tennis.* (There are only two sports.) *Swimming is one of my favorite sports. Another is tennis.* (There are more than two sports.)
Use third-person singular verb forms with *the other* and *another*.	*One of my children goes to college and the other works.*

3.1 Pronouns: *The Other, the Others, Others, Another (continued)*

B Use *the others* for two or more remaining members of a specific group. Use plural verb forms with *the others*.	*One of my children is in high school.* **The others** are *in college.* (I have at least three children: the one in high school and at least two in college.)
C Use *others* (without *the*) for additional members of a group or to contrast these members with previous ones. Use plural verb forms with *others*.	*Some people without jobs look for work every day.* **Others** look *once a week.* (Two contrasting groups of people.)

3.2 Reciprocal Pronouns: *Each Other, One Another*

A *Each other* and *one another* are reciprocal pronouns. Use them when two or more people or groups do the same thing. There is no difference in meaning. *Each other* is more common and more informal than *one another*.	*The teacher and the student respect* **each other**. *The teacher and the student respect* **one another**. (The teacher respects the student. The student respects the teacher.) *The five employees in my company help* **each other**. *The five employees in my company help* **one another**. (Each employee helps the other four employees.)

📊 Data from the Real World

Each other is more common than *one another* in conversation and academic writing. *One another* is slightly more common in academic writing than in conversation.

	Conversation	Academic Writing
Each other	▉▉▉	▉▉▉▉▉
One another	▉	▉

Reciprocal pronouns are less frequently used than personal pronouns (*I, you,* etc.).

🖱 Grammar Application

Exercise 3.1 *The Other, the Others, Others, or Another?*

A Complete the article about the benefits at two companies. Circle the correct words.

Some Great BENEFITS

Vacation time is often a key benefit that attracts people to a company.
The others are /(Another is) child care. Although many companies today are cutting
(1)
these types of benefits, **others are / the other is** still providing them.
(2)

Two California companies offer great benefits for their workers. One is Amgen.

Others are/The other is Google. One of the benefits employees at Amgen enjoy is 17 paid
(3)
days off and three weeks of paid vacation each year. **The others is/Another is** the cafeteria.
(4)
Many companies have on-site cafeterias, but **the others don't/the other doesn't** tend to
(5)
offer take-out breakfasts and lunches like Amgen does.

Free food is one of the perks that Google employees really love, and rightly so.

Another includes/Others include four gyms, free laundry machines, and on-site doctors.
(6)
Google also provides new parents with vouchers for take-out meals for three months so they

don't have to cook when they get home.

Some employees appreciate the free food and laundry services at companies like Google.

Others are/The other is looking for long, paid vacations. When you are looking for a job,
(7)
be sure to consider the benefits offered by the company, and not just the salary.

B Over to You What benefits do you look for in a job? On a separate sheet of paper,
complete the sentences. Then share your sentences with a partner.

There are two major benefits that I look for in a job. One benefit is

_____ . The other is _____ . There are

other benefits that I think would be nice. One is _____ .

Others are _____ and _____ .

There are two major benefits that I look for in a job. One benefit is health insurance.
The other is paid vacation days. There are other benefits that I think would be nice.
One is help with child-care costs. Others are flexible hours and a gym.

Exercise 3.2 *The Other, the Others, Others, or Another?*

Complete the information from a company website. Use *the other, another, each other,* or
one another. Sometimes more than one answer is possible.

Do you want your employees to respect ___*each other/one another*___ ?
(1)
TeamBuilders has several programs to help you and your staff trust _____ more and
(2)
work more productively together.

Read some of our reviews from our customers:

JM Corporation: My staff participated in five TeamBuilders activities, and we really enjoyed

them. One great activity was the Blindfold activity. _____ was the
(3)

"Say It Out Loud!" activity. With these activities, all 12 people on my team learned how to communicate with _____ . Thanks, TeamBuilders, for giving us the tools we need to
(4)
help _____ get the job done!
(5)

Big Buy Stores: Our company did a couple of TeamBuilders activities. Even though we'd only planned to do one activity called "Build-It," we had so much fun that we decided to do _____ . We enjoyed both activities, but we preferred "Build-It"
(6)
to _____ activity.
(7)

4 Indefinite Pronouns

Grammar Presentation

Indefinite pronouns (such as *everything, someone, anywhere, nobody*) are used when the noun is unknown or not important.	*The new boss wants to talk to everybody.* *Someone is moving into our office.*

4.1 Using Indefinite Pronouns

A Use *everybody, everyone, everything,* and *everywhere* to describe all members or things in a group. Use *everybody* or *everyone* for people. Use *everything* for things. Use *everywhere* for places.	*Everybody loves working here.* *Is everyone ready?* *He knows everything about this company.* *It seems you've looked everywhere for a job.*
B Use *somebody, someone, something,* and *somewhere* to refer to an unnamed person, place, or thing. Use indefinite pronouns with *some-* in questions to offer things or ask for things.	*Somebody is going to review our work today.* *Can I ask you something?* *I'd like to work somewhere really interesting.* *Would you like something to drink?*
C Use *anybody, anyone, anything,* and *anywhere* to refer to an unnamed person, place, or thing. Use indefinite pronouns with *any-* to ask questions and in negative sentences.	*"Can anybody receive financial help here?"* *"Sure. Anyone can ask for help."* *Do you need anything from the cafeteria?* *You can't take anything from this shelf.* *Have they advertised the product anywhere?* *I didn't go anywhere last night.*

4.1 Using Indefinite Pronouns (continued)

D Use *nobody, no one, nothing,* and *nowhere* to mean *none* or *not one* in affirmative statements.

No one likes this company. (= not one person)

She said *nothing* important in the meeting. (= not one thing)

There is *nowhere* I'd rather work. (= not one other place)

Grammar Application

Exercise 4.1 Indefinite Pronouns

Complete the interview between a career site and Ahn Nguyen, a corporate concierge for JM Corporation. Circle the correct indefinite pronouns.

INTERVIEW WITH A CORPORATE CONCIERGE

Interviewer First of all, what is a corporate concierge?

Ahn We're a lot like a hotel concierge, but instead of taking care of guests, we take care of employees. **Everybody** / **Somebody** needs a little extra help sometimes, especially people with high-pressure jobs.
(1)

Interviewer This is true **somewhere / everywhere**, not just at JM Corporation.
(2)

Ahn That's right. At JM, we're doing **something / anything** about it.
(3)
Somebody / Everyone at JM Corporation works very hard, and many travel a lot
(4)
for business. They can't take care of **something / everything** that they have to
(5)
do. I'm here to help.

Interviewer Can you give me some examples?

Ahn Sure. Imagine that **somebody / everyone** needs a suit cleaned for a business
(6)
trip. I'll take the suit to the dry cleaner and get it back in time for the trip.

Or **everyone / someone** might need a gift for a family member. I'll find
(7)
someone / something nice and have it wrapped and sent to the family member.
(8)

Interviewer Do you do **anything / nothing** else?
(9)

Ahn Sure. Let's say an employee wants to take a corporate guest

somewhere / everywhere nice for dinner. I'll recommend a restaurant and make
(10)
the reservations.

Interviewer Sounds like a fun job. Thanks very much for telling us a little bit about what the corporate concierge at JM Corporation does.

A Complete the conversation about vacations. Use *anyone*, *anything*, *anywhere*, *no one*, *nothing*, or *nowhere*.

Jane Are you going ___*anywhere*___ for your vacation this summer?
(1)

Adam No, we aren't doing _____ . We're too busy at this time of year.
(2)
_____ takes a vacation in the summer at my company.
(3)

Jane Wow! Does _____ complain about that?
(4)

Adam No. _____ complains because we get three weeks' paid vacation each
(5)
year. It's just that _____ can take it in the summer.
(6)

Jane Well, I wouldn't say _____ negative about that, either!
(7)

Adam What about you? Are you going _____ ?
(8)

Jane Well, _____ important happens at my company in the summer, so my
(9)
family is planning a two-week trip to the mountains. We went there last summer, too.
It's very beautiful and peaceful. There's _____ I'd rather be this summer
(10)
than in those mountains with my family.

Adam Sounds great!

B Listen to a continuation of the conversation in A. Then answer the questions.

1 On average, how many paid vacation days do people in these places get?

European Union: ___*25–30 days*___
Mexico: _____
The United States: _____
South Korea: _____
Japan: _____

2 Where do people get the most paid vacation time? _____

3 Where do people get the least paid time off? _____

C Pair Work Ask and answer the questions with a partner.

■ Are you going anywhere for vacation this summer?

■ Did you go anywhere last summer? If so, where did you go?

■ Are you doing anything special during your time off this year?

■ Does everyone in your family take off work at the same time for vacation?

5 Avoid Common Mistakes

1 **Use the plural pronoun *others* when talking about two or more people or things.**

others
Some managers value discipline; ~~other~~ believe in praise for good work.

2 **Use the object pronoun to form the reflexive pronouns *himself*, *itself*, and *themselves*.**

themselves
Valuable employees can solve problems ~~theirselves~~.

3 **Indefinite pronouns with *any-*, *every-*, and *no-* (such as *anyone*, *everyone*, and *no one*) take singular verb forms.**

gets
Everyone in the company ~~get~~ a performance review once a year.

Editing Task

Find and correct six more mistakes in the paragraphs about management styles.

Management styles can vary widely. At one end of the extreme are the authoritarian managers who make all the decisions and are very strict. At the opposite *others* end, there are ~~other~~ who permit their employees to solve problems and suggest ideas theirselves. Permissive managers are most effective when innovation and
5   problem solving are part of the work process, for example, in technology. Stricter ones are effective when people are inexperienced or need a lot of guidance, or where there is high turnover of staff.

Mr. Jones is an example of an authoritarian manager. He relies only on hisself to make decisions at the restaurant where he works. Everyone are expected to follow
10   his orders exactly. His style works because employees are constantly changing, so nobody need to understand the rules and regulations.

Ms. Taylor is more democratic. The agents at her real estate agency manage their client accounts theirselves. Some of her agents focus on business while other work with private real estate accounts. It would be impossible for her to know
15   what each agent is doing at any given time, so Ms. Taylor's style works well for her company.

There are different kinds of management styles ranging from very controlling to very open. Effective managers have a style of managing that is appropriate to the needs of their companies.

Getting an Education

1 Grammar in the Real World

A What can make attending college in the United States difficult? Read the article about the cost of attending college. What are some ways to make college more affordable?

B Comprehension Check **Answer the questions.**

1 Why do public colleges cost less than private colleges?

2 What is the difference between a grant and a loan?

3 What are two ways students can reduce or eliminate tuition costs?

C Notice **Find the sentences in the article and complete them.**

1 French students do not have to worry about _____ a lot for a college education because the government pays for it.

2 Some students want to avoid _____ loans, so they apply for grants, which they do not have to repay.

3 _____ a sport for a college team is one way to receive a scholarship.

What do the missing words have in common? In which sentence(s) does the missing word act as a subject? In which sentence(s) does the missing word act as an object?

The Cost of U.S. HIGHER EDUCATION

In many countries, the cost of a college education is not very high. In France, for example, university students pay an affordable $220 a year. French students do not have to **worry about**
5 **paying** a lot for a college education because the government pays for it. In the United States, however, college tuition[1] is more expensive. Many students **have difficulty affording** it, especially at private colleges.[2] In 2010, the average cost per
10 year of a private college in the United States was $35,000.

Public colleges[3] generally cost less because they depend on the government to help pay some of the expenses of education. However, if budget
15 cuts reduce that money, tuition can increase. This can **prevent** students **from attending** even a public college.

The tuition at community colleges is the least expensive, costing about $3,500–$4,000 a year.
20 Community colleges offer two-year programs with an associate's degree.[4] Other colleges and universities offer four-year programs and a bachelor's degree.[5] **Not attending** a four-year college right away is one option students use to
25 save money. Many students attend a community college for the first two years of college and then transfer to a more expensive school for the last two years.

To help pay for college, many students
30 apply for financial aid. Financial aid consists of loans, grants,[6] scholarships, and work-study programs. Students can apply for a student loan at a low interest rate. They must, however, **plan on repaying** the loan plus interest after they
35 graduate. Some students want to **avoid repaying** loans, so they apply for grants, which they do not have to repay. Scholarships are another form of financial aid that students do not have to repay. **Playing** a sport for a college team is one way to
40 receive a scholarship. Finally, students can apply for work-study programs. In these programs, students work at jobs at their school and receive a small salary to help pay for expenses.

For students **interested in getting** a higher
45 education in the United States, the cost can be high; however, there are ways to make it less expensive. Once students resolve the issue of money, they can **concentrate on having** the exciting experience of college life.

---

[1]**tuition:** the money students pay for education

[2]**private college:** a school that does not receive its main financial support from the government

[3]**public college:** a school that depends on some financial support from the government

[4]**associate's degree:** a two-year degree at a community college

[5]**bachelor's degree:** a four-year degree at a college or university

[6]**grant:** money that a university, government, or an organization gives to someone for a purpose, such as to do research or study

2 Gerunds as Subjects and Objects

Grammar Presentation

A gerund is the *-ing* form of a verb that functions as a noun. It can be the subject or object of a sentence.	*Attending college is important these days.* *I enjoy learning.*

2.1 Using Gerunds as Subjects and Objects

A Use a singular verb form when the gerund is the subject of the sentence.	*Studying in the morning is difficult for me.* *Completing my application has taken hours.*
B Use a gerund as the object after the following verbs: Time: *delay, finish* Likes and dislikes: *appreciate, dislike, enjoy, mind* Effort and interest: *avoid, keep, practice* Communication: *defend, discuss, propose* Thinking: *consider, imagine, suggest*	*I finished working on the project last night.* *My sister dislikes working in a bookstore.* *I enjoy teaching.* *Practice interviewing with a friend.* *Discuss applying for a loan with your parents.* *He considered transferring to another school.*
C Use *not* before a gerund to make it negative.	*Not attending a four-year college is one option for students with little money.*
D Do not confuse a gerund with the present progressive form of the verb.	PRESENT PROGRESSIVE GERUND *I am considering working at home.*

▶▶ Verbs Followed by Gerunds Only: See page A7.
▶▶ Verbs followed by Gerunds or Infinitives: See page A7.

Grammar Application

Exercise 2.1 Gerunds as Subjects and Objects

A Students are commenting on the process of applying for college in the United States. Use the words to write sentences with gerund subjects and objects. Use the simple present for the main verbs.

1 complete the college application / take / a long time
   Completing the college application takes a long time.

2 find the money for college / be / a problem for me
   _____

3 my counselor / suggest / borrow money for college

_____

4 not get into a good college / worry / me

_____

5 I / enjoy / discuss my future plans with my friends

_____

6 not have enough money for tuition / be / a concern

_____

7 go to interviews at schools / make / me nervous

_____

8 teachers / suggest / start the application process early

_____

B Pair Work Discuss the gerunds in A with your partner. Which are subjects? Which are objects?

Exercise 2.2 Gerunds as Objects

A Complete the web article about tips for starting the college application process. Use the correct forms of the verbs in parentheses.

TIPS for GETTING a COLLEGE EDUCATION

Do you want a college education? First, _____consider looking_____ (consider / look)
(1)
for the right college as soon as possible. If you are in high school or attending community

college, _____ (keep / study) hard so you'll have good grades.
(2)
Some schools require an essay on their college application. Many students in this position

_____ (dislike / write) the essay, but it's important, so
(3)
_____ (not delay / think about) it. Some schools require an on-site
(4)
interview, so _____ (practice / interview) with your friends or family.
(5)

Where will the money come from? Some students

_____ (consider / pay) for college
(6)
themselves. Other students _____
(7)
(not mind / borrow) money from their families, but not all families

can afford to pay for a college education. Sit down with your

family, and discuss all the options. _____ (discuss / work) at a part-time
(8)

job while you go to school, and _____ (imagine / work), studying, and
(9)

adjusting to a new lifestyle all at once. Is this really for you? If you think it is, then following these
tips will make the process easier.

B Group Work Answer the questions. Use gerunds in your sentences. Then share your ideas with the group.

- What should people in high school keep doing as soon as they decide to go to college?
- What should people consider doing when they need money for college?
- What should people try imagining before they make the final decision to go to college?

Exercise 2.3 More Gerunds as Objects

Use the words to write sentences about students and tuition costs. Use gerunds as objects
and the present progressive form of the main verbs.

1 Jack / consider / go to a community college to save money
   Jack is considering going to a community college to save money.

2 Bo / think about / apply for financial aid instead of working

   _____

3 Jane / avoid / borrow money by getting a part-time job at school

   _____

   _____

4 My parents and I / not discuss / get a loan

   _____

5 Tom / not enjoy / work while he goes to college

   _____

6 My friend / delay / go back to school until he saves more money

   _____

   _____

7 Lisa and Henry / discuss / take part in a work-study program

   _____

   _____

8 Mei-ling / not consider / start college without a part-time job

   _____

   _____

9 Naresh / avoid / apply to too many different institutions

   _____

3 Gerunds After Prepositions and Fixed Expressions

Grammar Presentation

The gerund is the only verb form used after prepositions and in certain fixed expressions.	*I am interested in studying art.* *I'm not in favor of skipping a year of college.*

3.1 Using Gerunds as Objects of Prepositions

Use a gerund as the object of prepositions after these common verb + preposition combinations:

Likes, dislikes, emotions: *be afraid of, care for, be excited about, be interested in, worry about (or be worried about)*

Are you afraid of failing?
Bryn is excited about applying to college.
I worry about not choosing the right school.

Interests and efforts: *be interested in, learn about, be responsible for, be successful at, take care of*

Many students are responsible for paying their own tuition.

Communication: *complain about, hear of, insist on, talk about, be warned of*

Some parents complain about having more than one child in college at the same time.
My friend insisted on visiting the school with me.
Did anyone talk about studying together tonight?

Thought: *be aware of, believe in, concentrate on, dream of, forget about*

I believe in sometimes staying up all night to study for a test.
My sister dreams of winning a scholarship.

Blame and responsibility: *admit to, apologize for, confess to, be guilty of*

We apologize for not contacting you sooner.

Other: *apply for, depend on, plan on, be used to*

I'm used to taking care of myself. I've lived alone for years.

▶▶ Verbs + Prepositions: See page A9.

3.2 Using Gerunds with Common Fixed Expressions

A Use a gerund after certain common fixed verb + noun expressions: *have a difficult time/have difficulty/have trouble, spend time/spend money, waste time/waste money*

She <u>had trouble</u> **finishing** her degree.
I <u>spent a lot of time</u> **helping** in the library.
Don't <u>waste time</u> **complaining**.

B Use a gerund after certain common fixed noun + preposition expressions: *an excuse for, in favor of, an interest in, a reason for*

There's <u>no excuse for</u> **being** late.
He has <u>a reason for</u> **choosing** this school.

▶▶ Expressions with Gerunds: See page A8.

Grammar Application

Exercise 3.1 Gerunds as Objects of Prepositions

A student is talking about his plans for going to college. Match the sentence parts.

1 Many students worry __*c*__

2 To pay for their education, they depend _____

3 I am very interested _____

4 I hope I will be successful _____

5 I'm not used _____

6 Fortunately, my parents want me to concentrate _____

7 They are planning _____

a in getting a college education.

b on applying for financial aid for me.

c̸ about being able to afford college tuition.

d on receiving scholarships and loans.

e on having an exciting college experience and not worrying about finances.

f at getting into the school of my choice.

g to studying and working at the same time.

Exercise 3.2 More Gerunds as Objects of Prepositions

A Complete the presentation on grants. Use the correct prepositions for the verbs in bold and the gerund form of the verbs in parentheses.

I know many of you are **excited** ___*about starting*___ (start) college soon. Also,
                                              (1)

many of you are **worried** _____ (pay) for school. I'm sure you have
                                      (2)

been **warned** _____ (take) out a lot of big loans. You have heard
                          (3)

some people **complain** _____ (owe) money for the rest of their lives.
                                (4)

Well, today, I'm going to **talk** _____ (apply) for three grants. Grants
(5)

aren't loans. You aren't **responsible** _____ (pay) them back.
(6)

    The first type is the Pell Grant. The Pell Grant is for students who are

going to college at least part-time and need financial aid. If you're **interested**

_____ (ask) for a Pell Grant, **insist** _____ (talk)
(7)   (8)

with a guidance counselor to find out more about this program.

    Are any of you **planning** _____ (major) in the areas of science
(9)

or mathematics? Then you might be **interested** _____ (try) for the
(10)

National Smart Grant. **Forget** _____ (get) this grant unless you
(11)

have maintained at least a 3.0 GPA in your first two years of college.

    Finally, I know some of you are **dreaming** _____ (become)
(12)

teachers. The TEACH Grant is for students who **plan** _____ (teach)
(13)

at least four years in a low-income public or private school after graduation.

    Now, are there any questions?

B Read about each person's situation and complete the advice. Use the words in parentheses
with the correct preposition and the gerund form of the verbs.

1 Chelsea wants to be an engineer, but she doesn't have a 3.0 GPA. She should not
   **depend on getting** (depend/get) a National Smart Grant.

2 Michael has completed two years of community college, but he doesn't
   have enough money to go to a four-year college. He should not
   _____ (be afraid/apply for) a Pell Grant.

3 Alison got a TEACH Grant, but she quit her teaching job after two years and got a
   high-paying job in computers instead. She must not _____
   (be worried/pay) back her loan.

4 Brandon goes to the community college, but he spends time partying and has a low
   GPA. He must not _____ (be interested/study).

5 Jorge got a TEACH Grant, taught for several years, and now is the head teacher at a
   private school. He must _____ (be successful/teach).

6 Sharon wants to major in computer science and get a National Smart Grant, but so
   far, her grades aren't that good. She should _____
   (concentrate/improve) her grades.

7 Rob's family can't help him pay for college, and he needs financial aid. He can
   probably _____ (depend/receive) a Pell Grant.

A Complete the conversations about college life. Use the correct forms of the fixed expressions in the box and the gerund forms of the verbs in parentheses.

(an) excuse for	have difficulty	in favor of	spend time
(an) interest in	have trouble	(a) reason for	waste time

Conversation 1

A   I've heard some crazy _excuses for not handing in_ (not / hand in) papers.
(1)

B   I don't think there's any good _____ (not / do) your
(2)
work once you're in college.

Conversation 2

A   You _____ a lot of _____ (study). Does
(3)   (3)
it help?

B   Yes, I would _____ (keep up) with my classes if I
(4)
didn't spend a lot of time studying.

Conversation 3

A   A lot of people _____ (party) in college. What do you
(5)
plan on doing after you leave this school?

B   I have _____ (get) a bachelor's degree, so I plan on
(6)
transferring to a four-year institution.

Conversation 4

A   What type of student is the Joe Olinsky Foundation
_____ (give) grants to?
(7)

B   We have money from a government fund that
we use for students who would otherwise
_____ (afford) a
(8)
two-year college.

B Listen and check your answers.

C Group Work **Answer the questions. Use gerunds when appropriate. Then compare your sentences in your groups.**

- What do you spend most of your time doing at school?
- What do you have the most trouble dealing with at school?
- What do you have an interest in doing after you leave this school?

Viet spends most of his time at school going to classes. I do, too. He has the most trouble dealing with parking. I have trouble dealing with the homework.

4 Gerunds After Nouns + *of*

Grammar Presentation

Gerunds are often used after nouns + *of*.	*The cost of getting an education is rising.* *I believe in the importance of studying hard.*

4.1 Nouns + *of* + Gerunds

The following nouns are often used in noun + *of* + gerund combinations:	
benefit of	A benefit of **going** to community college is cost savings.
cost of	The cost of **commuting** is rising because of gas prices.
danger of	There is a danger of **borrowing** too much money.
(dis)advantage of	What are some disadvantages of **taking** out loans for school?
effect of	The effects of **being** late are serious.
fear of	The fear of **being** jobless is what keeps me in school.
habit of	I'm in the habit of **not getting** up early.
idea of	The idea of **not going** to school is not an option.
importance of	It's impossible to underestimate the importance of **working** hard in school.
possibility of	The possibility of **not graduating** is worrisome.
problem of	The problem of **increasing** college costs affects a lot of students.
process of	He explained the process of **enrolling** in school.
risk of	She told me about the risks of **taking** out a loan.
way of	I'm thinking of a way of **paying** for school.

Exercise 4.1 Nouns + *of* + Gerunds

A Complete the conversations between Ms. Sparks, a community college counselor, and various families. Use the gerund form and the words in parentheses.

Conversation 1

Ms. Jones We are concerned about *the cost of paying* (the cost/pay) for our
(1)
son's education.

Ms. Sparks I understand _____
(2)
(the fear/not be able to) afford college.

Ms. Jones Of course, I want my son to have _____
(3)
(the possibility/get) the best education there is, but it's expensive.

Conversation 2

Mr. Allen What are _____ (the advantages/go)
(4)
to a community college?

Ms. Sparks _____ (the benefits/attend) a community
(4)
college are numerous. It's especially helpful for students who aren't sure of
their major.

Mr. Allen Is there _____ (a possibility/get) in this semester?
(4)

Ms. Sparks Yes, you can register today, if you like.

Conversation 3

Luisa _____ (the process/apply) to college is long!
(4)

Ms. Sparks I know it takes time, but you can reduce _____
(4)
(the risk/leave) something out by being organized. Here's a checklist to use.

B Over to You Write four sentences on a separate piece of paper about your family's and
your thoughts about going to school. Use some of the noun + *of* expressions in the box with
gerunds. Then share your sentences with a partner.

benefit of	effect of	habit of	idea of	possibility of	risk of	way of

One benefit of going to school when you are older is that you know what you want to do.

5 Avoid Common Mistakes ⚠

1 **Remember to use a gerund after a preposition.**

getting
Students often worry about ~~get~~ into college.

2 **As a general rule, when you use a verb as a subject, use a gerund.**

Paying
~~Pay~~ for a private college can be very expensive.

3 **Always use a singular verb with a gerund subject.**

is
Interviewing at several colleges ~~are~~ time-consuming.

Editing Task

Find and correct seven more mistakes in the paragraphs about study habits.

studying
All students start the semester with the intention of ~~study~~ hard; however, find
time to study can be challenging. Finding good places to study are one challenge.
Another is finding enough hours in the day and creating a schedule. Successful
students face these problems realistically.

5   Different people have different purposes and needs when it comes to doing
college work. Study in a quiet library works well for some people. At the same time, a
coffee shop or cafeteria can also be a good place to work for those who get energy
from be in a stimulating environment.

Then there is the question of time. Most students today are working, paying
10 bills, and taking classes at the same time, so they do not have the luxury of spend
many hours with their books. However, research offers hope. Studying for a few
minutes several times a day are a good way to learn new material.

Learn what works for you is the key to academic success.

Infinitives

Innovative Marketing Techniques

1 Grammar in the Real World

A What are some unusual types of advertising that you have noticed recently? Read the article on "guerrilla marketing." How do advertisers measure the success of a guerrilla marketing campaign?

B Comprehension Check **Answer the questions.**

1 What is guerrilla marketing? What is the purpose of guerrilla marketing?

2 How does guerrilla marketing get people's attention?

3 How is it different from traditional advertising?

C Notice **Find the sentences in the article and complete them.**

1 She wanted _____ it to raise money for her son's education.

2 The police tried _____ and destroy all of the signs.

3 A way to advertise with guerrilla marketing is _____ the environment in an unexpected way.

What do all the verbs you wrote have in common? Look at the words that come before these verbs. What kinds of words are they?

Advertising,
Guerrilla Style

Would you tattoo a website address on your body? One woman from Utah did just that. A company **got her to tattoo** its website address on her forehead for $10,000. She **wanted to**
5 **do** it to raise money for her son's education. The company **wanted her to do** it for cheap advertising space. They also got free publicity[1] because the story was on the news. This kind of extreme advertising – known as guerrilla
10 marketing – uses surprising ways to advertise a product and get people's attention.

A **way to advertise** with guerrilla marketing is **to use** the environment in an unexpected way. For example, a few years ago, a popular candy
15 company painted park benches so that they looked like giant chocolate bars. This creative ad[2] strategy got consumers' attention in a positive way.

For guerrilla marketing to be successful,
20 people must talk about the ads. A well-known sneaker company formed a partnership with Berlin's public transportation system. Every pair of sneakers was also a free pass to public transportation across the city for a whole year.
25 Anyone wearing the sneakers could ride the buses and trains at no extra cost. The news quickly spread on social media.

Not all guerrilla marketing works. A few years ago, an ad company **decided to place** signs with
30 flashing lights around different cities to advertise a television show. However, in Boston, the police thought the signs were bombs. The police **tried to find** and **destroy** all of the signs.

Unlike those who use traditional advertising
35 strategies, guerrilla marketers are not **afraid to shock** people. The idea is to **convince people to talk** about the products. However, it is **important** for companies **to consider** how people will react. Not all publicity is always good publicity.

---

[1] **publicity:** the attention received as a result of an activity meant to attract interest

[2] **ad:** advertisement; advertising

2 Infinitives with Verbs

Grammar Presentation

An infinitive is *to* + the base form of a verb. Some main verbs in a sentence are followed by an infinitive, not a gerund.	*I decided **to learn** about advertising.* *The company planned **not to use** traditional advertising.*

2.1 Verbs + Infinitives

Use an infinitive after the following verbs: Time: *hesitate, wait* Likes or dislikes: *care* Plans or desires: *decide, hope, need, plan* Efforts: attempt, *help, learn, manage* Communication: *agree, offer, promise* Possibility: *appear, seem, tend* Use *not* before the infinitive to show the infinitive is negative.	*We hesitated **to use** guerrilla marketing.* *I don't care **to see** boring ads on TV.* *The company is hoping **to buy** advertising space.* *Guerrilla marketers attempt **to get** your attention.* *Our company promised **not to waste** money.* *Guerrilla ads tend **to shock** consumers.*

▶▶ Verbs Followed by Infinitives Only: See page A7.

2.2 Verbs + Objects + Infinitives

A After some verbs, an object comes before the infinitive. The object performs the action of the infinitive. The following verbs are followed by an object + infinitive: *advise, allow, convince, encourage, get, persuade, prepare, teach, tell, urge,* and *warn.*	VERB + OBJ + INF *He got us **to try** a new advertising technique.* *The company didn't tell the salespeople **to educate** consumers.* *They urged the advertisers **not to surprise** people.*
B Some verbs can be followed by either an object + infinitive or an infinitive only. These verbs include *ask, choose, expect, help, need, promise, want,* and *would like.*	VERB + OBJ + INF *My department chose Sally **to create** the new ads.* (Sally will create the ads.) VERB + INF *My department chose **to create** the new ads.* (My department will create the ads.)

▶▶ Verbs + Objects + Infinitives: See page A8.

Data from the Real World

Research shows that these are the most common verbs + infinitives in academic writing:

appear, begin, continue, fail, seem, tend, try, want

Sales of the new product *continued to rise* last month.
The boss *failed to recognize* the company's problems.

Grammar Application

Exercise 2.1 Verbs + Infinitives

Complete the homework assignment about guerrilla marketing with the correct forms of the words in parentheses. Use the simple present form of the main verbs.

GUERRILLA MARKETING

Guerrilla marketing ___*attempts to reach*___ (attempt/reach) consumers
(1)

in unexpected or unusual contexts, such as public places. Guerrilla marketers

___hopes to shock___ (hope/shock) or surprise potential consumers.
(2)

Why is guerrilla marketing so popular? One reason for this is that it

___tend to cost___ (tend/cost) less than traditional marketing.
(3)

Guerrilla marketing usually ___manages to generate___ (manage/generate)
(4)

a lot of publicity for little money. It ___seem to be___ (seem/be) effective
(5)

for most products; however, several experts think that people are getting tired of it.

I ___hesitate to admit___ (hesitate/admit) this, but I agree.
(6)

Exercise 2.2 Verbs + Objects + Infinitives

A Complete the conversation about a nontraditional type of advertising called reverse graffiti. Use the words in parentheses. Use the correct form of the main verbs according to the context.

Dae Ho Our advertising consultants ___*are advising us to try*___ (advise/us/try) a type
(1)
of guerrilla marketing called reverse graffiti.

Erin What's reverse graffiti?

Luis It's a way to write an image on a dirty public surface by removing the dirt.
It _____ (get/consumers/notice)
(2)
a product. Do you think the managers will like the idea?

| Erin | Actually, I think the managers will _____ (3) (tell / us / not do) it. |

| Dae Ho | Why? I think we can probably _____ (4) (convince / them / try) it because it's cheap. |

| Luis | I bet we can _____ (5) (persuade / them / do) it. |

| Dae Ho | OK. We'll need help, though. |

| Luis | I'll _____ (6) (tell / Mike / create) a presentation. |

| Erin | OK, Luis, but you should _____ (7) (warn / him / prepare) for a lot of questions. Some people think it destroys property, so it's vandalism. It might not be legal. |

B Over to You **Answer the questions with information that is true for you. Include the verbs from A in your answers. Then share your sentences with a partner.**

■ What is your opinion of guerrilla marketing?

■ Does it work for you and your demographic (that is, people who are your age and have similar likes and dislikes)? Why or why not?

Guerrilla marketing tends to work well with people my age because my generation likes innovative ideas.

Exercise 2.3 Verbs + Infinitives and Verbs + Objects + Infinitives

Complete the report on quick response (QR) codes.[1] Use the words in parentheses with the simple present or simple past form.

Last week, Steve Green ___*asked me to look into*___ (ask / me / look into)
                                              (1)
QR codes, so I decided to interview people who use QR codes for marketing.

One way companies use QR codes is through smartphones. Consumers point their smartphones at QRs, and the code takes them immediately to a company or product website.

I _____ (choose / interview) two different people. Steve
      (2)
_____ (urge / me / interview) the manager from Dan's Gourmet
      (3)

Food for this report because his company uses QR codes. Dan said the QR codes

_____ (help/inform) consumers about the nutritional content of
(4)
the product and _____ (help/them/use) the product correctly.
(5)
Dan also _____ (want/consumers/find out) about
(6)
new products, so the QR code contains a link to Dan's company's website. The QR code

_____ (promise/become) an important marketing tool.
(7)

   After I interviewed the manager from Dan's, I _____
(8)
(prepare/visit) Liz Kurikova, the owner of a small flower shop. She was unable to meet

with me this week, but she _____ (encourage/me/contact)
(9)
a friend of hers who runs a small ice cream shop. I spoke with Ned Searby at Astoria

Ice Cream. Currently, they _____ (not need/offer) this
(10)
option to their customers. Once they start selling other products, however, they

_____ (expect/include) QR codes for products on the shelves.
(11)
They _____ (would like/use) this technology to expand their
(12)
business and promote their new products.

[1]**QR code:** an image like a bar code on products that contains links to text,
web addresses, and other types of information

3 Infinitives vs. Gerunds

Grammar Presentation

Some verbs can be followed by an infinitive or a gerund. Much of the time, the meaning is the same or very close, but sometimes there is a difference in meaning.

The woman stopped to read the ad.
(The woman saw the ad as she was walking and stopped. She read the ad.)
The woman stopped reading the ad.
(The woman was reading the ad. Then she stopped.)

3.1 Similar Meanings of Infinitives vs. Gerunds

After some verbs, you can use either a gerund or an infinitive without any change in meaning. Verbs that can be followed by either an infinitive or a gerund include *begin, can't stand, continue, hate, like, love, prefer,* and *start.*

Broadcasters love to get free publicity.
Broadcasters love getting free publicity.

When *begin, continue,* or *start* are in a progressive form, use an infinitive.

I'm beginning **to work** on the assignment now.
NOT *I'm beginning* ~~working~~ *on the assignment now.*

3.2 Different Meanings of Infinitives vs. Gerunds

A The following verbs can be followed by either an infinitive or a gerund, but the meaning is different:

Infinitives	Gerunds
Did you forget **to tell** *your assistant you'd be late today?* (You never told your assistant.)	*Did you* forget **telling** *your assistant you'd be late today?* (You told your assistant, but you do not remember it.)
I regret **to tell** *you that our sales have dropped.* (I'm sorry that our sales have dropped, but I'm telling you about it.)	*I* regret **telling** *you that our sales have dropped.* (I told you our sales had dropped, but I wish I hadn't.)
They remembered **to email** *the sales figures.* (They almost forgot, but then they sent the email.)	*They* remembered **emailing** *the sales figures.* (They sent the email. Later, they thought about it again.)
People stopped **to look** *at the colorful signs.* (People stopped and looked at them.)	*People* stopped **looking** *at the colorful signs.* (People were looking at them but then stopped.)
The mayor tried **to change** *the town's name, but the citizens didn't want to.* (This was an experiment to see if he could do it. The mayor didn't succeed. He couldn't change the name.)	*The mayor* tried **changing** *the town's name, but it didn't help tourism.* (The mayor made an effort to do this, and he succeeded. He changed the name.)

B Note that the meaning of *tried* is only different in the past.

I tried **to pay** *with a credit card, but the store only accepted cash.* (I wanted to pay with a credit card, but they wouldn't let me.)
≠ *I* tried **paying** *with a credit card, but I didn't like it.* (I did pay with a credit card.)

I will try **to call** *you tomorrow.*
= *I will* try **calling** *you tomorrow.*
(= Tomorrow I plan to call you, but it may not work.)

▸◂ Verbs Followed by Gerunds or Infinitives: See page A7.

⌨ Grammar Application

Exercise 3.1 Meanings of Infinitives vs. Gerunds

A Rewrite the sentences about paying people to promote products through social media. Replace the infinitives in bold with gerunds. Replace the gerunds in bold with infinitives. Then label the sentence *S* (if the meaning is the same) or *D* (if the meaning is different).

1 Companies have begun **to pay** people to blog about their products.

   Companies have begun paying people to blog about their products.   *S*

2 LP Social Friends regrets **to tell** the media that they pay people to be "friends."

3 I stopped **to read** the article about social media marketing.

4 Alison forgot **mentioning** GamerWorld in her blog yesterday.

5 Upside Energy Drinks continues **to pay** fans on social networking sites.

6 People have started **questioning** Upside Energy Drinks' marketing strategy.

7 A lot of people can't stand **reading** blogs that are full of ads.

8 GamerWorld tried **to pay** me to write about them in my blog.

9 I tried **changing** the privacy settings since I don't want messages from advertisers.

B Pair Work In which sentences in A does the meaning change? Explain the difference in meaning to a partner.

A Listen to a discussion of the results of a focus group.[1] The focus group watched a reality TV show called *Jake's Life* and tried to remember a product that they saw in the show. Match the sentence parts.

1 Bo regrets _____e_____   a to push the button when Jake drank soda.
2 Bo tried _____   b to get a snack.
3 Jocelyn doesn't regret _____ c to stop reading.
4 Participant 1 stopped _____   d seeing Jake drink anything.
5 Participant 2 stopped _____   ≠ to say that the product placement isn't working.
6 Participant 3 didn't remember _____   f watching after the third episode.
7 Nobody forgot _____   g doing things differently this time.
8 Jocelyn told Bo _____   h hiring Bo.

[1]**focus group:** a group of people whose opinions help marketers

B Listen again and check your answers.

4 Infinitives After Adjectives and Nouns

Grammar Presentation

| Infinitives can also follow some adjectives and nouns. | The consumers were **happy to see** some interesting advertising.
 The advertisers needed more **time to educate** the community. |

4.1 *Be* + Adjectives + Infinitives

| Use infinitives after the following adjectives: *afraid, amazed, difficult, easy, embarrassed, fun, interesting, lucky, necessary, ready, sad, shocked, sorry, surprised, (un)likely, upset.* | Some companies are _afraid_ **to use** new marketing techniques.
 The police were _ready_ **to destroy** the ads.
 The advertisers were _sorry_ **to cause** a problem. |
| *It + be* is frequently used with many of these words. | _It would be fun_ **to surprise** people with guerrilla advertising. |

▸▸ Be + Adjectives + Infinitives: See page A9.

4.2 Nouns + Infinitives

| Use infinitives after the following nouns: *ability, chance, decision, time, way.* | Some ads have the _ability_ **to excite** the public.
 It was a great _chance_ **to learn** something new.
 It's _time_ **to be** more creative in advertising. |

Grammar Application

Complete the article about tracking technology. Use the adjective + infinitive combinations in the box.

difficult / avoid	fun / go	necessary / use	~~surprising / know~~
easy / acquire	interesting / read	shocked / find out	unlikely / change

Who is watching you as you visit Internet pages? It may be

surprising to know that advertisers are following you as you surf
(1)

the Web. Many Internet users would be _____
(2)

how much companies know about them through tracking technology

such as cookies, which allow websites to identify visitors and

their web page preferences. Today, because of tracking technology, it is

_____ data on people's habits and tastes. Most websites
(3)

have this technology, so it is _____ . Companies believe
(4)

that it is _____ tracking because it helps consumers
(5)

find out about products that they like.

Here is an example of what companies can learn through tracking.

Maria thinks it is _____ to websites and comment
(6)

on movies she has seen. She also thinks it is _____
(7)

about health issues on several sites. She notices that ads pop up on topics

that she has done searches on, but she is _____ her
(8)

search habits because of this.

Complete the conversations about using nontraditional marketing. Use the words in parentheses to write sentences.

1 **A** We're going to do a survey on how well guerrilla marketing really works.

  B (that/be/a good way/get/information)

    That's a good way to get information.

2 **A** Our survey shows that product placement isn't working.

  B (it/be/time/do/something different now)

3 **A** Are you going to use QR codes or reverse graffiti?

  B (we/make/the decision/use/QR codes/yesterday)

4 **A** Why should I hire your advertising agency?

  B (we/have/the ability/attract/the 18- to 24-year-old demographic)

5 **A** Why are you considering paying sports bloggers to write about your product?

  B (it/be/a chance/introduce/our product to athletes)

6 **A** Why doesn't guerrilla marketing work, in your opinion?

  B (it/not/be/the best way/get/messages across/to older demographics)

7 **A** Why is the character holding the soda can so we can see the brand?

  B (it/be/a chance/sell/the product to viewers)

Group Work **Think about the different types of marketing below. Evaluate each strategy in terms of how it works with children, teens, adults, and seniors (people over age 65). Compare and discuss your ideas with your group members. Use an infinitive + adjective and noun in each statement.**

Guerrilla marketing may not be an effective way to attract seniors because it may be too shocking for some of them.

- Traditional advertising (TV commercials, magazine ads)
- Guerrilla marketing
- Product placement (placement of products in movies and TV shows)
- Viral marketing (paying bloggers and people with social networking sites)

5 Avoid Common Mistakes ⚠

1 **With the verb *want*, use verb + object + infinitive, not verb + *that* clause.**

to
The advertisers want ~~that~~ you∧buy their products.

2 **Use the correct word order when using the negative form of an infinitive.**

not
The company decided∧to ~~not~~ pay bloggers to write about their products.

3 **Do not confuse the preposition *to* with an infinitive *to*.**

PREP + GERUND
seeing
I look forward to ~~see~~ the new dragon movie.

VERB + INFINITIVE
see
Many people like to ~~seeing~~ familiar places and objects in a movie.

4 **Use an infinitive (*to* + the base form of verb), not *for* + base form of verb, where appropriate.**

to
It is important ~~for~~ make sure the advertisement targets the right audience.

Editing Task

Find and correct the mistakes in the paragraphs about advertising in movies.

Product placement in movies is a type of advertising that is popular today.
to
Advertisers want ~~that~~ consumers∧see their products in movies so that their products will
seem more appealing. That's why advertisers pay filmmakers for place their products in
movies. For example, in one movie, a director arranged to using a pair of famous brand-
5   name sunglasses for make his characters appear fashionable. In another movie, the plot
required a certain type of luxury car. The filmmakers used the car in their film, but in this
case, they did not receive any money from the auto's manufacturers. For the automaker, it
was an easy way to not pay for advertising. Filmmakers seem to not mind the advertising
because they can earn extra money. Moviegoers do not seem to mind it, either.
10   In my opinion, product placement in movies is acceptable, but I want that
advertisers use product placement carefully. If directors expect to making a film that
is believable, then everything in the film must fit the story. Otherwise, the movie will
seem more like an advertisement. This would be terrible. I hope that filmmakers
continue to making wise decisions and use products that look natural on screen.

Negative Questions and Tag Questions

Geographic Mobility

1 Grammar in the Real World

A Have you moved very often in your life? If so, why did you move? Read the interview about geographic mobility. What are some of the reasons why people move?

B Comprehension Check **Answer the questions.**

1 What are some reasons why people move long distances?

2 What are some reasons why people stay nearby when they move?

3 Why is the mobility rate in Russia lower than in the United States?

C Notice **Find the sentences in the article and complete them.**

1 Professor, you **have been** interested in geographic mobility for

a long time, _____ you?

2 Mobility **isn't** easy to explain, _____ it?

Look at the verbs you wrote and the verbs in bold. What do you notice about the use of *not*?

Geographic Mobility
ACROSS CULTURES

Interviewer Today we're speaking with two specialists in geographic mobility. They will discuss some reasons why people move from one place to another. Professor O'Neill is from
5 Carlow University in the United States, and Professor Tabenkin is from Zala University in Russia. Let's start with Professor O'Neill. Professor, you have been interested in geographic mobility for a long time,
10 **haven't you**?

O'Neil Well, yes. When I was a boy, my best friend moved away, and that affected me deeply. As I grew older, I saw more people move away. I noticed that the population
15 decrease affected local businesses. As a result, I got interested in the choices people make about moving.

Interviewer People are very mobile and are moving a lot. But most people aren't moving long
20 distances, **are they**? **Isn't** that curious?

O'Neil Yes. That's interesting. In fact, I've been studying the connection between moving and distance recently. Every year, about 11.6 percent of people in the United States
25 move, and of these, about 14.8 percent move to a different state.

Interviewer **Doesn't** that surprise you?

O'Neil No, not really. Often, people who change jobs have to move long distances. On
30 the other hand, people looking for better housing usually stay near their original home. And people who relocate[1] for family reasons may move far away or stay nearby.

Interviewer So, I guess it depends on the situation,
35 **doesn't it**?

O'Neil That's right. It's more complicated than you may think. For example, my wife was living in California when we met. When we got married, she moved a long distance to live
40 with me in Chicago. Now her sister, who lives near Chicago, is expecting a baby. She and her husband plan to move a short distance to be closer to us.

Interviewer Professor Tabenkin, people in Russia have
45 the same issues, **don't they**?

Tabenkin To a certain extent, yes. It's harder to find housing in Russia, so people tend to move less frequently. In fact, the mobility rate in Russia is less than 2 percent. In my
50 research, I found that young people often decide not to move because available, affordable housing would take them further from family.

Interviewer OK. But **don't** people sometimes have to
55 move long distances for economic reasons?

Tabenkin Yes, that's true. Personally, I had to move a very long distance ten years ago because there were no jobs nearby. However, my experience doesn't seem to be the norm.[2]

Interviewer 60 Mobility isn't easy to explain, **is it**? Thank you both for your thoughts on this issue.

---

[1]**relocate:** move to a new place   [2]**norm:** an expected situation or a situation considered to be typical

2 Negative Questions

Grammar Presentation

Negative questions are similar to *Yes/No* questions in that they begin with an auxiliary verb, a modal, or a form of *be*.	*Haven't you moved recently?* *Aren't there many reasons why people move?*

2.1 Forming Negative Questions

A Negative questions usually begin with a contraction.	*Don't you live around here?* *Can't you help me move?* *Wasn't he living in Chicago?*
B The full form of *not* in negative questions is very formal. The word *not* comes between the subject and the main verb.	*Were they **not** living in Chicago?* *Have you **not** moved recently?*
C With a contraction, use *are* instead of *am* with *I*. Use *am* when you use the full form.	*Aren't I correct?* *Am I not correct?*

2.2 Using Negative Questions

A Use negative questions when you think the information is true and you expect people to agree.	*Don't people often move when they change jobs?* (My experience tells me people often move when they change jobs.) *Isn't it unusual for people to move in Russia?* (I've read that it's unusual to move in Russia.)
B Use negative questions to show surprise or disbelief.	*"Tom has changed his major to English."* *"Really? Isn't he still planning to work at a bank?"*
C Use negative questions to show annoyance or anger.	*Didn't you say you would call me?* (I'm angry that you didn't call me.) *Shouldn't Bob have finished that report by now?* (I'm annoyed because Bob hasn't finished the report.)

2.3 Answering Negative Questions

Respond to a negative question just as you would a regular *Yes/No* question. Typically, we answer negative questions with *yes* or *no* and an explanation.	*"Don't you want to move?"* (Do you want to move?) *"**Yes**, I do. I'd like to live somewhere else."* *"**No**, I don't. I really want to stay here."*

Grammar Application

Exercise 2.1 Negative Questions

A family is packing for a big move. Complete the negative questions with the correct form of the words in parentheses.

1 _____*Didn't I tell*_____ (I told) you to be careful with that lamp?

2 _____ (you have been listening) to what I've been saying?

3 _____ (you can stop) texting and help me?

4 _____ (you should have bought) bigger boxes?

5 _____ (I am) correct that you promised to help?

6 _____ (you were going to take) the baby to the neighbor's?

Exercise 2.2 More Negative Questions

Read the sentences about moving and migration. Then write negative questions with the information in parentheses. Use contractions when possible.

1 A lot of people left Ireland in the 1800s.
   Didn't a lot of people leave because of a famine?
   (You heard that a lot of people left because of a famine.)

2 Hope of employment brings a lot of immigrants to rich countries.
   _____
   (You heard that good schools have made rich countries more attractive, too.)

3 Some people move great distances.
   _____
   (You heard that some people move great distances to reunite with family members.)

4 Some corporations require their employees to move to another country.
   _____
   (You think that this is happening more because of globalization.)

5 People are able to move around more freely because of globalization.
   _____
   (You heard that the laws are changing to allow even more movement.)

Pair Work Read the chart on migration in the United States. Study it for 30 seconds. Then cover it. What details can you remember? Ask your partner negative questions. Then switch roles and answer your partner's negative questions.

A *Haven't 60 percent of men moved?*

B *Yes, that's right.*

A *And haven't 50 percent of college graduates moved?*

B *Actually, no, 77 percent of college graduates have moved.*

People Who Move: Percentages of people who have moved at least once in their lifetimes		
	% of People Who Have Moved	**% of People Who Have Never Moved**
Total	63	37
By Gender		
Men	60	40
Women	65	35
By Education		
College graduates	77	23
High school graduates	56	44

▶ www.pewsocialtrends.org/2008/12/17/who-moves-who-stays-put-wheres-home

3 Tag Questions

Grammar Presentation

Use tag questions to confirm information or ask for agreement.	*You're a professor, **aren't you**?* *He hasn't been studying, **has he**?*

3.1 Forming Tag Questions

A The verb in a tag question is an auxiliary verb, a modal, or a form of *be*.	*Your parents have never moved, **have** they?* *She got the job, **didn't** she?* *You can't stay, **can** you?*

3.1 Forming Tag Questions *(continued)*

B The pronoun in a tag question agrees with the subject.	*The students* will be on time, won't **they**? *Your sister* lives close by, doesn't **she**?
Use *it* when the subject is *that* or *something*.	*That's* amazing information, isn't **it**?
Use *they* when the subject is *someone* or *everyone*.	*Someone* recorded the interview, didn't **they**? *Everyone* respects the professor, don't **they**?
C Use an affirmative tag with a negative statement.	NEGATIVE STATEMENT AFFIRMATIVE TAG They *don't live* in Chicago, **do they**? You*'re not* from Russia, **are you**?
Use a negative tag with an affirmative statement.	AFFIRMATIVE STATEMENT NEGATIVE TAG Geography *is* interesting, **isn't it**? Her sister *moved* to Chicago, **didn't she**?

3.2 Answering Tag Questions

A In negative tags, we expect the listener to answer *yes*, but it is possible to answer *no*.	"They moved from Miami to Chicago, *didn't they*?"
	    "**Yes**, they got jobs in Illinois." (That's right, they moved.)
	    "Actually, **no**." (That's not right. They didn't move.)

B In affirmative tags, we expect the listener to answer *no*, but it is possible to answer *yes*.	"They didn't move from Miami to Chicago, *did they*?"
	    "**No**, they decided to stay." (You're right, they didn't move.)
	    "**Yes**, they had to move for work." (Actually, they did move.)

C You cannot answer *Yes . . . not*.	"They didn't move from Miami to Chicago, *did they*?" "**Yes, they did.**" OR "**No, they didn't.**" NOT "~~Yes, they didn't.~~"

Grammar Application

Exercise 3.1 Tag Questions

Match the statements and tags about a friend who is moving.

1 Erica and her family are moving overseas, __*d*__   a do they?

2 You knew about their move, _____   b didn't you?

3 Erica's company is relocating to London, _____   c aren't you?

4 Erica's husband won't get a new job, _____   d̸ aren't they?

5 They don't have a place to live yet, _____   e don't I?

6 Erica will get an international driving permit, _____   f isn't it?

7 I have a lot of information about their move, _____   g will he?

8 You're giving them a going-away party, _____   h won't she?

Exercise 3.2 Tags

Complete the questions about the stresses of moving. First underline the subject and circle the auxiliary verb in each sentence. Then write the correct tag.

1 <u>Moving</u> (can) be stressful as well as expensive, __*can't it*__ ?

2 People can sometimes deduct moving costs from their income taxes, _____ ?

3 Things have sometimes disappeared from a moving truck, _____ ?

4 Your friends will give you boxes, _____ ?

5 Everyone should read reviews of a moving company before hiring one, _____ ?

6 Marta has been disorganized since the move, _____ ?

7 Vinh and Ahn weren't moving today, _____ ?

8 It's been a stressful time for you, _____ ?

Exercise 3.3 Statements in Tag Questions

Complete the questions about people who are moving. Use the words in parentheses with the correct verb forms.

1 _____ *Mary is retiring to Florida* _____ , isn't she?
    (Mary / retire / Florida)

2 _____ , hasn't he?
    (Raul / relocate / London)

3 _____ , didn't she?
    (Annette / attend school / France)

4 _____ , won't they?
    (Miriam and Amir / turn down the promotion / New York)

5 _____ , did you?
(You / like / the air quality / Hong Kong)

6 _____ , will he?
(Bernard / take the children / with him / Texas)

Exercise 3.4 Answering Tag Questions

Complete the conversations with the expected answers.

Conversation 1

Paolo I'm interviewing for a job in New York.

You grew up there, didn't you?

Luis _____Yes, I did_____ . What do you want
(1)
to know?

Paolo Well, I'm worried about housing. Apartments
aren't cheap there, are they?

Luis _____ . They're also hard to find.
(2)

Conversation 2

Phoebe You've read the article on migration patterns for class today, haven't you?

Alex _____ . It was interesting.
(3)

Phoebe Oh, good. You don't have time to tell me about it before class, do you?

Alex _____ . But I can send you a link to the article.
(4)

Conversation 3

Claudia I heard the company is moving to Dallas, Texas. Some of us will have to move,

won't we?

Jun _____ . I'll know exactly who next week.
(5)

Claudia You have family there, so you won't mind moving, will you?

Jun _____ . My family's excited.
(6)

Conversation 4

Fen There are a lot of new families moving into the neighborhood, aren't there?

Bin _____ . I'm glad to see new faces.
(7)

Fen It's nice to see a lot of young children around again, isn't it?

Bin _____ . It's wonderful!
(8)

Use rising intonation in the tag when you are not certain your statement is true.	"Moving wasn't difficult, **was it**?" ↗ "Yes, it was!" "There won't be a quiz tomorrow, **will there**?" ↗ "No, there won't."
Use falling intonation when you expect the listener to agree with you.	"His research is really boring, **isn't it**?" ↘ "Yes, it is." "You didn't go to class, **did you**?" ↘ "No, I didn't."

A Listen and repeat the questions in the chart above.

B Listen to the conversations about a student moving far away to attend college. Draw the intonation pattern above the tag. Then write *U* if the speaker is uncertain of the information or *E* if the speaker is expecting agreement.

Conversation 1

1 You're not still thinking about going to college in Pennsylvania, are you? ↗ ___U___

2 But that college doesn't offer the major you want, does it? _____

Conversation 2

3 Your son is thinking of going to college far from home, isn't he? _____

4 Duquesne University is in Pittsburgh, isn't it? _____

Conversation 3

5 You're excited about moving to Pennsylvania for college, aren't you? _____

6 You're not worried about moving so far from home, are you? _____

Conversation 4

7 Your son is worried about moving so far from home, isn't he? _____

8 But you and your wife feel OK about him moving so far away, don't you? _____

C Pair Work Find out information about your partner by asking tag questions. Use both intonation patterns. Use rising intonation when you are uncertain and falling intonation when you expect agreement.

A *You're from Egypt, aren't you?*

B *Yes, I am. You're studying culinary arts, aren't you?*

A *Actually, no. My major is geography.*

4 Avoid Common Mistakes ⚠️

1 **In negative questions, use the auxiliary verb + *not*.**

Didn't she
~~She no~~ call you?

2 **Answer negative questions the same way as regular *Yes/No* questions.**

"Aren't you coming with us?"

No, I'm not.   *Yes, I am.*
"~~Yes.~~" (I'm not coming.)   "~~No.~~" (I'm coming.)

3 **In tag questions, remember to use an auxiliary verb + a pronoun in the tag.**

wasn't it
The research was old, ~~no~~?

4 **In the tag, use an auxiliary verb that agrees with the main verb + the correct pronoun for the subject.**

aren't they
They are still living in their hometown, ~~isn't it~~?

Editing Task

Find and correct six more mistakes in the conversation about economic mobility.

A   That article on economic mobility in America was really interesting, ~~no~~? *wasn't it*

B   It sure was. Some of the facts were surprising, isn't it? I was especially surprised that there is more economic mobility in countries like France and Germany.

A   I was, too. I thought there was more mobility here. By the way, don't you have a class
5   right now?

B   Yes. I'm finished for today. I'm free for the evening.

A   But you're working tonight, no?

B   No, I quit my job.

A   Really? Why? You no like it?

10 B   The job was fine. The truth is I'm moving to Florida with my family at the end of the semester, so I'm really busy.

A   You're kidding! Why? Your family no like it here?

B   They like it here, but there aren't many good jobs. We're moving where the jobs are.

A   But you only have one semester left, isn't it?

15 B   That's right, but I have to go with them.

1 Grammar in the Real World

A Is it possible to identify "typical" American values? Theories exist about the values Americans hold today – and why. Read the article about one view of American values. Do you agree with the writer's point of view?

B Comprehension Check **Match the two parts of the sentences.**

1 According to some historians, the difficulty of living on the frontier led to _____

2 Survival under difficult circumstances may have led to _____

3 The lack of towns and traditions may have led to _____

a optimism.

b the value of hard work.

c individualism.

C Notice **Find the sentences in the article and complete them.**

1 Many Americans _____ they must work hard in order to be happy.

2 Traditionally, American children _____ they are responsible for their own lives.

3 Not all historians _____ frontier life influenced modern American values.

How many subjects are in each of these sentences? What word connects the two clauses?

U.S. Cultural Values

Values are beliefs held in common by members of a group. They often come from shared experiences. For example, some historians assert[1] **that the settlement of the American**
5 **West in the nineteenth century shaped many American values. These include the importance** of hard work, optimism, and individualism.

Countless U.S. children have learned in school **that hard work is essential**. In fact,
10 many Americans believe **that they must work hard in order to be happy**. How did this belief develop? According to some researchers, as Americans moved deeper into the continent, they discovered **that the West was mostly**
15 **wilderness**.[2] Their lives were difficult, and they had to work hard to survive. Some historians are convinced **that their success helped form a general belief in the value of hard work**.

Furthermore, many Americans believe **that**
20 **they should have a positive view of the future**. A few historians suggest **that this perspective helped put men on the moon**. What is the origin of this optimism? Some research suggests **that struggles on the frontier[3] encouraged this**
25 **attitude**. People found **that they could survive, even in difficult situations**.

Another common belief about Americans is **that they are individualistic**. Traditionally, American children have learned **that they are**
30 **responsible for their own lives**. This way of thinking supports the idea **that every person can succeed through hard work**. In addition, Americans tend to believe **that they can start over when they make mistakes**. Why
35 do they feel this way? It is the belief of some historians **that this idea developed as a result of frontier life**. Because there were few towns and traditions, settlers created their own rules. Each new settlement developed its own ways
40 of getting things done. When settlements faced problems, they had no choice but to try new and different approaches.

Not all historians agree **that frontier life influenced modern American values**.
45 Furthermore, the United States is becoming more and more culturally diverse all the time. Undoubtedly, this is already affecting the values held by its citizens. In what way might American values change?

---

[1]**assert:** to state an opinion

[2]**wilderness:** an area of land that has not been farmed or had towns and roads built on it

[3]**frontier:** the western area of the United States that did not have many white settlers from the eastern part of the United States

2 *That* Clauses

Grammar Presentation

Noun clauses function like nouns in sentences. They often begin with the word *that*.	*Many people believe that they must work hard in order to be happy.*

2.1 Forming *That* Clauses

A *That* clauses have their own subject and verb.

MAIN CLAUSE	THAT CLAUSE
SUBJECT VERB	SUBJECT VERB

Many Americans think that anyone can succeed.

B In conversation and informal writing, *that* is often omitted. In academic writing, *that* is usually not omitted.

Most people recognize cooperation is important. (informal)

Most people recognize <u>that</u> cooperation is important. (formal)

2.2 Using *That* Clauses

Use *that* clauses after the following verbs that express mental activity:

assume, believe, decide, discover, expect, feel, find (out), guess, hear, hope, imagine, know, learn, notice, read, realize, recognize, say, see, show, suppose, think, understand

Can we <u>assume</u> that the core values have remained basically the same?

Some people <u>believe</u> that hard work brings happiness.

I've <u>discovered</u> that some cultures don't have a positive view of the future.

I <u>read</u> that American values developed during the colonial period.

Grammar Application

Exercise 2.1 Forming *That* Clauses

Combine the sentences about employees in the United States. Use *that* clauses.

1 Many Americans notice something. They are working harder but have less money.

   <u>*Many Americans notice that they are working*</u>
   <u>*harder but have less money.*</u>

2 In fact, recent research has found something. Hard work doesn't always lead to wealth.

   _____

   _____

3 Many older Americans are realizing something. They are unable to retire after working hard all their lives.

_____

_____

4 Many employees assumed something. Their companies would reward them for their hard work.

_____

_____

5 Researchers recently reported something. Job satisfaction has declined in recent years.

_____

_____

6 Employers are beginning to understand something. It is important to give people some freedom at work.

_____

_____

Exercise 2.2 Using *That* Clauses Without *That*

Over to You Do you believe that money makes people happy? Why or why not? Write five sentences. Use *that* clauses but do not use *that* in your sentences. Then share your sentences with a partner.

A *I don't think money makes people happy because having money causes many problems.*

B *I disagree. I believe you need a certain amount of money to feel secure, and this makes people happy.*

Exercise 2.3 Using *That* Clauses

A Write statements with *that* clauses using the words in parentheses.

1 Europeans work fewer hours than Americans. (I / understand)

   I understand that Europeans work fewer hours than Americans.

2 The average European gets about two months' vacation every year. (Michael / read)

   M_____

3 The average American works 46 weeks per year. (international labor statistics / show)

   _____

4 Culture may be one reason for the difference in attitudes toward work. (some experts / believe)

   _____

5 Europeans tend to value leisure more highly than Americans.
(a group of scholars / found)

_____

6 Americans tend to value earning money more highly than Europeans.
(some scholars / believe)

_____

7 Many Americans seem to use possessions as a measure of success.
(a professor at Gradina University / wrote)

_____

B Group Work As a group, talk about differences between Americans and Europeans. You may also include another culture that you know about. Discuss the following questions, or use your own ideas.

■ How much vacation time do Americans usually get?

■ How much vacation time do Europeans usually get?

■ How much vacation time do people from other cultures usually get?

■ Who tends to relax on vacation?

■ Who tends to bring work to do on vacation?

Use the following verbs in your discussion:

believe	hear	imagine	read	see	suppose	think

A *I've heard that Americans get less vacation time than Canadians.*
B *I think that's true. My brother lives in Canada, and he told me the same thing.*

3 Agreement Between *That* Clauses and Main Clauses

Grammar Presentation

Use a past form in a *that* clause when the verb refers to a past event. When it refers to a present event or state, use a present form.	*Some historians believe that American values developed a long time ago.* (present belief about a past action)
	Some historians believe that early American history explains certain American values. (present belief about a present state)

3.1 *That* Clauses in Sentences with Present Verbs in the Main Clause

A When the main clause is in the present, use a present form in the *that* clause to express a fact or general truth.	*Many Americans <u>feel</u> that nothing <u>is</u> impossible.*
	Some cultures <u>think</u> that cooperation <u>is</u> very important.
B When the main clause is in the present, use a past form in the *that* clause to describe a past event.	*Some historians <u>don't think</u> that early American history <u>influenced</u> American culture.*
C When the main clause is in the present, use a future form in the *that* clause to describe a future event.	*I <u>assume</u> that you <u>are going to do</u> more research.*

3.2 *That* Clauses in Sentences with Past Verbs in the Main Clause

A When the main clause is in the past, use a past form in the *that* clause to describe an event or idea that happened at the same time as the event in the main clause.	*Nineteenth-century Americans <u>knew</u> that hard work <u>was</u> necessary.*
	My professor <u>noticed</u> that many students <u>were writing</u> about the nineteenth century.
B When the main clause is in the past, use a present form in the *that* clause to express a universal truth or a fact that applies to the present.	*Who <u>discovered</u> that the Earth <u>is</u> round and not flat?*
	Scientists <u>discovered</u> that DNA <u>holds</u> the code for life.
	When I started living on my own, I <u>found out</u> that life <u>is</u> sometimes very hard.
C Use the past perfect or past perfect progressive when the event in the *that* clause happened before the event in the main clause.	*I <u>discovered</u> that she <u>had been copying</u> my history research for years!*
	I <u>heard</u> that she <u>had failed</u> the test.

D Use *would* or *was/were* going to when the event of the *that* clause happened after the event of the main clause.

I <u>heard</u> that a famous historian <u>would be speaking</u> at the conference.

We <u>discovered</u> that we <u>were going to study</u> twentieth-century history.

Grammar Application

Exercise 3.1 *That* Clauses in Sentences with Present Verbs in the Main Clause

Complete the sentences about the influence of Latin American cultures on mainstream U.S. culture. Use a *that* clause with the correct verb form. Sometimes more than one answer is possible.

1 Anthropologists agree / there be / links between Latin American cultures and U.S. culture (present for general truth)

   Anthropologists agree that there are links between Latin American cultures and U.S. culture.

2 Research / shows / contemporary Latin American cultures / have / roots in African, European, and indigenous cultures (present for general truth)

   _____

3 Sociologists / believe / Latin American cultures / influence / world culture as well as U.S. culture (past event)

   _____

4 Many musicologists / agree / modern U.S. music / be / derived in part from Latin American cultures (present for general truth)

   _____

5 Many language experts / assert / Spanish speakers / contribute / a great many words to the English language (past event)

   _____

6 Most sociologists / agree / Latin American cultures / continue / to influence U.S. culture (future for future action)

   _____

Exercise 3.2 *That* Clauses in Sentences with Past Verbs in the Main Clause

Listen to part of a lecture on westward movement in nineteenth-century North America. Complete the sentences with the words you hear.

In the nineteenth century, many people __*believed that*__ Americans __*had*__ the right
                                                              (1)   (2)
to expand across the continent. John Quincy Adams, the sixth president of the United States,

_____ one large country _____ good for all Americans.
        (3)   (4)

However, some people _____ the westward
expansion _____ some negative consequences.
(5)   (6)
For example, some people _____ westward
(7)
expansion _____ a negative impact on Native
(8)
American culture. In fact, some Americans at the time
_____ the U.S. government _____
(9)   (10)
Native American land unfairly. They also _____
(11)
westward expansion _____ many wars, such as the Mexican-American War of
(12)
1836. Most people _____ Americans _____ native plants and
(13)   (14)
wildlife as well.

Exercise 3.3 Agreement Between *That* Clauses and Main Clauses

Group Work **Do Internet research on how a culture, such as Irish-American or Latin American culture, has influenced culture in the United States or Canada. Write statements with *that* clauses. Use simple present for general truths, simple past for past events, and future for future action. Share your sentences with your group members. Use the following phrases in your sentences:**

- I learned / discovered / found that . . .
- Another area that . . .

- For example, . . .
- A recent study showed / found that . . .

I learned that Indian culture has influenced American culture. One area that Indian culture has influenced is entertainment. Many film specialists agree that Bollywood movies are influencing American movies.

4 *That* Clauses After Adjectives and Nouns

Grammar Presentation

That clauses can follow some adjectives and nouns.	I'm sure *that a cultural group shares at least some values.* I have the feeling *that our values are quite different.*

4.1 *That* Clauses After Adjectives

A You can use a *that* clause after adjectives that express certainty or emotion.	I'm <u>certain</u> *that I haven't read enough about American culture.* The conference organizers were <u>pleased</u> *that he accepted the invitation.*

4.1 *That* Clauses After Adjectives *(continued)*

B You can use *that* clauses after
It + be + certain adjectives. These
adjectives often express emotions or
degrees of certainty. They include:

*certain, clear, evident, (un)fortunate,
interesting, (un)likely, surprising,
understandable*

It is evident that many other cultures have influenced
U.S. culture.

It is unfortunate that many students don't know more
about their country's history.

It is unlikely that we'll finish the unit by the
next class.

It is understandable that historians disagree about the
development of cultural values.

4.2 *That* Clauses After Adjectives

A You can use *that* clauses after nouns
that express thoughts and ideas, such
as *belief, feeling, impression,* and
possibility.

It was our impression that the historian was wrong.

There was no possibility that he was going to
convince us.

B You can use noun + *be* + *that* clauses
with these commonly used nouns:
*concern, difference, hope, idea,
impression, point, problem, saying,*
and *views.*

The concern was that we would never find out the truth.

The point is that the United States is a very large
country.

The problem is that very individualistic people can find
it hard to work in a group.

📊 Data from the Real World

Research shows that the following nouns frequently occur with *that* clauses:

assumption, belief, claim, conclusion, doubt, fact, hope, idea, impression, possibility, report, suggestion, view	*Is it your assumption* that we cannot find jobs in other companies? *We came to the conclusion* that he would never understand our point of view.

🖱 Grammar Application

Exercise 4.1 *That* Clauses After Adjectives

Complete the magazine interview with a cultural studies expert. For each item, use the words
in parentheses with the correct form of *be* and a *that* clause.

U.S. CULTURE AND THE WORLD

Interviewer Some experts are studying culture, and they have expressed some concerns. What are they concerned about?

Dr. Green *They are concerned that U.S. culture may have a negative impact on global culture.*
(1. they / concerned / U.S. culture may have a negative impact on global culture)

Interviewer Why are they worried?

Dr. Green Some people are worried that
(2. some people / worried / Americanization is making everything the same)

Interviewer Why do they think this?

Dr. Green They are aware that Hollywood
(3. they / aware / Hollywood and fast-food chains are influencing culture)

Interviewer What's your opinion?

Dr. Green I am convinced that culture
(4. I / convinced / culture is a two-way street)

Interviewer Why do you think that?

Dr. Green I am positive that ...
(5. I / positive / other cultures influence U.S. culture as much as U.S. culture influences them)

Interviewer Can you give some examples?

Dr. Green A lot of people are surprised that the
(6. a lot of people / surprised / the French invented movies)

Interviewer What else?

Dr. Green They are surprised that
(7. they / surprised / the British invented one of the original fast foods, fish and chips)

Interviewer So what can we conclude?

Dr. Green I am sure that
(8. I / sure / we all benefit from global cultural exchange)

A Group Work Complete the answers to these questions about the spread of U.S. culture worldwide. Explain your answers.

1 Is the exportation of U.S. culture to the rest of the world a good thing?

It is my belief that *the exportation of U.S. culture is in some ways a good*
thing and in some ways a bad thing   .

2 Survey your group members: Do you think that most people outside of the United States have a favorable opinion of U.S. popular culture?

It is our feeling that _____

_____ .

3 Does your group think that most people outside of the United States have good feelings about American fast-food restaurants opening up in cities around the world?

It is our group's impression that _____

_____ .

B Over to You Read the results of a survey about the exportation of U.S. culture. Write three sentences about the survey results. Use the following adjectives: *amazed, disappointed, glad, pleased, relieved, surprised*. Discuss your reactions with a partner.

What is your opinion of U.S. popular culture, such as music, TV shows, and movies?

Very favorable	21%
Somewhat favorable	39%
Somewhat unfavorable	25
Very unfavorable%	14%
No Answer	1%

I'm not surprised that most people have mixed feelings about U.S. culture.

5 Avoid Common Mistakes ⚠

1 Do not use a comma before a *that* clause.

Their parents are pleased/ that they are getting married.

2 Remember that *that* clauses need a **complete verb**.

was
I noticed that she∧leaving.

3 *That* clauses must have a subject.

many settlers
Records show that∧hoped to return east later.

4 In academic writing, do not omit *that*.

that
Some cultures believe∧individuals should put other people first.

Editing Task

Find and correct six more mistakes in the paragraphs about a famous American of the mid-nineteenth century.

Settlers from the east who traveled across the American West in the

that
mid-nineteenth century understood ∧ they faced a difficult journey across deserts and

would
mountains. They knew ⨯ that the trip would take years and that some people ∧lose their

lives. However, they were optimistic.

5　　Michael T. Simmons was one of those determined travelers. Someone told him

to go to the Pacific Northwest for new opportunities. He sold his business to pay

for the supplies that he and his family needed. He knew that the area was largely

unknown. He also knew that was dangerous. This did not stop him.

　　When Simmons and his group reached Oregon, he announced that *he* was

10　going to continue north. The Hudson's Bay Trading Company heard the news, and

they discouraged him. However, Simmons was certain ⨯ that the trip *was* ̶going to be

successful, and he did not listen. Instead, he continued north as planned. After he

arrived, he helped to establish the first settlement in the territory that is now known

as Washington State. Documents show that Simmons built the first mill using water

15　from the Tumwater waterfall for power. For this, he is sometimes called the father of

Washington industry.

⨯ = no comma

16

Noun Clauses with *Wh-* Words and *If/Whether*

Inventions They Said Would Never Work

1 Grammar in the Real World

A Have you ever thought of inventing something? If so, what was it? Read the article about inventors. What obstacles did Edison and the Wright brothers face?

B Comprehension Check **Answer the questions.**

1 Why did people doubt Thomas Edison?
2 How did Edison convince the world of his accomplishment?
3 What were the obstacles the Wright brothers faced?

C Notice **Find the sentences in the article and complete them.**

1 No one knew exactly _____ .

2 Second, the success of inventors often depended on

_____ .

3 He could not predict _____ .

Look at the sentences again. Answer the questions.

1 In sentence 1, what type of question is the missing clause similar to?

   a an information question   **b** a *Yes/No* question

2 In sentences 2 and 3, what type of question is the missing clause similar to?

   a an information question   **b** a *Yes/No* question

INVENTIONS PEOPLE SAID WOULD NEVER WORK

Throughout history, new ideas have often faced skepticism[1] from society. Skepticism, however, has never stopped the creation of new inventions. Three important American inventors, Thomas Edison and
5 Orville and Wilbur Wright, faced strong public doubt, but they persevered,[2] and the results were the invention of the electric light bulb and the airplane.

While Edison may now be considered a brilliant inventor, in his lifetime he faced much criticism. Most
10 inventors in his day would not announce an invention until they had a model. Edison, however, stated that he had invented the light bulb, but he had no actual evidence for it. Thus, scientists doubted **what he said**. Also, most inventors had a schedule
15 for their projects, but Edison did not. No one knew exactly **when he would complete it**. Moreover, his experiments failed repeatedly, and this added to the skepticism. However, in 1882, Edison succeeded in lighting up an entire New York neighborhood,
20 and the world finally understood **what he had accomplished**.

Many inventors in the early 1900s wondered **whether it was possible to fly**. The Wright brothers proved **what others doubted** by inventing the first

25 airplane. However, they faced many obstacles along the way. First, most inventors were highly educated, but the Wright brothers had little formal education. Second, the success of inventors often depended on **whether they had financial support**. The
30 Wright brothers had none. Finally, most inventors publicized their research, but the Wright brothers did not. No one knew exactly what they were doing. Consequently, the public did not believe that the Wright brothers would succeed. Wilbur himself was
35 not sure **what would happen**. He could not predict **if their airplane would fly or not**. Then, in 1903, the Wright brothers flew their airplane for 12 seconds in Kitty Hawk, North Carolina. No one could believe **what they were seeing**. Five years later in France,
40 they flew another plane higher and longer.

Inventors almost always face public disbelief. Some people have trouble believing that new ideas are possible, but they certainly are. No one can be sure about **what the future holds**.

---

[1]**skepticism:** doubting the truth or value of an idea or belief
[2]**persevere:** continue doing something in a determined way despite difficulties

2 Noun Clauses with *Wh-* Words

Grammar Presentation

Noun clauses with *wh-* words can act as subjects, direct objects, or objects of prepositions.

What they wanted was financial support.
The inventor understood how we should build the machine.
I learned about how many inventions are made every year.

2.1 Forming Noun Clauses with *Wh-* Words

A Noun clauses with *wh-* words use statement word order (subject + verb).

I've just realized what he did!
I don't know when Edison invented the light bulb.

B When noun clauses with *wh-* words *who*, *what*, and *which* act as subjects, they take a singular verb.

What happened next is going to surprise you.

2.2 Using Noun Clauses with *Wh-* Words

A Noun clauses with *wh-* words often appear after the following verbs:

Thoughts and opinions: *consider, know, remember*

Learning and perception: *figure out, find out, see, understand, wonder*

Emotions: *care, doubt, hate, like, love*

I don't remember who invented the airplane.

We need to figure out why our invention failed.

Our professor cares how we do our work.

B Noun clauses with *wh-* words often follow verbs + prepositions, including *care about, decide on, find out about, forget about, know about, learn about, read about,* and *see about.*

We shouldn't forget about which inventions succeeded and which didn't.
I read about where Edison grew up.

2.3 Reduced Noun Clauses with Infinitives

Noun clauses with *wh-* words can often be reduced to *wh-* word + infinitive. Common infinitives used this way include *to ask, to consider, to decide, to figure (out), to find (out), to forget, to know, to learn, to remember, to say, to see, to show, to understand,* and *to wonder.*

We're not sure who/whom[1] <u>to ask</u> for information.
= We're not sure who/whom[1] *we should ask for information.*

I don't know what <u>to say</u> about your invention.
= I don't know what *I can say about your invention.*

[1]The use of *whom* is infrequent, except in very formal writing.

Grammar Application

Exercise 2.1 Noun Clauses with *Wh-* Words

A Listen to the conversation among a group of students doing Internet research on recent inventions and inventors. Complete the sentences with the noun clauses you hear.

Peter OK, let's start with Randi Altschul.

Larry I don't know ___*who Randi Altschul is*___ .
(1)

Paula Neither do I. I don't know ___what she invented___.
(2)

Peter I know ___who she is___ . She invented the disposable
(3)
cell phone.

Paula I'm impressed! I wonder ___why she invented___.
(4)

Larry I don't know.

Peter Got it! It says here her cell phone wasn't working well, and she felt like throwing it away.

Larry Let's find out ___when she invented___ .
(5)

Peter It says here she got a patent for it in 1999.

Larry I just found out ___where she is living___ at the
(6)
time. It was Florida.

Paula I wonder ___to see cell phon looks like___ .
(7)

Peter It says here that it was only 2 inches by 3 inches – kind of like a credit card.

Larry I wonder ___what is made of___ .
(8)

Peter It was made of recycled paper.

PHONE-CARD-PHONE™
Working Model

B Pair Work With a partner, talk about what you know or don't know about other inventions. Use the verbs in A with *wh-* noun clauses.

I know when the smartphone was invented. It was in 2007. I remember what company first made it, but I don't know who invented it.

Exercise 2.2 Reduced Noun Clauses with *Wh-* Words + Infinitives

Some college students are talking to a business adviser about their new product. Rewrite the sentences with *wh-* words + infinitives.

1 We don't know where we should start.

   We don't know where to start.

2 Amy wonders where she could find a good patent lawyer.

   _____

3 I don't know how I can find a manufacturer for our product.

   _____

4 Binh is wondering who he can ask for money for our invention.

   _____

5 I'll figure out who we can contact for financial advice.

   _____

6 I wonder what we should charge for our product.

   _____

3 Noun Clauses with *If/Whether*

Grammar Presentation

Noun clauses can begin with *if* or *whether*. These noun clauses are similar in some ways to *Yes/No* questions, but they follow statement (subject + verb) word order.	I'm not sure *if the Wright brothers invented the airplane*. He doesn't know *whether we will get money for our experiment*.

3.1 Forming Noun Clauses with *If / Whether*

A Use statement word order (subject + verb) for noun clauses with *if/whether*.	*I don't know **if the public will accept our idea**.* *I don't know **whether Edison really invented the light bulb**.*
B You can use the words *or not* at the end of both *if* and *whether* clauses.	*The scientist didn't know **if/whether you would understand her invention or not**.*
Or not can immediately follow *whether*, but not *if*.	*The scientist didn't know **whether or not you would understand her invention**.* NOT *The scientist didn't know if ~~or not~~ you would understand her invention.*
C You can use *if/whether* to introduce two options.	*We don't know **whether the new phone or the new tablet will come out first**.*

3.2 Using Noun Clauses with *If / Whether*

A You can use noun clauses with *if/whether* after the following verbs: Thoughts and opinions: *decide, know, remember* Learning and perception: *figure out, find out* Emotions: *care, doubt, matter, mind*	*I <u>haven't decided</u> **if I'm going to write a report about the Wright brothers**.* *He can't <u>find out</u> **if Edison first tried the light bulb in New York**.* *They <u>doubted</u> **whether anyone would steal their idea**.*
B You can also use noun clauses with *whether* after verbs + prepositions, including *care about, decide on, find out about, forget about, know about,* and *read about.* You cannot use *if* after prepositions.	*You should <u>forget about</u> **whether you'll make a lot of money with that invention**.* NOT *You should forget about ~~if you'll make a lot of money with that invention~~.*
C You can use an infinitive with *whether.* You cannot use an infinitive with *if.*	*He didn't know **whether <u>to share</u> his discovery**.* (= He didn't know whether he should share his discovery.) NOT *He didn't know ~~if to share his discovery~~.*

> ### 📊 Data from the Real World
>
> Noun clauses with *if* are much more frequent than noun clauses with *whether*. *Whether* is more frequent in writing than in speaking.

Grammar Application

Combine the sentences. Use a noun clause with *if* or *whether*. Sometimes more than one answer is possible.

1 Scientists have not decided something. Is time travel possible?

Scientists have not decided whether time travel is possible.

2 Many people don't know something. Do some robots think like humans?

F.

3 Many people don't know this. Can we invent a non-polluting fuel?

if we can

4 We can't remember this. Has anyone invented a self-cleaning house?

... iF/whether anyone has ...

5 Many people don't know about this. Are hybrid cars good for the environment?

whether hybrid ...

6 Scientists haven't figured this out. Are there other planets humans can live on?

... Figured out iF/whether there are other...

A Read the inventor's list of questions about her invention. Rewrite the questions as sentences. Use noun clauses with *if* or *whether*.

1 Can I really invent a solar-powered car?

I don't know if I can really invent a solar-powered car.

2 Will it take a long time to invent it?

3 Am I smart enough to do it by myself?

4 Do people really want solar-powered cars?

5 Will a solar-powered car work on cloudy days?

I don't Know iF a solar-powered car will work on cloudy days.

6 Is my car going to be too expensive?

B Read more questions from the inventor in A. Rewrite the questions as sentences. Use *whether or not* with an infinitive.

1 Should I get some help?

   I can't decide whether or not to get some help.

2 Should I take out a loan from the bank?

   _____

3 Should I patent my idea first?

   _____

4 Should I see a lawyer?

   _____

4 Noun Clauses in Direct and Indirect Questions

Grammar Presentation

Wh- noun clauses and noun clauses with *if* and *whether* can be used in direct and indirect questions.	Do you know **when New York got electricity**? (direct question) I was wondering **when New York got electricity**. (indirect question)

4.1 Forming Direct and Indirect Questions

A Direct questions with noun clauses have question word order and end with a question mark. Common phrases include: *Do you know . . . ? Can you tell me . . . ? Would you know . . . ?*	Do you know **who invented the first calculator**? Are you trying to find out **if Edison was born in this country**? Can anyone tell me **if Edison was born in Scotland**?
B Indirect questions with noun clauses have statement word order and end with a period. Common phrases include: *I want to find out . . . I'd like to know . . . I don't know why . . .*	I have been wondering **what a patent is**. My group really needs to find out **if the Wright brothers had financial support for their invention**. I'd like to know **if people need to get patents for their inventions**.

▸▸ Verbs and Fixed Expressions that Introduce Indirect Questions: See page A10.

Exercise 4.1 Direct and Indirect Questions

Complete the interview with artist and inventor Crispiano Columna. Rewrite the questions in parentheses as noun clauses in direct and indirect questions. Sometimes more than one answer is possible.

ArtOnline	I'm wondering *if you are both an artist and an inventor* .
	(1 Are you both an artist and an inventor?)
Crispiano Columna	Yes, I'm both.
ArtOnline	I'd like to know _____ .
	(2 What is your most famous invention?)
Crispiano Columna	I make sculptures that you can wear as gloves.
ArtOnline	I was wondering _____ .
	(3 Can you show us an example?)
Crispiano Columna	Yes, I'm wearing a pair right now.
ArtOnline	I was wondering _____ .
	(4 Did you study art in college?)
Crispiano Columna	No. In fact, I studied literature.
ArtOnline	I'd like to know _____ .
	(5 How did you become an artist?)
Crispiano Columna	I taught myself. I learned about color and drawing from books.
ArtOnline	I'd like to know _____ .
	(6 What was your first invention?)
Crispiano Columna	I invented a toy airplane for my nephew when I was a teenager.

Exercise 4.2 More Indirect Questions

A Look at the pictures of inventions. Write one indirect question about each picture. Use the following phrases:

I wonder / I'm wondering . . .   I'd like to know . . .   I'm interested in knowing. . .

| The hair protector | The food cooler | The baby mop | The butter stick |

I wonder who invented the hair protector.

1 _____
2 _____
3 _____
4 _____

B Pair Work Take turns reading your questions.

5 Avoid Common Mistakes ⚠

1 **Remember that a noun clause with a *wh-* word follows statement word order.**

will

No one knows what ~~will~~ the next great invention ∧ be.

2 **Be careful to spell *whether* correctly.**

whether

The success of the invention depended on ~~wether~~ people would buy it.

3 **Do not confuse *whether* and *either*.**

whether

The newest electronic devices will always tempt us, ~~either~~ we like them or not.

Editing Task

Find and correct the mistakes in the paragraphs about the importance of the Internet.

Many inventions make life more convenient, but the Internet is the most essential one today. The Internet is a part of daily life. Although some people worry

whether

about ~~wheather~~ this fact is harmful or not, many agree that they do not know what would they do if they could not go online.

5   First of all, the Internet helps people communicate instantly with family and friends who are far away. In the past, people had to write a letter or pay for a long-distance call to find out how were they doing. While they waited, they worried about whether their loved ones were all right. Now there are many ways to contact people and find out if they are well.

10   In addition, the Internet helps people find information. If we want to know what is the temperature in Seoul today, we only have to type the question. Also, it is very easy to look for employment, research solutions to a problem, and even find out wether a movie is playing nearby.

It is too early to tell either the Internet causes serious long-term problems for

15 society or not. To me, it seems extremely valuable because it connects me to people I care about and to information I need.

Direct Speech and Indirect Speech

Human Motivation

1 Grammar in the Real World

A What makes people work hard at their jobs? Read the article about employee motivation. What type of reward is particularly effective in motivating workers?

B Comprehension Check Complete the chart. Check (✓) whether each reward is external or internal.

	External Reward	Internal Reward
1 Pay raise		
2 Feeling successful		
3 Freedom to work independently		
4 Good salary		
5 Good grades		

C Notice Find similar sentences in the article and complete the sentences below.

1 Lionel Messi _____ , "Money is not a motivating factor… My motivation comes from playing the game I love."

2 Daniel Pink, the author of a book on motivation, _____ an audience once that Google was a great example of a company that supported autonomy.

3 Pink _____ the audience that Google News and Gmail had been created during this free time.

Each sentence tells what someone says. Which sentence gives the actual words of the speaker? How do you know?

WORKPLACE MOTIVATION

Motivation is the desire to do something. Soccer star Lionel Messi **said**, "Money is not a motivating factor… My motivation comes from playing the game I love." Messi meant that he enjoys playing soccer more
5 than making millions of dollars. Can that be true? What other factors are important in motivating people?

Many psychologists believe that there are two types of rewards that affect motivation: external rewards and internal rewards. External rewards are rewards that
10 someone gives you. A pay raise is a common external reward. A good grade at school is also an example of an external reward. Internal rewards are connected to the feelings people have about the work they do. The satisfaction you get when you do something well is
15 an internal reward. Researcher Frederick Herzberg (1923–2000) studied motivation in the workplace for many years. Herzberg **said that** employers must think about factors that affect employees' feelings of satisfaction. Herzberg **explained that** working
20 conditions and relationships among co-workers affect workers' motivation. Therefore, employers need to create an environment that makes employees feel safe, valued, and accepted.

Some studies on workplace motivation have
25 focused on autonomy, which is the freedom to work independently. This is an important internal reward. Daniel Pink, the author of a book on motivation, **told** an audience once **that** Google was a good example of a company that supported autonomy. One day each
30 week, Google engineers focus on their own ideas. Pink **informed** the audience **that** Google News and Gmail had been created during this free time.

Research also shows that appreciation is a powerful reward. In his book *The 1001 Rewards and*
35 *Recognition[1] Fieldbook*, Bob Nelson described a study on the effects of appreciation on motivation. The study **asked**, "What motivates you?" Workers ranked the importance of 65 motivating factors. Nelson **indicated that** appreciation for their work ranked first for
40 the workers.

The subject of worker motivation is complex. People expect fair pay for their work. However, research **shows that** people find internal rewards more meaningful than a high salary.

---

[1]**recognition:** special positive attention

2 Direct Speech

Grammar Presentation

Direct speech repeats people's exact words.	Lionel Messi said, "Money is not a motivating factor. … My motivation comes from playing the game I love."

2.1 Forming Sentences with Direct Speech

A Direct speech consists of a reporting clause and a person's exact words.	REPORTING CLAUSE Lionel Messi said, "Money is not a motivating factor."
The most common reporting verb is *said*. Use a comma after the verb.	Our manager said, "Treat the customers like family, and they will come back."
To quote speech, use quotation marks and a capital letter to begin the direct speech. End the direct speech with punctuation inside the quotation marks.	My colleague said, "We are going to lead the company in sales next year!"
B The reporting clause can also come at the end or in the middle of direct speech. Notice that the verb can also come before the subject in the reporting clause when the reporting clause comes at the end or in the middle.	"The company pays its workers fairly," the president said. "We didn't do well this year," said Liz, "so we won't get a sales bonus."
C Use the verb *asked* to quote a question.	Mr. Smith asked, "What do you hope to accomplish in this job?"

Grammar Application

Exercise 2.1 Statements in Direct Speech

A Rewrite the quotations about motivation as direct speech. Sometimes more than one answer is possible.

1 in my experience, there is only one motivation, and that is desire –Jane Smiley

   Jane Smiley said, "In my experience, there is only one motivation, and that is desire."

2 the ones who want to achieve and win championships motivate themselves
–Mike Ditka

_____

_____

3 the ultimate inspiration is the deadline –Nolan Bushnell

_____

_____

4 motivation is the art of getting people to do what you want them to do because
they want to do it –Dwight D. Eisenhower

_____

_____

5 I'm a great believer in luck, and I find the harder I work, the more I have of it
–Thomas Jefferson

_____

_____

6 great work is done by people who are not afraid to be great –Fernando Flores

_____

_____

7 nothing great was ever achieved without enthusiasm –Ralph Waldo Emerson

_____

_____

8 you miss 100 percent of the shots you don't take –Wayne Gretzky

_____

_____

9 the journey of a thousand miles begins with a single step –Lao Tzu

_____

_____

B Over to You Choose two of the quotations, and write a sentence that explains what
each one means.

*When Jane Smiley said, "In my experience there is only one motivation, and that
is desire," she meant that the only real motivation is wanting to do something.*

C Pair Work Share your sentences with a partner. Discuss whether you agree or disagree
with your partner's interpretation.

A Read the transcript of an online discussion about motivating employees. Then rewrite each question as a direct speech question. The information in parentheses tells you where to put the reporting clauses – at the beginning or end of the sentences.

Working Today

Today, motivational expert Camila Valdez is here to answer your questions.

Claire **Is money the best way to get employees to work harder?**
(1)
Camila No. Studies show that appreciation and recognition are the best ways.

Pedro **Do you have guidelines for rewarding employees?**
(2)
Camila Try to match the size of the reward to the size of the accomplishment.

Roxana **When should you give the rewards?**
(3)
Camila It's really best to give them as soon as possible after employees have

accomplished something.

Hong **What are some ways to motivate employees?**
(4)
Camila Give rewards that fit your employees' working style.

Chelsea **Can you give an example of what you mean?**
(5)
Camila Certainly. For example, give a more flexible schedule to working parents.

They will feel more focused at work because they will be able to take care

of their home-related responsibilities.

---

1 (beginning) *Claire asked, "Is money the best way to get employees to*

work harder?"

2 (end) _____

3 (beginning) _____

4 (end) _____

5 (beginning) _____

B Over to You Ask two classmates these questions: Would money motivate you to work harder? Why or why not? Then write a short report on your interviews with direct speech statements and questions.

I talked to Anne and Mike. I asked, "Would money motivate you to work harder?"
Anne said, "No, it wouldn't." I asked, "Why not?" Anne said, "I work to please myself.
That's my reward." Then I asked Mike, "Would money motivate you to work harder?"
Mike said, "Yes, it would."

3 Indirect Speech

Grammar Presentation

Indirect speech tells what someone says in another person's words. Indirect speech is also called reported speech.

Lionel Messi said, "Money is not a motivating factor." (direct speech)

Lionel Messi said that money was not a motivating factor. (indirect speech)

3.1 Forming Indirect Speech

An indirect speech statement consists of a reporting verb such as *say* in the main clause, followed by a *that* clause. The word that is optional and is often omitted when speaking.

She said, "The boss is angry." (direct speech)

She **said (that)** the boss was angry. (indirect speech)

3.2 Tense Shifting in Indirect Speech

A After a past verb in the reporting clause, the verb form in indirect speech usually changes. The verb shifts to express a past time.

DIRECT SPEECH	INDIRECT SPEECH
She said, "The boss is angry."	She said that the boss was angry.
He said, "She is enjoying the work."	He said that she was enjoying the work.
They said, "The store closed last year."	They said that the store had closed last year.
The manager said, "The group has done good work."	The manager said that the group had done good work.

B The following forms usually change in indirect speech.

DIRECT SPEECH	INDIRECT SPEECH
He said, "The department will add three new managers."	He said that the department would add three new managers.
She said, "They are going to hire more people soon."	She said that they were going to hire more people soon.
The teacher said, "The students can work harder."	The teacher said that the students could work harder.
Their manager said, "Money may not be very important to them."	Their manager said that money might not be very important to them.

3.2 Tense Shifting in Indirect Speech (continued)

C The forms of *should, might, ought to,* and *could* are the same in direct and indirect speech.

DIRECT SPEECH *The boss said, "He should go home."*	INDIRECT SPEECH *The boss said that he should go home.*

D Do not change the form of verbs in general truths or facts.	*She said, "Martin Luther King, Jr. was a great man."* *She said (that) Martin Luther King, Jr. was a great man.* NOT *She said that Martin Luther King Jr. had been a great man.*

▸▸ Tense Shifting in Indirect Speech: See page A11.

Grammar Application

Exercise 3.1 Tense Shifts in Indirect Speech

Read the quotes about a psychology course. Then rewrite each quote as indirect speech. Sometimes more than one answer is possible.

1 The professor said, "Psychology 101 includes a unit on motivation."

   The professor said that Psychology 101 included a unit on motivation.

2 A student said, "The class is discussing motivation and personality this week."

   _____

   _____

3 The professor said, "The class is reading about Abraham H. Maslow's theories on motivation."

   _____

   _____

4 One student said, "I'm learning a lot in the class."

   _____

   _____

5 Another student said, "I don't understand the lectures."

   _____

   _____

6 The teaching assistant said, "The readings have great practical value."

   _____

   _____

Exercise 3.2 Modals and Future Forms in Indirect Speech

Read the excerpt from a lecture on how to motivate adult learners. Then complete the email. Rewrite each sentence from the lecture as indirect speech. Sometimes more than one answer is possible.

Welcome to Motivating Adult Learners. This class is for people who teach adults. Participants in the course are going to learn all about motivating adult learners. The course will rely heavily on participants' own experiences. Students should come to class prepared to discuss their own experiences. We may occasionally have guest speakers. The course will include presentations, homework, and weekly quizzes. There will be three papers and two oral presentations. Participants can substitute an oral presentation for one of the papers.

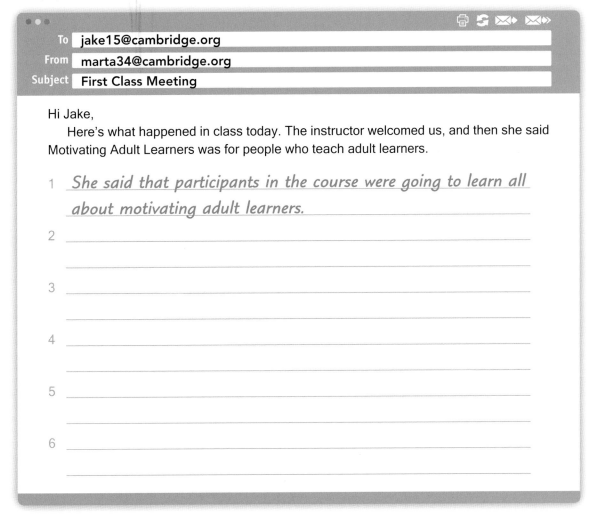

To   jake15@cambridge.org
From   marta34@cambridge.org
Subject   **First Class Meeting**

Hi Jake,
    Here's what happened in class today. The instructor welcomed us, and then she said Motivating Adult Learners was for people who teach adult learners.

1   *She said that participants in the course were going to learn all about motivating adult learners.*

2   _____

3   _____

4   _____

5   _____

6   _____

4 Indirect Speech Without Tense Shift

Grammar Presentation

Indirect speech usually includes a shift in verb tense. However, in some cases the form of the verb does not change.

*The president announced that she **was going** to start an employee program next year.*

*The president announced that she **is going** to start an employee program next year.*

4.1 Keeping the Original Tense in Indirect Speech

You may use the tense in the original direct speech clause when you report statements that are still true now, such as:

Facts or general truths

*He said, "A pay raise **is** a common reward."*

*He said that a pay raise **is** a common reward.*

Habits and routines

*Leo said, "Our meetings always **begin** on time."*

*Leo said that their meetings always **begin** on time.*

Actions in progress

*Eve said, "I'm **studying** hard for the exam."*

*Eve said that she **is studying** hard for the exam.*

▶▶ Tense Shifting in Indirect Speech: See page A11.

4.2 Using Present Tense Reporting Verbs

Use a present tense verb in the reporting clause when what was said relates to the present and is still important at the moment of speaking. Keep the same tense as in the quote.

*Everybody always **says**, "Employees **need** to be motivated."*

*Everybody always **says** that employees **need** to be motivated.*

Grammar Application

Exercise 4.1 Keeping the Original Tense in Indirect Speech

Read the quotes from a business meeting. Then rewrite the quotes as indirect speech. Use the same tense as the direct speech. Sometimes more than one answer is possible.

1 "We are trying to improve our new marketing plan."
   –the marketing manager

   The marketing manager said that we are trying
   to improve our new marketing plan.

2 "The client loves it." –the manager

_____

3 "We have always solved these problems in the past." –Janet

_____

4 "Staff satisfaction has been very important." –Janet

_____

5 "Tomorrow, we are going to have a half-day training session on giving constructive feedback." –Rodrigo

_____

_____

6 "We will all work together, as a team." –Rodrigo

_____

Exercise 4.2 Using Present Tense Reporting Verbs

A **Complete the sentences. Use the correct form of the verbs in parentheses.**

1 My father always says that money __*makes*__ (make) the world go round.

2 My friend Amanda insists that a good night's sleep _____ (be) more important than studying.

3 My aunt says that she _____ (enjoy) doing the work more than making money.

4 My friend says that he _____ (enjoy) having autonomy at work.

5 My colleague says that it _____ (not/be) always easy to stay motivated.

6 My manager says that you _____ always _____ (should/ask) questions if something is not clear.

B Pair Work Discuss the sentences in A. Do you agree with the statements?

5 Other Reporting Verbs

Grammar Presentation

Although *say* is the most common reporting verb, many other verbs can introduce indirect speech.	The president *explained* that our company's workers deserved higher pay. The president *told us* that our company's workers deserved higher pay.

5.1 Other Reporting Verbs

A *Tell* is a common reporting verb. Always use a noun or object pronoun after *tell*.	The president *said* that he was doing a great job. The president *told him* that he was doing a great job.
B You can use these verbs in place of *say*: *admit, announce, complain, confess, exclaim, explain, mention, remark, reply, report, state,* and *swear*.	"The workers need recognition," *said* the manager. The manager *admitted* that the workers needed recognition.
When used with an object, the object comes after *to*.	He *swore* <u>to us</u> that he'd be on time in the future.
C You can use these verbs in place of *tell*: *assure, convince, inform, notify,* and *remind*. Always use a noun or object pronoun with these verbs.	The president *told the managers*, "All workers need to be creative." The president *reminded them* that all workers need to be creative.

▶▶ Reporting Verbs: See page A11.

📊 Data from the Real World

Commonly used reporting verbs in formal writing include *claim, explain, find, show, state,* and *suggest*.	The author **claimed that** internal motivation was more effective than external motivation. The results of the study **showed that** money was not always an effective way to motivate employees.

Grammar Application

Complete the excerpt from an email about a presentation on cultural differences in motivation. Circle the correct verbs.

Wei **said** /**told** me that he had attended a presentation on the cultural
(1)
differences that affect motivation. He **said** / **told** that an expert on motivation
(2)
gave the presentation. He **said** / **told** me that the expert was Dr. Ghosh.
(3)
He **reminded** / **mentioned** me that we had read one of her articles in class.
(4)

Anyway, Dr. Ghosh **said** / **informed** the group that the typical workplace
(5)
included people with various cultural backgrounds. She **explained** / **reminded**
(6)
that these workers had different expectations. She **informed** / **explained** the
(7)
group that these workers often had different motivations.

At the same time, Dr. Ghosh **reminded** / **remarked** that there was no one
(8)
way to motivate all workers. She **admitted** / **reminded** that in multicultural
(9)
settings, it was even more complicated.

She **stated** / **reminded** the group that managers shouldn't make
(10)
generalizations about cultures. She **assured** / **remarked** that the "human touch,"
(11)
getting to know employees as individuals, was the best way to motivate them.

A Listen to the conversation about a presentation on cultural differences in classrooms. Complete the sentences with the words you hear.

David   What happened in class today?

Mira   We had a guest speaker. He _told us_ about the importance of motivation in
(1)
the language classroom. He _____ there are two kinds of
(2)
motivation: intrinsic and extrinsic.

David   Right. Last week, the professor _____ there were two different
(3)
types, and she gave examples.

Mira   Yes. So anyway, the speaker _____ he had done a study of
(4)
students in Japan and students in the United States. He _____
(5)
both groups had native-speaking English teachers. He _____
(6)
the purpose of the study was to see whether the teachers' remarks had a negative
effect on the motivation of the Japanese students.

David   What did he find out?

Mira   He _____ the study found four ways in which the teachers'
(7)
behavior had a negative effect on Japanese students' motivation.

David   Did he give any examples?

Mira   He _____ classroom discussion is one area where there are
(8)
key differences. He _____ in the Japanese classroom, students
(9)
generally listen more and talk less.

David   And as we know from our reading, Porter and Samovar _____
(10)
in the U.S. classroom, some students speak up spontaneously, and that a lot of
teachers encourage discussion.

Mira   Right. So, he _____ when a teacher criticizes a Japanese group
(11)
for not participating, it has a bad effect on motivation.

B Listen again and check your answers.

C Over to You Compare the behavior of American and Japanese students to students from another culture that you are familiar with. Use sentences with indirect speech.

The speaker said that in the Japanese classroom, students listen more and talk less. That is true in my culture, too. Students show respect that way.

6 Avoid Common Mistakes ⚠

1 **For verbs such as *admit*, *announce*, *complain*, *explain*, and *mention*, the object pronoun comes after the preposition *to*.**

to us
He explained ~~us~~ the objective.

2 **Change the form of the verb in indirect speech in most cases.**

had
He claimed that they followed the directions.

3 **Use beginning and ending quotation marks with direct speech.**

The director said, "All designers may work from home on Fridays."

Editing Task

Find and correct the mistakes in the paragraphs about a memorable event.

One of the highlights of my life happened through an experience at work.
to us
It started when my manager announced ~~us~~ some interesting news. He said, I am
starting a company band. Then he asked, "Who wants to join?" I mentioned him that
I had played guitar for many years. He said, You should definitely try out.

5   On the day of tryouts, I was a little nervous because everyone played extremely
well. After I auditioned, the manager thanked me and explained me that he will let
me know soon.

I forgot about it, so I was very surprised when I got a phone call from my
manager a few days later. He said, You can play lead guitar. I said, Wow! That's great!

10   After that, the band practiced a few times a week. A few months later, we played
at the company party. We were nervous, but we played well. The president of the
company spoke to me later and said I have a lot of talent. I was embarrassed by his
compliment, but I said I am proud to play for the company. I will never forget
that experience.

18 Indirect Questions; Indirect Imperatives, Requests, and Advice

Creative Problem Solving

1 Grammar in the Real World

A When you have to solve a problem, what strategies do you use? Read the article about brainstorming. Would you prefer traditional brainstorming or "brainwriting"?

B Comprehension Check **Answer the questions.**

1 What are the four rules of brainstorming?

2 Why does Michalko believe that brainwriting may be more productive than brainstorming?

3 According to the writer, who can use brainstorming?

C Notice **Find the sentences in the article and complete them.**

1 First, he told participants _____ other people's ideas.

2 Therefore, he asked participants _____ even unusual ideas.

What are the forms of the missing verbs?

BRAINSTORMING
as a Problem-Solving Tool

There is more than one way to solve a problem. One method many people use is brainstorming. Brainstorming is an activity designed to produce a number of ideas in a short time. Alex Osborn
5 invented the word in 1939. In his book *Unlocking Your Creative Power*, Osborn said that the word *brainstorm* means using the brain to solve a problem creatively. Although he **said that groups should brainstorm** in a particular way, variations
10 on his technique have also become popular.

Osborn's original brainstorming method had four rules. First, he **told participants not to judge** other people's ideas. Second, he welcomed all ideas, even wild ideas. Osborn said that crazy
15 ideas could get people thinking along new lines and could lead to effective solutions. Therefore, he **asked participants to shout out** even unusual ideas. Third, Osborn **asked group members to produce** a large number of ideas. He thought that
20 the group would find a few really good ideas if

many different ones were available. Finally, Osborn **asked the brainstorming group if they could improve** the ideas that had been suggested.

One alternative to brainstorming is
25 brainwriting. Brainwriting is a silent version of brainstorming. With brainwriting, participants write down their ideas instead of shouting them out. In his book *Thinkertoys*, creativity expert Michael Michalko suggests that brainwriting may be more
30 productive than traditional brainstorming. This is because people often think of additional ideas as they write. He also asserts that this method is better for quieter individuals because they do not have to express their ideas out loud.

35 Brainstorming and brainwriting are flexible methods. Anyone can use them because they do not require a lot of training or expensive materials. These processes are all effective tools for creative problem solving in professional, academic, and
40 personal situations.

2 Indirect Questions

Grammar Presentation

Indirect questions tell what other people have asked. There are two kinds of indirect questions: *Yes/No* questions and information questions.	He asked, "Are your jobs satisfying?" He asked if our jobs were satisfying. The director asked, "Which technique do you prefer?" The director asked us which technique we preferred.

2.1 Forming Indirect Questions

A Use asked in the reporting clause and *if* to introduce an indirect *Yes/No* question.	"Will we start attending brainstorming sessions?" Mia *asked*. Mia *asked if* we will/would start attending brainstorming sessions.
Use *asked* in the reporting clause and the same *wh-* word to introduce an indirect information question.	"When will the training begin?" our manager *asked*. Our manager *asked when* the training will/would begin.
B Use statement word order in the indirect question.	He asked if Rita was one of our most productive employees.
C After *ask*, you can use a direct object. The direct object can be a noun or pronoun.	She *asked the students* if they understood. She *asked me* when I wanted to leave the company.

Grammar Application

Exercise 2.1 Forming Indirect Questions

Read the interview between Joanna and Dr. Martin, a critical thinking expert. Then rewrite each of Joanna's questions as an indirect question.

 Dr. Martin, why is creative thinking in the business world so important?

 Companies need very creative people to help design and market new products.

5 Why will creative thinking be even more important in the future?

 Competition is getting stronger. You have to be creative to stay competitive.

 What techniques have worked to get people to think creatively?

 One technique that really works is to move the body. I tell people who are

10 sitting at a desk to move into the conference room or take a walk outside.

Joanna	How does moving promote creativity?
Dr. Martin	Moving stimulates the brain.
Joanna	Are there any other ideas like this?
Dr. Martin	Of course. Try putting colorful pictures on the wall. Never try to be creative in an empty room.
Joanna	Do objects and colors stimulate creative thinking?
Dr. Martin	They definitely do.

15

1 What did Joanna ask Dr. Martin about creative thinking in the business world?

Joanna asked Dr. Martin why creative thinking in the business world was important.

2 What did Joanna ask Dr. Martin about the future?

3 What did Joanna ask about creative techniques?

4 What did Joanna ask about moving?

5 What did Joanna ask about other ideas?

6 What did Joanna ask about stimulating creative thinking?

Exercise 2.2 More Forming Indirect Questions

Read the conversation about a company's creativity exercises. Then rewrite each of Ahmet's questions as an indirect question.

Ahmet	How was your creativity session yesterday?
Irina	It was fun, and we had some really good ideas, too.
Ahmet	Was the session here?
Irina	Yes, it was here.
Ahmet	Who was your leader?
Irina	It was Dr. Martin, a creativity expert. She gave us a problem to solve. Then she gave us large pieces of white paper and markers in a lot of different colors.
Ahmet	What did you do with the paper and the markers?
Irina	We drew pictures of things that we wanted to say, that is, the solutions we had for the problem.
Ahmet	Interesting. How long were you drawing pictures?

5

10

Irina	We did that for about an hour. Then we had a thing called "incubation." We stopped working, had lunch, and then watched a TV show!
Ahmet	Why did you watch TV in the office?
15 Irina	The idea was to forget about everything and then come back to the problem. When we went back to work, we then found the best solution.

1 What did Ahmet ask Irina about yesterday?

He asked her how her creativity session was.

2 What did Ahmet ask Irina about the location?

3 What did Ahmet ask Irina about the leader?

4 What did Ahmet ask Irina about the paper and the markers?

5 What else did Ahmet ask Irina about the activity with the paper and markers?

6 What did Ahmet ask Irina about watching TV in the office?

Exercise 2.3 Using Indirect Questions

Group Work **Ask and answer the questions about creativity with two students. Then share your answers with the whole class.**

- What are some situations in which people have to be creative?

- Why is creativity difficult for some people?

- When you have to be creative, do you have any techniques to stimulate your thinking? What are they?

3 Indirect Imperatives, Requests, and Advice

Grammar Presentation

Imperatives, requests, and advice are usually made indirect with an infinitive.	*"Please sit down."* He asked us *to sit down.* *"Would you please turn off your phones?"* He asked us *to turn off* our phones.

3.1 Indirect Imperatives, Requests, and Advice

A Use an infinitive in indirect imperatives. Use *not* + infinitive in negative indirect imperatives. You can use *tell* or *say*.	*"**Don't make** a lot of noise," said Mr. Jung.* *Mr. Jung said **not to make** a lot of noise.*
Use an infinitive in indirect requests. You can use *ask*, *tell*, or *say*.	*"**Please turn off** your phones," said Mr. Cho.* *Mr. Cho told us **to turn off** our phones.*
Use an infinitive to report advice given with modals such as *should*. Use *not* + infinitive to report advice with *should not*. You can use *tell* or *say*.	*"You **shouldn't reject** any ideas," Carl said.* *Carl told us not to reject any ideas.*
B Always use an object after *tell*.	*Ms. Ali **told us** to work quietly.* NOT *Ms. Ali told to work quietly.*
Use a pronoun or noun after *ask* to show the person who is the object of the request.	*Sam **asked her** to share her ideas with the group.*

Grammar Application

Exercise 3.1 Indirect Imperatives and Requests

Read the directions that a trainer gave to a group of employees. Then rewrite the steps with infinitives and the words in parentheses.

1 "Get into groups of three or four."
2 "Don't get into a group with someone you usually work with."
3 "Cut out pictures from magazines that show your ideal working environment."
4 "Don't criticize your group members' choices."
5 "Present your picture to the other groups."
6 "Comment on the other groups' pictures, but don't criticize people's choices."
7 "Discuss the emotions that the pictures suggest."

   I attended a problem-solving session with Dr. Martin yesterday. The goal was to help us get along better with each other. She helped us a great deal. Here's what she did:

1 (First / she / tell) *First, she told us to get into groups of three or four.*
2 (Then / she / say) _____
3 (She / tell) _____
4 (Dr. Martin / say) _____
5 (Then / she / tell) _____
6 (After that / she / say) _____
7 (Finally / Dr. Martin / say) _____

Listen to the marriage counseling session. Then answer the questions. Use the words in parentheses and *ask*, *say*, or *tell*.

1 What did the therapist tell the husband and wife to do?

The therapist told them to take a pad
of paper and a pencil.
(take a pad of paper and a pencil)

2 What did the husband ask?

_____

_____
(take a different pencil)

3 What did the wife ask?

_____
(use her own pen)

4 What did the therapist say?

_____
(write for 15 minutes without stopping)

5 What did the therapist tell the clients?

_____
(not look at each other's writing during the activity)

6 What did the therapist say?

_____
(not talk to each other)

7 What did the therapist tell the clients?

_____
(be prepared to read their descriptions to each other)

8 What did the husband ask?

_____
(have a little more time to write)

A Over to You Think of some good and bad advice you or people you know have received. What was the advice? Write six sentences.

Good Advice

My father's doctor told him not to eat meat and to exercise more.

1 _____

2 _____

3 _____

Bad Advice

Economists told Americans in 2015 to buy real estate because prices would increase.

4 _____

5 _____

6 _____

B Group Work Compare your answers with your group members. Discuss why the advice was good or bad. Take notes on your group members' answers.

A *My father's doctor told him not to eat meat and to exercise more. This was good advice because it helped him to get into better shape.*

B *Many economists told their clients to buy real estate because prices would increase. This was bad advice because real estate prices went down.*

4 Avoid Common Mistakes ⚠

1 **Use infinitives in indirect imperatives.**

         to
The leader asked us ~~that we~~ write for 5 minutes about the topic.

2 **In indirect *Yes/No* questions, remember to use an *if* clause.**

       if   *wanted*
He asked me ~~did I want~~ to be the group leader.

3 **Remember to use an object pronoun or noun after *tell*.**

   them
I told∧my ideas, and we ended up using two of them in the project.

Editing Task

Find and correct the mistakes in the paragraph about a brainstorming session.

                                                        if   *wanted*
When my psychology professor asked our class ~~did~~ we ~~want~~ to try brainstorming as part of our next group project, I had no idea that the experience would be so challenging or successful. First, when we started, one of our members asked many unimportant questions. When the team leader asked her that she asks the questions

5 later, that person began complaining. Then the team leader asked the person did she want to be the group leader. The rest of us told this was a bad idea, and there was an argument. A different problem arose when we met the second time. The leader asked one student that he takes electronic notes, but he forgot. As a result, when we met the third time, the leader had to tell the information again. She asked me that

10 I write the notes this time, and I did. Aside from these minor problems, the group generated a lot of ideas and finally came up with a successful proposal for a project. So, if someone asked me do I want to work as a group again, I would say yes because even though it is hard to work as a group, the outcome can be better.

The Passive (1)

1 Grammar in the Real World

A Should everyone speak English? Why or why not? Read the article on the use of English around the world. Why is English important to learn?

B Comprehension Check Answer the questions.

1 Where is English being spoken?
2 When do people around the world speak English?
3 What might be some disadvantages of English being a global language?

C Notice Match the sentences in A with the sentences in B that mean the same thing.

A	**B**
_____ 1 International companies **ask** their employees to learn English for their jobs.	a How **is** English **used** by nonnative speakers?
_____ 2 In addition, English **dominates** the Internet.	b Employees of international companies **are** often **asked** to learn English for their jobs.
_____ 3 How do nonnative speakers **use** English?	c In addition, the Internet **is dominated** by English.

Look at the forms of the verbs in bold in each of the matched sentences. How are the verbs in column B different from the verbs in column A?

ENGLISH IS SPOKEN HERE

An Italian businesswoman in Russia speaks English in meetings. Teenagers from Argentina, Turkey, and Japan chat online – in English. Learning English is clearly important in today's world. David
5 Crystal, a linguist[1] who studies the English language, believes that English has become a global language, although it is not an official language in many countries. According to Crystal, no other language **has been spoken** in so many countries and by so
10 many speakers. Currently, over 360 million people speak English as a first language around the world, and approximately one billion speak it as a second language. This means that there are more nonnative speakers of English than native speakers. How **is**
15 English **used** by nonnative speakers? Employees of international companies **are** often **asked** to learn English for their jobs. In addition, the Internet **is dominated**[2] by English. Some experts say that more than half of the information on the Internet is
20 in English. Also, English **has** long **been viewed** as a common language among travelers from different countries. The use of English worldwide appears to have clear benefits for everyone.

Does this increase in the use of English worldwide
25 have any disadvantages? Some say that cultures may lose some of their identity if people use English instead of their native languages. For example, much of a culture's identity **is reflected** in its music and literature. Would these songs and stories be
30 as effective in English? Others say that the English language itself could change. In fact, this is happening now. When English **is spoken** by a group of people whose native language is not English, words from the native language **are** sometimes **mixed in**, and
35 the pronunciation of words is different from British or American English. This means that dialects[3] and different forms of English **are being spoken** in various areas around the world. Sociologists **are** currently **studying** this phenomenon. The loss of
40 cultural identity and the creation of varieties of English are two areas of interest for sociologists and linguists.

English **is being used** worldwide more and more, and for many people, learning it is necessary for their personal and professional lives. There are obvious
45 advantages to learning English. The disadvantages remain unclear. It is clear that varieties of English will continue to evolve. How will this affect how English is **taught**? In the future, will greater numbers of people have to decide which variety of English they learn?

---

[1]**linguist:** someone who studies languages and their structures

[2]**dominate:** control a place or person, want to be in charge, or be the most important person or thing

[3]**dialect:** a local variety of language that differs in its pronunciation and word usage

2 Active vs. Passive Sentences

Grammar Presentation

A passive sentence and an active sentence have similar meanings, but the focus of the sentences is different. In the passive sentence, the focus is on the action or on the person or thing receiving the action.

The president asked the employees to speak English. (active)

The employees were asked to speak English. (passive)

2.1 Passive Sentences with *By* + Agent

A In active sentences, the agent (or doer of the action) is in subject position. In passive sentences, the object of the active sentence becomes the subject. The word *by* comes before the agent.	AGENT OBJECT *People spoke English at the meeting.* (active) *English was spoken by people at the meeting.* (passive)
B The agent is not always necessary.	*English was spoken at the meeting.* (We assume people were doing the speaking.)
C Use the *by* + agent phrase if the agent is important or if the meaning of the sentence would be unclear without it.	*The Internet is dominated by English.* NOT *The Internet is dominated.* (By who or what?)

2.2 Present and Past Forms of the Passive

A For the simple present form of the passive, use the present form of *be* + the past participle of the main verb.	*Some international companies ask their employees to learn English.* (active) *Employees are asked to learn English by some international companies.* (passive)
B For the present perfect form of the passive, use *has / have* + *been* + the past participle of the main verb.	*The company has told the employees to speak English.* (active) *The employees have been told to speak English.* (passive)
C For the present progressive form of the passive, use the present form of *be* + *being* + the past participle of the main verb.	*These days, people around the world are speaking many dialects of English.* (active) *These days, many dialects of English are being spoken by people around the world.* (passive)

2.2 Present and Past Forms of the Passive (continued)

D For the simple past form of the passive, use the past form of *be* + the past participle of the main verb. This form is the most common.	*Years ago, people did not consider English a global language.* (active) *Years ago, English was not considered a global language.* (passive)
E For the past progressive form of the passive, use the past form of *be* + *being* + the past participle of the main verb. This form is rare.	*Ten years ago, fewer people were using English online.* (active) *Ten years ago, English was being used by fewer people online.* (passive)
F In passive sentences, do not use a form of *do* in questions and negative statements in the simple present and simple past.	*Do most travelers speak English?* (active) *Is English spoken by most travelers?* (passive) *Turkish teenagers didn't use English to chat online two decades ago.* (active) *English wasn't used by Turkish teenagers to chat online two decades ago.* (passive)

📊 Research shows that the simple present, present perfect, and simple past forms of the passive are much more frequent than the present progressive, past progressive, and past perfect forms of the passive.

▶▶ Irregular Verbs: See page A1.
▶▶ Passive Forms: See page A12.

📊 Data from the Real World

Research shows that in academic writing, these are the most common verbs used in the passive:

analyze, calculate, carry out, collect, determine, expect, find, measure, observe, obtain, prepare, see, set, show, test, and *use*

🖥 Grammar Application

Exercise 2.1 Active and Passive Sentences

A Complete the online interview with a reporter from BusinessTimes Online and the CEO of an international company. Circle the correct verb forms.

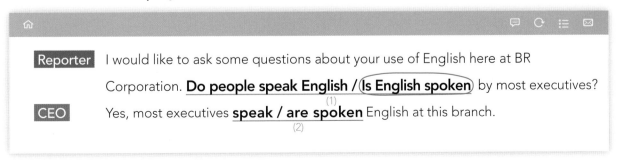

Reporter   I would like to ask some questions about your use of English here at BR Corporation. **Do people speak English / (Is English spoken)** by most executives?
(1)

CEO   Yes, most executives **speak / are spoken** English at this branch.
(2)

Reporter	Do only executives speak English? I mean, do lower level employees **use / are used** English here, too?
	(3)
CEO	No, English **isn't used / doesn't use** by them much.
	(4)
Reporter	Why is English necessary for some employees?
CEO	English **is needed /needs** by executives who travel. Also, we
	(5)
	are expected / expect them to read technical documents in English.
	(6)
Reporter	**Does BR Corporation support / Is BR Corporation supported** English language learning?
	(7)
CEO	Yes, BR Corporation **is offered / offers** onsite English courses.
	(8)
Reporter	**Are the courses taught / Do the courses teach** by native English speakers?
	(9)
CEO	Yes, native speakers **are conducted /conduct** all of our English classes.
	(10)
Reporter	Thank you for speaking with me today.

B Pair Work Which sentences in A are in the passive? Rewrite them as active sentences.
Do most executives speak English?

C Group Work Rewrite the active sentences in A as passive sentences. In which sentences is the *by* + agent phrase necessary? Share your answers with the group.

Exercise 2.2 Present Forms of the Passive

Complete the article about foreign-language teaching. Use the simple present or present perfect form of the passive with the verbs in parentheses. Sometimes more than one answer is possible.

> English *has been taught* (teach) in many countries all over the world for years.
> (1)
> It _____ currently _____ (speak), at least to some degree, by
> (2)   (2)
> one–quarter of the world's population. Schools in the United States also recognize the
> importance of learning other languages. For some time, languages other than English
> _____ (include) in these schools' programs. Recently, a growing number of
> (3)
> languages has become available. Which languages _____ (offered) by U.S.
> (4)
> high schools nowadays? The results may surprise you.
>
> French is one of the most popular foreign languages for high school students.
> It _____ (teach) in most U.S. high schools for many years. Arabic
> (5)
> is becoming more and more popular. In fact, Arabic _____ (offer) at many
> (6)

Massachusetts public schools these days. Chinese is also beginning to gain popularity.

An increase in the number of students learning Chinese _____
(7)

(report) for several years in various states across the country. It _____
(8)

(estimate) that more than 200,000 U.S. school children are now enrolled in

Mandarin Chinese classes.

Exercise 2.3 Past Forms of the Passive

A Read the active sentences about language. First underline the object in each sentence. Then rewrite the sentences as passive sentences. Sometimes more than one answer is possible.

1 At one time, many people used Latin as a global language.

At one time, Latin was used as a global language by many people.

2 The ancient Romans spoke Latin.

_____

3 Ancient Roman authors wrote many important manuscripts.

_____

4 For many centuries, the Romans conquered neighboring nations.

_____

5 These conquered groups spoke versions of Latin.

_____

6 Conquered people from Britain to Africa used Latin.

_____

7 People were still speaking Latin after the Roman Empire fell.

_____

8 Scholars and scientists were using Latin until the eighteenth century.

_____

B Read the sentences in A again. In which sentences are the agents not important? Discuss the reasons for your answers with a partner. Then rewrite these sentences in the passive without the agent.

A *In the first sentence,* many people *isn't important because we know that only people use language.*

B *You're right. The sentence could be* At one time, Latin was used as a global language.

3 Verbs and Objects with the Passive

Grammar Presentation

Transitive verbs (verbs that take an object) can occur in the passive. Intransitive verbs (verbs that do not take an object) cannot occur in the passive.	Someone *saw* her at the conference. (transitive) She *was seen* at the conference. I *fell* asleep. (intransitive)

3.1 Transitive and Intransitive Verbs

A Some common transitive verbs that occur in the passive are *call, concern, do, expect, find, give, know, left, lose, make, put, see, take,* and *use.*

Improvement of your language skills *is expected.*
I *was given* a new English textbook.
The reasons for his success *were not known.*

B *Born* is the past participle of *bear. Born* is used almost exclusively in the passive.

I *was born* in a small town.
Where *were* you *born*?

C Some common intransitive verbs, which have no passive form, include *appear, arrive, come, die, fall, go, happen, live, look, occur, sit, smile, stay, wait,* and *walk.*

When *did* your symptoms first *appear*?
NOT ~~When were your symptoms first appeared?~~
Globalization of some languages *happens* over time.
NOT ~~Globalization of some languages is happened over time.~~

3.2 Passive Forms with Direct and Indirect Objects

Some verbs, such as *give, offer, show,* and *tell,* can have two objects: a direct and an indirect object. In passive sentences, either the direct object or the indirect object can become the subject. Use *to* before an indirect object that is not in subject position.

INDIRECT OBJ   DIRECT OBJ
The team gave *the manager* *the report*.
The manager **was given** *the report* by the team.
The report **was given** *to the manager* by the team.

Grammar Application

Read the sentences about "dead" languages. Underline the verb in each sentence. If the sentence can occur in the passive, write the passive sentence on the line. Do not use an agent. Write **X** if a passive form is not possible.

1 People in Ancient Rome spoke Latin.
   Latin was spoken in Ancient Rome.

2 People don't use Latin for everyday communication today.
   _____

3 Some languages die.
   _____

4 This occurred with Dalmatian.
   _____

5 People spoke Dalmatian in Croatia. _____

6 Dalmatian speakers lived in coastal towns of Croatia. _____

7 Groups in different regions developed dialects of Dalmatian.
   _____

8 Native speakers didn't record the grammar of Dalmatian.
   _____

A Over to You Answer the questions about a language you know. Use the underlined verbs in your answers. Use passive sentences when possible. Use the indirect object as the subject of the passive sentence when possible. Write sentences that are true for you.

1 What is a computer called in this language?
   A computer is called "bilgisayar" in Turkish.

2 What English words are used in this language?
   _____

3 Do any other foreign words occur in this language? If so, what are they?
   _____

4 Is this language spoken by more people or fewer people than it was 50 years ago?
   _____

5 What advice is frequently given by teachers to people learning this language?
   _____

6 Do speakers of this language tell their children traditional stories?
   _____

B Group Work Share your sentences with your group members.

A Read the sentences about Esperanto, a language that was created as a global language. Underline the agents.

1 The first book about Esperanto was published by <u>a company</u> in 1887.
2 Esperanto was invented by L. L. Zamenhof.
3 Esperanto was created by its inventors to be a very easy language to learn.
4 The grammar was designed by Zamenhof to be simple and clear.
5 It is spoken by about 10,000 people.
6 It is being used by people in about 115 countries.
7 It has not been recognized as an official language by any country.
8 The language is used by some international travelers.

B Pair Work   Read the sentences in A again. Circle the direct objects. Compare your answers with a partner.

4 Reasons for Using the Passive

Grammar Presentation

The passive is used to describe processes and to report news events. The agent is not important. The focus is on the action or on the person or thing receiving the action.	*First, the students were shown a video in English.* *A "dead" language has been brought back to life in one community.*

4.1 Reasons for Using the Passive

A Use the passive to describe a process or a result. Common verbs to describe a process or a result are *compare, develop, examine, make, measure, study,* and *test.*	*First, the information was studied.* *Then recommendations were made.* (process) *Therefore, English was made the official language of the company in 2010.* (result)
B Use the passive when you don't know who performed the action. You can also use the passive to avoid directly blaming or criticizing someone.	*The report was poorly written.* (We don't know, or we don't want to say, who wrote the report.)
C Use the passive to report news events.	*Recommendations for the teaching of languages were published today.*

Grammar Application

Exercise 4.1 Describing Processes and Results

 A Listen to a report on a language study of English as a Second Language (ESL) students. Then complete the answers to the questions. Use the passive and the words in parentheses.

1 How many groups of students were there? (put into)

The students *were put into two groups*   .

2 What was the assignment at the beginning of the semester? (give)

Students in each group _____ .

3 What did group 1 study? (teach)

Group 1 _____ .

4 What did group 2 study? (teach)

Students in group 2 _____ .

5 Who read the essays? (read)

The first and final essays _____ .

6 What did the judges do with all of the final essays? (put)

All of the final essays from group 1 and group 2 _____

_____ .

7 How did the judges rate all the final essays? (rate)

The essays _____ .

8 What rating did the essays produced by group 1 receive? (give)

Most of the final essays produced by group 1 _____ .

9 What did the results seem to indicate? (include)

ESL students' writing improves when grammar and writing instruction

_____ .

B Listen again and check your answers.

Read the sentences about preserving two Native American languages. Then rewrite each sentence in the passive. Do not use an agent. Sometimes more than one answer is possible.

1 In 2009 in Minnesota, the legislature established a volunteer group to preserve Native American languages.

   In 2009 in Minnesota, a volunteer group was established to preserve Native American languages.

2 The legislature recognized the importance of preserving the Native American languages.

3 The volunteer group collected data on the use of the Ojibwe and Dakota languages.

4 In Minnesota, many Native American people no longer spoke the Ojibwe and Dakota languages.

5 The volunteer group developed a strategy to teach the Ojibwe and Dakota languages in schools.

6 The group is developing teacher-training programs.

7 In 2011, a nonprofit business released software for teaching the Ojibwe language.

8 The preservation of the languages will strengthen the Native Americans' cultural identities.

Read each classroom scenario and pretend you are the teacher. Then write passive statements to avoid directly blaming or criticizing someone. Use the underlined sentences in your answers. Sometimes more than one answer is possible.

1 Someone stole some valuable equipment from the classroom. You think that someone in the class is responsible, but you aren't sure. You tell the class:

   Some valuable equipment was stolen from the classroom.

2 One student's essay contained plagiarized material. The student copied some material in his essay from the Internet. You tell the student:

3 A hacker broke into the school's e-mail system last night. No one knows who is responsible, but you must inform the students. You tell the class:

_____

4 A student hands in the second draft of an essay. You see a lot of grammar mistakes. The student did not edit the paper carefully. You tell the student:

_____

5 Avoid Common Mistakes ⚠

1 **Remember to use a form of _be_ in passive sentences.**

is
English∧spoken at most airports.

2 **Always use the past participle form of the verb in passive sentences.**

translated
The words have been ~~translating~~ into Spanish, Arabic, Chinese, and Urdu.

3 **Do not use the passive form when the subject is the doer of the action.**

studying
I have been ~~studied~~ English for five years.
Most students have ~~been~~ used an English dictionary.

4 **With questions, remember to put _be_ before the subject.**

was
Why∧he ~~was~~ given an award?

Editing Task

Find and correct the mistakes in the paragraphs about English spelling.

Even good writers will tell you that English spelling has ~~been~~ confused them at one time or another. The same sound spelled many different ways. For example, the words _lazy_ and _busy_ are pronouncing with a /z/ sound, but they are not consistent in their spelling because of strange rules that are being related to the vowels.

5 Why English is written this way? English is an ancient language that contains old spelling rules. Also, other languages have been contributed many words to English.

Some experts who have been studied the English language for years would like to see English spelling simplified. They ask important questions: Why so much time is wasted on spelling lessons? Why is literacy lower in English-speaking countries than

10 in countries with simplified spelling? They point to the fact that many other languages simplified successfully. They suggest that in places such as Sweden, France, and Indonesia, changes to the written form have helped make learning to read easier.

The Passive (2)

1 Grammar in the Real World

A What do you know about genetically modified food? Read the article about genetically modified food. What are some genetically modified foods?

B Comprehension Check **Answer the questions.**

1 What are genetically modified foods?

2 What are some advantages of genetically modified foods?

3 What are some concerns about genetically modified foods?

C Notice **Find the sentences in the article and complete them.**

1 For example, those in favor of GM foods believe that crops _____ to resist insects.

2 Opponents insist that the problem of world hunger _____ by producing more food.

3 However, _____ extra care _____ until the long-term risks are known?

What verb comes after modals in passive verb forms?

GENETICALLY Modified Food

Genetically modified[1] (GM) foods come from plants that **have been changed** in a laboratory. This technology alters the genes[2] of the plants. It was developed so that food could have specific, desirable
5 traits. For example, the first GM crop in the United States consisted of tomatoes that were genetically changed to stay firmer longer.

Many people have strong opinions about the potential[3] benefits and risks of GM agriculture.
10 For example, those in favor of GM foods believe that crops **should be designed** to resist insects. They point to the example of sweet corn. They say that sweet corn **used to be destroyed** by pests. This created serious problems. Farmers lost money. Crops **got damaged**
15 and **could not be eaten**. Therefore, they say that a great benefit **can be found** in GM sweet corn, which has been modified to resist insects that cause damage. People who oppose GM foods see the issue differently. They cite[4] a study that links GM corn to organ[5] damage
20 in rats. They claim that the safety of these crops has not been tested adequately.[6]

GM supporters see GM soybeans as another beneficial crop. These crops are not harmed by a powerful weed-killing chemical. This chemical kills
25 weeds the first time it is applied, so farmers use less of it. Supporters say that this improves air and water quality since fewer pollutants enter the environment. Critics argue that the weeds are no longer affected by the weed killer, and new "superweeds" are growing.
30 Therefore, farmers have to use more chemicals to save their crops.

Finally, those in favor of GM foods say that better control of pests and weeds has made it possible for GM crops to produce more food in a shorter time.
35 They believe this increased production will help feed a world population which is expected to grow to 9 billion by 2050. Opponents insist that the problem of world hunger **will not be solved** by producing more food. They argue that farmers grow enough food now
40 and that global hunger is a result of unequal food distribution, not the result of a food shortage.[7]

Clearly, there are pros and cons to this debate. GM foods seem to have the potential to benefit the world. However, **should** extra care **be taken** until the long-
45 term risks are known?

---

[1]**modify:** change something in order to improve it

[2]**gene:** a code that controls the development of particular characteristics in a plant or animal

[3]**potential:** possible but not yet achieved

[4]**cite:** mention something as an example or proof of something else

[5]**organ:** a vital part of the body, like the heart, lungs, and kidneys

[6]**adequately:** good enough but not very good

[7]**shortage:** a lack of something needed

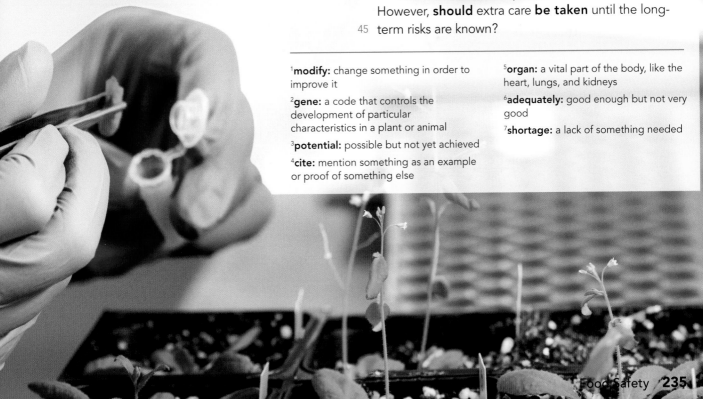

2 The Passive with *Be Going To* and Modals

Grammar Presentation

You can use the passive with *be going to* and modals.	GM foods **will replace** natural foods. (active) Natural foods **will be replaced** by GM foods. (passive)

2.1 Forming the Passive with *Be Going To* and Modals

A For the passive with *be going* to, use *be going to* + *be* + the past participle of the main verb. *Not* comes before *be going to* in the negative form.	Only natural foods **are going to be served** *in our house.* *The food* **is not going to be eaten** *immediately.* **Is** *more GM food* **going to be grown** *in the future?*
B For the passive with modals, use a modal + *be* + the past participle of the main verb. *Not* follows the modal in the negative form.	People **could be harmed** by GM food. People **must be informed.** Food **should not be eaten** if it isn't fresh. **Will** questions about GM food **be answered** by scientists?

▶▶ Passive Forms: See page A12.

Grammar Application

Exercise 2.1 The Passive with *Will* and *Be Going To*

Complete the interview about plans for a food conference. Circle the passive form of the verbs.

> **Reporter** A conference called **The Future of Food** will hold /(will be held) at
> Bay City Tech next week. Issues concerning the food industry
> (1)
> **will be discussed / will discuss** by experts from a variety of fields.
> (2)
> We interviewed two participants, Dr. Fred Bell, a biologist, and Deniz
> Martin, the president of the Traditional Food Society. First, what major
> issues **are going to address / are going to be addressed** at next week's
> (3)
> conference?
>
> **Dr. Bell** Policies on food aid **are going to debate / are going to be debated** in
> (4)
> one session.
>
> **Reporter** What are the issues there?

Dr. Bell	Well, GM plants **are going to be promoted / are going to promote** as the main solution to hunger in poor nations.
Reporter	World hunger is a serious problem. What's your opinion as a biologist? Will the situation **improve / be improved** by GM plants?
Dr. Bell	No, the problem of world hunger **will not solve / will not be solved** by GM crops, in my opinion.
Reporter	Don't some experts believe that GM food will help increase crop production?
Dr. Bell	In my opinion, crop production **will not be increased / will not increase** by GM plants. In fact, there is no proof of this so far.
Reporter	Ms. Martin, what Traditional Food Society issues **will be presented / will present** at the conference?
Ms. Martin	The issue of sustainable food production – growing food without harming people or the environment – **will address / will be addressed** . For example, ways to improve organic farming methods **will be demonstrated / will demonstrate** .
Reporter	Thank you both for your time.

(5)
(6)
(7)
(8)
(9)
(10)
(11)

Exercise 2.2 The Passive with Modals

A Read the facts that a student collected for a report on pesticides.[1] Rewrite the facts as passive sentences. Sometimes more than one answer is possible.

1 Pesticides can harm humans, animals, and the environment.

   Humans, animals, and the environment can be harmed by pesticides.

2 Pesticides can cause air pollution.

   _____

3 In the United States, scientists can find pesticides in many streams.

   _____

4 Pesticides may have harmed some farm animals.

   _____

5 Pesticides may have affected meat from farm animals.

   _____

6 Pesticides in water could affect fish.

   _____

7 In some cases, pesticides can affect humans.

   _____

[1]**pesticide:** a weed-killing chemical

Exercise 2.3 More Passive with Modals

Complete the web article about a government recall. Rewrite the steps as passive sentences with modals. Use the indirect object as the subject of the passive sentence when possible. Sometimes more than one answer is possible.

NOTICE to Purchasers of Sunny Farm Eggs

We regret to inform you that Grade A eggs from Sunny Farm sold in the last two weeks have been making customers sick. If you have recently purchased eggs or are concerned about the situation, you can take the following steps:

1 You must check the date and plant number on the container first.

The date and plant number on the
container must be checked first.

2 You must not open the package.

_____

3 You must not consume the product.

_____

4 You can return the product for a refund.

_____

5 Store management may ask you questions about the product you bought.

_____

6 Store management might offer you a similar product.

_____

Exercise 2.4 Using Passive Forms of Modals

Group Work **Discuss the questions about GM food. Use passive sentences with modals.**

- Should food be genetically modified? Why or why not?

- In your opinion, can people be harmed by eating genetically modified food? If yes, in what ways?

- Should genetically modified food be labeled in the United States? Why or why not?

A *In my opinion, food should not be genetically modified because we don't know the dangers.*

B *I disagree. I think food should be genetically modified because it's the best way to end world hunger.*

3 Get Passives

Grammar Presentation

Passive sentences with *get* instead of *be* are more informal and are often used to express stronger emotions.	*The storm **destroyed** the crops.* (active) *The crops **got destroyed** by the storm.* (passive)

3.1 Forming *Get* Passives

A For the *get* passive, use a form of *get* + the past participle of the main verb.	*He **is getting transferred** to the research department.* *Our orange trees **got damaged** last night.*
B For negative statements and questions in the simple present and simple past, use a form of *do* + *get* + the past participle of the main verb.	*In my opinion, food **doesn't get inspected** carefully enough.* *Did your crops **get damaged** in the hurricane?*

3.2 Using *Get* Passives

We often use *get* passives to talk about negative situations or situations we think are beyond our control.	*Some food companies **are getting fined** for using unsafe equipment.*

The *get* passive is more common in speaking than in general writing. In formal academic writing, the *get* passive is very infrequent.

speaking	
general writing	
formal academic writing	

Say: "She *got arrested and charged* with murder."
Write: She *was arrested and charged* with murder.

🖥️ Grammar Application

Complete the interview about food contamination. Write *get* passives with the words in parentheses. If there is a line through the agent, do not use it in the passive.

Alternative **REVIEW**

Interviewer There's been another case of contaminated[1] lettuce. How does this happen? An anonymous lettuce grower agreed to be interviewed if we did not mention his name. So, I hear *you're getting investigated by the FDA*
(1 the FDA[2] is investigating you)
for problems with food safety. What happened?

Grower _____ .
(2 ~~Something~~ contaminated our lettuce)

Interviewer _____ ?
(3 Did the FDA recall the lettuce)

Grower Yes, _____ .
(4 ~~The FDA~~ recalled it)

Interviewer What happened, exactly?

Grower I'm not sure. As you know, _____
(5 ~~workers~~ pick our produce)
right here on the farm. _____ here.
(6 ~~Workers~~ also pack it)
_____ . This can cause contamination.
(7 ~~Workers~~ sometimes mishandle it)

[1]**contaminated:** less pure and potentially harmful | [2]**FDA:** Food and Drug Administration, a U.S. government agency

| Interviewer | Don't you have strict procedures? |

| Grower | Yes, but it's been very hot lately. Working conditions have been difficult.

Perhaps _____ .
(8 ~~something~~ distracted the workers) |

| Interviewer | _____ before it goes to
(9 Doesn't ~~someone~~ check your produce)

the stores? |

| Grower | No, _____ . That's our responsibility,
(10 ~~people~~ don't inspect it)

and my company is very sorry that we didn't catch it. |

| Interviewer | I see. Well, thank you very much for agreeing to be interviewed. |

Exercise 3.2 More *Get* Passives

A Over to You **Look at the following statements about food safety. Check (✓) the statements you agree with.**

☐ **1** When a restaurant gets inspected, the results should be posted on the restaurant's front door.

☐ **2** Food recalls get publicized too much. This hurts farmers, and a lot of perfectly good food gets thrown away.

☐ **3** If a supermarket sells spoiled food, the manager should get fired.

☐ **4** If a restaurant gets temporarily shut down for food safety problems, no one should ever eat there again.

☐ **5** All foreign fruit and vegetables should get inspected before entering the country.

B Group Work **Compare your answers with your group members. Discuss your reasons. Use *get* passives.**

A *I think that when a restaurant gets inspected, the results should be posted on the restaurant's front door.*

B *I disagree. If a restaurant gets inspected and receives a low rating, it's bad for business.*

4 Passive Gerunds and Infinitives

Grammar Presentation

<table>
<tr>
<td>Gerunds and infinitives can occur in the passive.</td>
<td>

Some people worry about genetically modified food *harming* them. (active)

Some people worry about *being harmed* by genetically modified food. (passive)

Consumers should expect food companies *to give* them accurate information about their food. (active)

Consumers should expect *to be given* accurate information about their food. (passive)
</td>
</tr>
</table>

4.1 Forming Passive Gerunds

<table>
<tr>
<td>

A To form passive gerunds, use *being* + the past participle of the main verb.
</td>
<td>

Consumers are afraid of food companies harming them. (active)

Consumers are afraid of being harmed by food companies. (passive)
</td>
</tr>
<tr>
<td>

B Common verbs that are followed by passive gerunds include *avoid, consider, dislike, enjoy, like, miss, quit,* and *remember.*
</td>
<td>

I remember being given information about GM foods in the supermarket.
</td>
</tr>
<tr>
<td>

C Common verbs + prepositions that are followed by passive gerunds include complain *about,* keep on, succeed in, and worry about.
</td>
<td>

The restaurant worried about being closed by the food inspectors.
</td>
</tr>
<tr>
<td>

D Common adjectives + prepositions that are followed by passive gerunds include *afraid of, aware of, concerned about, content with, interested in, tired of,* and *worried about.*
</td>
<td>

The company was interested in being seen as a socially responsible company.
</td>
</tr>
</table>

▸▸ Verbs Followed by Gerunds Only: See page A7.
▸▸ Verbs Followed by Gerunds or Infinitives: See page A7.
▸▸ Verbs + Prepositions: See page A9.
▸▸ Adjectives + Prepositions: See page A10.

4.2 Forming Passive Infinitives

A To form passive infinitives, use *to be* + the past participle of the main verb.	*Food companies are not likely **to solve** the problem of world hunger.* (active) *The problem of world hunger is not likely to be solved by food companies.* (passive)
B Common verbs followed by passive infinitives include *ask, expect, hope, manage, refuse, seem,* and *want*.	*The manager of the restaurant expected **to be told** that the restaurant passed the inspection.*

▸▸ Verbs Followed by Infinitives Only: See page A7.
▸▸ Verbs Followed by Gerunds or Infinitives: See page A7.

Grammar Application

Exercise 4.1 Passive Gerunds and Infinitives

Complete the sentences about restaurant food safety. Circle the correct passive forms of the verbs.

1 Customers at Corner Café recently complained about (being)/ to be served undercooked food.
2 The manager of the café was concerned about **to be / being** inspected.
3 The owners were afraid of **to be / being** told they must close the cafe if the problems were not corrected.
4 The owners expected **being / to be** cited by the county food safety bureau.
5 The staff hoped **to be / being** paid for the time that the restaurant was closed.
6 The manager was not happy about **being / to be** told to close the restaurant.

Exercise 4.2 More Passive Gerunds and Infinitives

A Listen to an interview with consumers about food labeling. Write the passive gerund or infinitive forms you hear.

> **Reporter** Hello to everyone. Today I'll be asking people their thoughts on food labeling. First, let's talk to Andrew. Andrew, do you read food labels?
>
> **Andrew** I refuse ___*to be forced*___ to do so much work when I go shopping! I just want
> (1)
> _____ decent, healthy food. No, I don't read them.
> (2)
> **Reporter** I can understand that. Al and Mei?

Al	We expect _____ the truth by food companies,

Al   We expect _____ the truth by food companies,
      <small>(3)</small>
      but we know labels aren't always accurate.

Mei   You have to inform yourself. All consumers have to start _____
      <small>(4)</small>
      better _____ , so we always read them.
      <small>(4)</small>

Reporter   OK. And you, Roxana, do you read food labels?

Roxana   Yes, because I'm a pretty informed consumer. I'm not too concerned
      about _____ by food companies, but I'm not
      <small>(5)</small>
      interested in _____ , either!
      <small>(6)</small>

Reporter   Thank you, Roxana. And finally, Jessica. What do you think?

Jessica   It's sometimes easy _____ by product labeling, so I
      <small>(7)</small>
      don't read them much because they don't matter. Take the word
      natural, for example. You expect it _____ for food that
      <small>(8)</small>
      has few or no artificial ingredients. However, the word *natural* can be
      used for genetically modified food products.

Reporter   Thanks to you all. It appears that consumers are tired of
      _____ by food companies.
      <small>(9)</small>

B Over to You **Complete the sentences about food labeling with passive gerunds or infinitives and the verbs in the box. Write sentences that are true for you.**

~~confuse~~	give	lie to	tell
do	inform	sell	use

1 I'm tired of *being confused by food labels* _____ .

2 I expect _____ .

3 I'm (not) concerned about _____ .

4 I hope _____ .

5 It's (not) easy _____ .

C Pair Work Compare your answers with a partner.

    A *I'm tired of being confused by food labels. I don't want to be told something is "organic" when it really isn't.*

    B *Well, I know what you mean, but actually, I'm tired of being told to eat organic and healthy food all the time. Why can't I enjoy a candy bar once in a while?*

5 Avoid Common Mistakes ⚠

> **1**   **In passive sentences, use a past participle after *be*, not the base form of the verb.**
>
>   *produced*
>   *Unintended side effects can be ~~produce~~ by new technologies.*

> **2**   **Don't forget to use *be* + the past participle to express a passive meaning.**
>
>   *be caused*
>   *An allergic reaction can ~~cause~~ by many different kinds of foods.*

Editing Task

Find and correct seven more mistakes in the paragraph about some GM food concerns.

                                                                           made

    It is certain that many advances in technology will be ~~make~~ in the twenty-first century. Although many of these advances will improve our future, others may do as much harm as good. GM foods are one example. Currently, many new foods are creating by scientists. For instance, many people suffer from food allergies. Certain

5 GM foods may help avoid this problem; the food's DNA has been change so that the food no longer causes allergic reactions. Also, one day, the world's growing population may be feed with GM foods that grow quickly. This will make it possible for more food to be produce. These new foods can be use to feed more people. However, GM foods have another side. Because these foods have not existed very

10 long, scientists do not know all their effects. For example, some people fear that cancer can cause by GM foods. This is especially troubling because GM foods might not mark as such, so consumers may not know what they are buying. When they develop new foods, scientists should be aware of the concerns that consumers have. In my view, we should be careful with any new technology.

Subject Relative Clauses (Adjective Clauses with Subject Relative Pronouns)

Alternative Energy Sources

1 Grammar in the Real World

A What are some alternative sources of energy (other than oil or coal)? Read the article about one type of alternative energy. Is "people power" an efficient energy source? Why or why not?

B Comprehension Check Answer the questions.

1 What are some ways that people can make energy?
2 How can "people power" help the environment?
3 What are some problems with people power?

C Notice Find the sentences in the article and complete them. Then draw an arrow from each missing word to the word that it refers to.

1 Professional athletes, _____ **exercise routines** can last for several hours, could help power a house!

2 This heat, _____ **is sent** to a nearby building, cuts the energy bill by 25 percent.

3 However, people _____ **support** green energy are confident that this technology will catch on in the near future.

Look at the words in bold that follow the words you wrote. What parts of speech are the words in bold?

EXERCISING for ELECTRICITY

Much of the world's energy comes from sources like oil and coal, **which cannot be replaced when used up.** Renewable sources – water, wind, and the sun – are better for the environment. However, these alternative
5 sources of energy have not always been sufficiently explored for political and economic reasons. People **who care about the environment** are looking for more alternative sources that might appeal to people who make decisions about these things. One source **that is**
10 **becoming popular** uses energy **that is generated by humans**, sometimes called "people power."

With people power, people create electricity through exercise. People exercise in green gyms, **which contain special treadmills.** These machines
15 convert human energy into electricity that helps run the lights and air-conditioning. People power also helps prevent air pollution. Someone **who exercises for one hour** can feel good about the fact that he or she is helping prevent carbon dioxide from going into the air.
20 Professional athletes, **whose exercise routines can last for several hours,** could help power a house!

Exercise is not the only way people can make energy. One company has created surfaces **which are powered by humans.** People dance or walk on special
25 dance floors and sidewalks. This movement generates electricity, **which can light up the dance floor or power street lamps.** Body heat is used for power, too. One system in Sweden gathers the body heat from commuters in a train station. This heat, **which is sent to**
30 **a nearby building,** cuts the energy bill by 25 percent.

People power is not perfect, though. Large gyms need a lot of energy to run. People power, **which only generates a part of the total electricity needed,** does not lower the gym's electric bill much. Also, the use
35 of this technology is moving slowly. Business leaders, **who must focus on making a profit,** do not always want to be the first to create new products. They are afraid to spend money on technology **which might not be successful.** However, people **who support green**
40 **energy** are confident that this technology will catch on in the near future.

People power is not a major energy source yet, but it could be soon. Meanwhile, this "green energy" encourages people to exercise, and it makes people
45 more aware of the environment. It is one kind of technology **that helps people and the planet** at the same time.

2 Identifying Subject Relative Clauses

Grammar Presentation

Relative clauses modify – define, describe, identify, or give more information about – nouns. In a subject relative clause, the relative pronoun is the subject of the clause. An identifying relative clause gives essential information about the noun it modifies.	SUBJECT I go to a gym. *The gym creates its own electricity.* RELATIVE PRONOUN I go to a gym *that creates its own electricity.*

2.1 Forming Identifying Subject Relative Clauses

A The subject of an identifying subject relative clause is the relative pronoun. The relative pronoun refers to the noun before it. Use *who* or *that* for people, and *which* or *that* for things.	RELATIVE NOUN PRONOUN *Nowadays, people often drive cars that don't use a lot of gas.*
Do not add a second subject to the clauses.	*People that exercise can use special machines to create electricity.* NOT *People that they exercise can use special machines to create electricity.*
B The information in an identifying subject relative clause is essential. Do not add a comma before this type of clause.	*People who care about the environment often recycle their garbage.* (The relative clause tells which people.) *The school uses the electricity that comes from the exercise machines in the gym.* (The relative clause tells which electricity.)
C The verb in the relative clause agrees with the noun that the relative pronoun modifies.	SINGULAR NOUN SINGULAR VERB *Someone that supports the environment recycles.* PLURAL NOUN PLURAL VERB *Many people that support the environment recycle.*

▶▶ Relative Clauses: See page A13.

2.2 Using Identifying Subject Relative Clauses

A Use an identifying relative clause to give essential information about a noun. These clauses are also called restrictive subject clauses.	*People power is a kind of energy.* (What kind of energy? What is important about it?) *People power is a kind of energy that creates electricity.* (The relative clause gives essential information.)
B Use an identifying relative clause in definitions, especially with words such as *anyone, people, someone,* or *something*.	*Green energy is something which doesn't hurt the environment.* *Environmentalists are people who care about the environment.*

Grammar Application

Exercise 2.1 Subject Relative Pronouns

A Complete the article about people power. Use *who* or *which* and the simple present form of the verbs in parentheses.

Silvia is a student at Bay City University (BCU) __who works out__ (work out) at the campus gym every day. Today, she is exercising on a bike __which connect__ (connect) (1) to a power grid. Silvia is possibly producing the energy __who keeps__ (keep) the (3) gym lights on or __which power__ (power) a professor's laptop in another part of the (4) campus. BCU and Bay City Tech are just two educational institutions __which uses__ (5) (use) human energy as power.

We interviewed Mark Sandoval, a BCU employee __who runs__ (run) campus (6) operations. He said, "This is not a program __which save__ (save) the university (7) money. It's more of an experiment __which illustrate__ (illustrate) to the (8) students how they affect their environment." GreenGo is a Bay City human energy company __which prov..__ (provide) BCU with the exercise equipment. Rita Crane, a GreenGo (9) spokesperson, said, "We enjoy working with students and faculty __who takes__ (take) (10) their impact on the environment very seriously."

 B Listen to the article and check your answers.

A Complete the energy definitions with *who or that* and the correct form of the verbs in parentheses. Sometimes more than one answer is possible.

1 Geothermal energy is heat ___*that comes*___ (come) from inside the earth.
2 Renewable energy is something *that doesn't disappear* (not/disappear).
3 Ecologists are people *who studies* (study) the relationship between organisms and the environment.
4 A green politician is someone *who puts* (put) environmental issues ahead of other issues.
5 A sustainable engineer is anyone *who designs* (design) objects to protect the environment.

B Complete the energy definitions with subject relative pronouns and the words in the box.

> chemicals/trap/heat in the atmosphere
> ~~fuel/come/from vegetable oil or animal fat~~
> people/be/part of a political group focused on good environmental policy
> someone/work/to protect the environment
> structures/not have/a large negative impact on the environment
>
> a type of energy/come/from human exercise
> a type of energy/use/the sun as its source
> a vehicle/use/two sources of power to run

1 Biodiesel is a kind of ___*fuel that/which comes from vegetable oil or animal fat*___ .
2 A conservationist is _____ .
3 "Greens" are _____ .
4 Greenhouse gases are _____ .
5 A hybrid car is _____ .
6 Solar energy is _____ .
7 People power is _____ .
8 Green buildings are _____ .

A Combine the sentences from an alternative energy company's advertisement. Use *who, that,* or *which* in subject relative clauses. Sometimes more than one answer is possible.

1 GreenGo is a company. It develops renewable energy systems.

   ___*GreenGo is a company that/which develops renewable energy systems.*___

2 GreenGo developed a technology. The technology turns exercise machines into power generators.

   _____

   _____

3 GreenGo builds machines like exercise bikes. These exercise bikes let exercisers generate electricity from their workouts.

_____

_____

4 The electricity connects to a power grid. The power grid covers a large geographic area.

_____

_____

5 Sachiko Hanley is the woman. The woman invented this technology.

_____

6 Many GreenGo clients are colleges and other institutions. The institutions have on-site gyms.

_____

_____

7 GreenGo provides an energy source. The energy source is good for the environment.

_____

8 "We are proud to work with institutions. They have the same environmental goals that we do."

_____

_____

B In each of the sentences you wrote in A, underline the subject relative clause and draw an arrow from the relative pronoun to the noun in the main clause it refers to.

GreenGo is a company that develops renewable energy systems.

3 Nonidentifying Subject Relative Clauses

Grammar Presentation

Nonidentifying subject relative clauses have the same form as identifying clauses. Unlike identifying clauses, nonidentifying clauses provide additional, not essential, information about the nouns they modify.

Biodiesel fuel, **which often comes from plants,** is an economical source of energy. (Where the fuel comes from is extra information. It is not essential information about _Biodiesel fuel._)

3.1 Forming Nonidentifying Subject Relative Clauses

A Like identifying subject relative clauses, the subject of a nonidentifying subject relative clause is the relative pronoun. The relative pronoun refers to the noun before it.

Use *who* for people and *which* for things. Do not use *that* in a nonidentifying clause.

People power, which is a way to create energy, is popular.

NOT *People power, ~~that~~ is a way to create energy, is popular.*

B Use commas before and after the nonidentifying subject relative clause. The commas indicate that the information is not essential to the meaning of the noun. It is extra information.

Hybrid cars, which are better for the environment, use less gas.

3.2 Using Nonidentifying Subject Relative Clauses

A Use a nonidentifying subject relative clause to give nonessential information about a noun. These clauses are also called nonrestrictive clauses.

People power, which is a way to create energy, is popular with environmentalists.

B Nonidentifying relative clauses are more common in writing and formal speaking than in informal speaking.

3.3 Identifying vs. Nonidentifying Subject Relative Clauses

A Identifying relative clauses provide essential information about the noun. The information in the clause identifies or distinguishes the noun.

Renewable energy that comes directly from the sun is called solar energy. (The information identifies a particular type of renewable energy – not all types of renewable energy.)

My sister who lives in Maine loves being outside. (The information distinguishes this sister from the other or others; it implies there is more than one sister.)

B Nonidentifying clauses give extra information about a noun. The information is not essential. In speaking, use a short pause before and after the clause. In writing, separate the clause between commas.

Renewable energy, which releases fewer greenhouse gases, is becoming more popular. (The information does not identify the type of renewable energy; it gives more information about it.)

My sister, who lives in Maine, loves being outside. (The information is extra, not essential; it also implies the speaker has only one sister.)

Grammar Application

A Read the news report on building affordable green homes in New Orleans. Underline the relative clauses. Label each of the relative clauses *I* (for identifying) or *NI* (for nonidentifying).

As the environment changes, hurricanes and other severe storms have become a serious problem in the United States and Latin America. Hurricanes, <u>which primarily attack</u> *NI* <u>southern and southeastern parts of the United States</u>, have been increasing in severity. The hurricane that did the most damage in recent history was Hurricane Katrina. Since
5 then, a great number of Americans, including many celebrities, have helped the people of New Orleans rebuild their homes.

The celebrity who is best known for building homes in New Orleans is Brad Pitt. Pitt, who created a foundation called Make It Right, helps build new "green" homes in New Orleans. The goals of this foundation are admirable. Make It Right volunteers, who work for
10 free, want to build 150 new green homes in the Lower 9th Ward.

The foundation is not simply providing new homes. Make It Right homes have many features which are environmentally sound. For example, Make It Right homes have metal roofs which absorb heat and keep them cool. It is possible that Make It Right homes will inspire new home builders not only in New Orleans but around the world as well.

B Pair Work Compare your answers with a partner. Discuss the reason for each of your answers.

The relative clause which primarily attack southern and southeastern parts of the United States *is nonidentifying, because it is not essential to understanding the sentence. You can say* Hurricanes have been increasing in severity, *and the idea is complete.*

Combine the facts and the additional information about green architecture. Use nonidentifying relative clauses.

1 **Fact:** Green architecture is becoming more common.

   Additional Information: Green architecture considers both design and the environment.

   Green architecture, which considers both design and the environment, is becoming more common.

2 **Fact:** The Turning Torso building uses only renewable energy.
   Additional Information: The Turning Torso building is located in Malmö, Sweden.

3 Fact: The Turning Torso building was inspired by a sculpture of a twisting human being.
Additional Information: The Turning Torso building is the tallest building in Sweden.

_____

_____

4 Fact: The Burj al-Taqa will be a wind- and solar-powered green skyscraper.
Additional Information: The Burj al-Taqa will be in Dubai.

_____

_____

5 Fact: Eckhard Gerber has also designed a green building in Riyadh.
Additional Information: Eckhard Gerber designed the Burj al-Taqa.

_____

_____

6 Fact: Architect Eric Corey Freed believes that people will pay more for green buildings.
Additional Information: Eric Corey Freed has written several books on building green structures.

_____

_____

4 Subject Relative Clauses with _Whose_

Grammar Presentation

Subject relative clauses that begin with the pronoun _whose_ show possession.	_In Sweden, there are train commuters. The commuters' body heat supplies energy for a building._ _In Sweden, there are train commuters whose body heat supplies energy for a building._

4.1 Forming Relative Clauses with _Whose_

A The pronoun _whose_ shows a possessive relationship between the noun before and after it.	_They are the scientists whose research has won awards._ (The research belongs to the scientists.) _That is the product whose inventor attended this college._ (The product is related to the inventor.)

4.1 Forming Relative Clauses with *Whose* (continued)

B The verb in the relative clause agrees with the noun following *whose*.

WHOSE + SINGULAR NOUN + SINGULAR VERB

He's the scientist **whose** newest idea is often quoted.

WHOSE + PLURAL NOUN + PLURAL VERB

He's the scientist **whose** ideas are often quoted.

4.2 Using Relative Clauses with *Whose*

Relative clauses with *whose* can be identifying or nonidentifying subject relative clauses.

IDENTIFYING RELATIVE CLAUSE

They are the journalists **whose articles have explained green energy.** (The information in the clause identifies which journalists.)

NONIDENTIFYING RELATIVE CLAUSE

Brad Pitt, **whose movies are well known,** gives a lot of money to environmental causes. (The information about his movies is not essential to identifying Brad Pitt.)

Grammar Application

Exercise 4.1 Subject Relative Clauses with *Whose*: Identifying or Nonidentifying?

A Read the article about a human-powered vehicle. Underline the subject relative clauses. Add commas when necessary.

Meet Charles Greenwood, the inventor of a new type of car. Greenwood, whose human-powered car can go up to 60 miles per hour, is an engineer. This inventor whose dream is to sell the cars to the public has also started a business to manufacture it. A car whose power source is human energy is obviously good for the environment. How does

5 it work? The car whose main power source is human-operated hand cranks[1] also runs with a battery. It's not expensive, either. The car – the HumanCar Imagine PS – will sell for about $15,000. A hybrid car whose selling price will only be about $15,000 should be very popular with energy-conscious consumers.

10 There are other benefits to a human-powered car. A car whose power source is human energy might also help drivers stay fit. In addition, owners expect to save money operating the HumanCar. The HumanCar whose main source of power is human-operated hand cranks gets the

15 equivalent of 100 miles to the gallon of gas in a regular car.

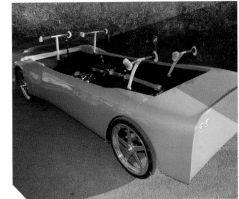

[1]**crank:** a handle or bar on a machine that you can turn to make another part turn

B Pair Work Compare your answers with a partner. Discuss whether each subject relative clause is identifying or nonidentifying.

The relative clause whose human-power car can go up to 60 miles per hour *is nonidentifying because it is not necessary for identifying Greenwood.*

Exercise 4.2 *That, Who, or Whose?*

Complete the article about green awards. Use *that*, *who*, or *whose*. Sometimes more than one answer is possible.

AWARDS for Being Green

There are many organizations ___*that*___ offer awards to companies _____ practices
(1)   (2)
help the environment and society. Some organizations recognize the work of companies

_____ focus on environmentally responsible practices. The Evergreen Award program
(3)
honors companies _____ create environmentally friendly products. An award in 2010
(4)
went to Play Mart Inc., a maker of plastic playground equipment _____ products were
(5)
made from jugs and bottles from landfills.

The One Show is another awards organization, _____ Green Pencil award
(6)
celebrates environmentally conscious advertising. In 2009, Häagen-Dazs received the

award for their advertisements _____ raised awareness about the disappearance of
(7)
honeybees. Häagen-Dazs, _____ ice-cream is well known, also donates money to
(8)
research _____ studies honeybees. People _____ buy certain flavors of
(9)   (10)
Häagen-Dazs ice-cream help support this research.

Exercise 4.3 Subject Relative Clauses with *Whose*

Pair Work Answer the questions. Use subject relative clauses with *whose* in your sentences. Then compare your answers with a partner.

■ What are the benefits of human-powered vehicles and flying machines?

■ What are the disadvantages to these inventions?

A *I said, "A vehicle whose power source is human energy is good for the environment."*

B *I said, "A vehicle whose power source is human energy probably won't go very far or very fast."*

5 Avoid Common Mistakes ⚠

1   Use *which* or *that* for things, not *who*.

Scientists are looking for new energy sources ~~who~~ don't harm the environment.
                     which/that

2   Use *who* or *that* for people, not *which*.

Governments support researchers ~~which~~ are trying to develop alternative approaches to energy.
     who/that

3   Don't use *who's* when you mean *whose*.

An inventor ~~who's~~ innovative technology solves the energy crisis will help all of us.
      whose

4   Don't include a second subject in the relative clause.

A fuel that ~~it~~ is renewable will help solve the world's pollution problems.

Editing Task

Find and correct eight more mistakes in the paragraph about an alternative renewable energy source.

       People think renewable energy only comes from water, wind, or the sun, but there
                                which/that

is another renewable energy source: biofuels. Biofuels are fuels ~~who~~ are derived from

oils in plants. Farmers who's fields were once planted with food crops can now grow

energy on their land. The most commonly used example of this is ethanol, a biofuel who

5   is usually made from corn and added to gasoline. However, ethanol has been criticized.

Some critics say that the world, who's population continues to grow, needs all of its corn

for food production. Others have argued that it takes too much energy to produce corn

ethanol. Recently, scientists which do biofuels research have been working to overcome

these problems. For example, some scientists have produced a genetically modified

10   tobacco that it contains more oil than usual. Other scientists have produced genetically

modified tobacco plants that they produce a lot of oil. This oil can be made into ethanol.

In fact, some scientists have produced ethanol from inedible grass that it grows in the

wild. The scientists which made these inventions hope that biofuels will become an

important part of our renewable energy future.

22

Object Relative Clauses (Adjective Clauses with Object Relative Pronouns)

Biometrics

1 Grammar in the Real World

A What are some techniques that the police use to solve crimes? Read the article about how the police analyze evidence. What are some modern techniques for analyzing evidence?

B Comprehension Check **Answer the questions.**

1 What are some types of forensic evidence?
2 What is one way that police can identify someone?
3 Why can forensic evidence sometimes be inaccurate?

C Notice **Match the first part of the sentence from the article on the left with the second part on the right.**

A	**B**
1 The victim shows the police the room _____	a **that** thieves leave behind.
2 Traditional forensic techniques include collecting and analyzing evidence _____	b in **which** the theft occurred.
3 This evidence includes dust, hair, or fibers _____	c **that** police find at the crime scene.

Do the words in B in bold act as the subjects or objects of the clauses they are in?

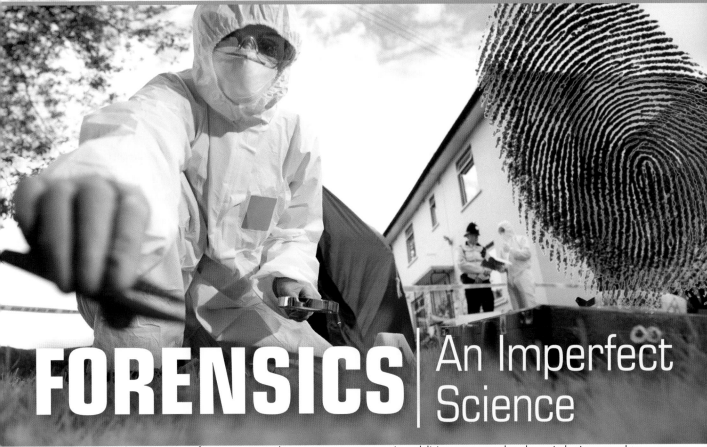

FORENSICS | An Imperfect Science

Someone steals a painting from a private home. The victim shows the police the room **in which the theft occurred**. Police collect clothing fibers and dirt left on the carpet. Experts then use the fibers
5 and dirt to identify the thief. The thief is caught, and the art is returned. The use of scientific tests to investigate crimes like this one is called forensics. Traditional forensic techniques include collecting and analyzing evidence **that police find at the crime**
10 **scene**. This evidence includes dust, hair, or fibers **that thieves leave behind**. Police sometimes use dogs to investigate a crime. Scents **that dogs are trained to recognize** include the scents of people, drugs, and explosives. Police also look for fingerprints, **which**
15 **they often find on hard surfaces**. Unfortunately, fingerprints are often incomplete. However, new techniques use computer programs to help police identify suspects or missing people. Computer programs can produce a list of matches for partial
20 fingerprints. This kind of list, **which police use to narrow a large field of suspects**, helps investigators work efficiently.

In addition, new technology is being used to analyze other evidence. New video cameras can
25 automatically identify a face **whose image police have on film**. Police can compare the faces of suspects to the image of the criminal and find the actual person more quickly. There is also a new way **in which police can identify someone who may be**
30 **a "missing person."**[1] This new technology compares a digital image of the person's iris[2] with the irises of people who are listed as missing in a database.

Forensic evidence **that police collect** is not always accurate. For example, fiber matching is inconclusive.[3]
35 Currently, fibers **that investigators analyze** can only be matched to a type of cloth. The fibers may not be from clothes **that the suspect owns**. Another concern is that there are no strict training standards for forensic dogs. Therefore, agencies like the FBI have only a few
40 dog teams **whose work they trust.**

Combining technology with traditional methods is changing the way **that criminal investigations are done.** Forensic science is not perfect, but it is still an important tool in investigations.

---

[1]**missing person:** someone who has disappeared
[2]**iris:** the colored part of the eye
[3]**inconclusive:** not leading to a definite result or decision; uncertain

2 Identifying Object Relative Clauses

Grammar Presentation

In an object relative clause, the relative pronoun is the object of the clause. An identifying object relative clause gives essential information about the noun it modifies.

OBJECT

*Evidence is sometimes inaccurate. Police collect **this evidence**.*

RELATIVE
PRONOUN

*Evidence **that** police collect is sometimes inaccurate.*

2.1 Forming Identifying Object Relative Clauses

A The object relative pronoun follows the noun it replaces and comes at the beginning of the relative clause. In an object relative clause, the relative pronoun is the object of the clause.	*Humans aren't aware of <u>smells</u>. A dog can recognize <u>smells</u>.* NOUN RELATIVE PRONOUN *Humans aren't aware of smells <u>that</u> a dog can recognize.*
B Use the relative pronouns *who*, *that*, or *whom* with people. Use *which* or *that* for things.	*Detectives are <u>people</u> who / that / whom I respect tremendously.*
These pronouns are frequently omitted in speaking, but not in formal writing.	*Forensic evidence is something <u>which / that</u> police count on.* (in writing) *Forensic evidence is something police count on.* (in speaking)
When referring to people, *that* is more common than *who*. The pronoun *whom* is very formal and is much less common than *that* or *who* in conversation.	least formal *Detective Paula Cho is a person **that** I admire very much.* *Detective Paula Cho is a person **who** I admire very much.* most formal *Detective Paula Cho is a person **whom** I admire very much.*
C Use *whose* + a noun to show possession. *Whose* cannot be omitted.	*The person <u>whose car</u> the thieves stole was a friend of mine.*

▸▸ Relative Clauses: See page A13.

2.2 Using Identifying Subject Relative Clauses

Use an identifying relative clause to give essential information that defines or identifies the noun it modifies.	*Evidence **that criminals leave at the crime scene** is called forensic evidence. (That criminals leave at the crime scene identifies the evidence.)*

Grammar Application

Complete the sentences about forensic technology.
Use *who* or *which* and the verbs in parentheses.

1 *Biometrics* refers to the techniques __*which*__
   people ___*use*___ (use) to identify individuals by
   their physical or behavioral characteristics.
2 Biometric information _____ experts
   _____ (analyze) includes DNA,
   fingerprints, eyes, and voice patterns.
3 People _____ the police _____
   (suspect) of a crime can be excluded with the use
   of biometrics.
4 Biometric technology can match fingerprints with
   ones _____ the police _____
   (have) on file.
5 One type of biometric technology _____
   people _____ (utilize) for security is the fingerprint scanner.
6 For example, people _____ Disney World _____ (admit) to the park must
   have their fingerprints scanned.
7 The fingerprint scanners _____ Disney World _____ (use) help to stop
   people from entering the park without a proper ticket.

Complete the web interview about forensic technology. Rewrite the sentence pairs in
parentheses as single sentences with object relative clauses. Sometimes more than one
answer is possible.

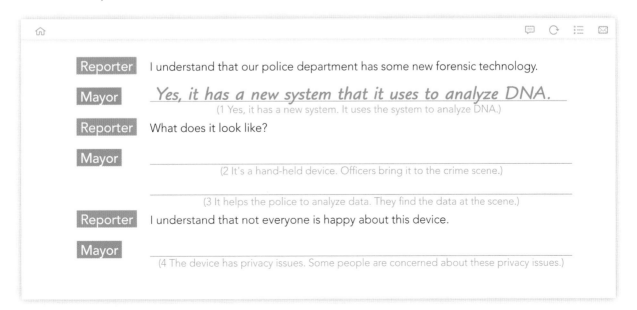

Reporter I understand that our police department has some new forensic technology.

Mayor *Yes, it has a new system that it uses to analyze DNA.*
(1 Yes, it has a new system. It uses the system to analyze DNA.)

Reporter What does it look like?

Mayor _____
(2 It's a hand-held device. Officers bring it to the crime scene.)

_____
(3 It helps the police to analyze data. They find the data at the scene.)

Reporter I understand that not everyone is happy about this device.

Mayor _____
(4 The device has privacy issues. Some people are concerned about these privacy issues.)

Reporter	Why is this a concern?
Mayor	_____
	(5 Well, the DNA might get the person in trouble. The device collected this DNA.)
	_____
	(6 For example, many people have health issues. They want to keep these issues private.)
Reporter	Oh, I see. This is certainly a lot to think about. Thank you for the interview.

Exercise 2.3 Sentence Combining

A Rewrite the reporter's notes on local crimes. Use identifying object relative clauses with the relative pronouns in parentheses.

Recent Crime Reports

1 A man was arrested for theft. Police raided his house last night. (whose)

A man *whose house police raided last night was arrested for theft* .

2 The detectives made their report. The police sent the detectives to the crime scene. (whom)

The detectives _____ .

3 Several valuable items had been stolen. The police recovered the items. (that)

Several valuable items _____ .

4 The man has not been identified. Burglars invaded the man's home. (whose)

The man _____ .

5 Detectives have visited the house. The thief broke into the house yesterday. (which)

Detectives _____ .

6 The man is in good condition. A car hit him last night. (that)

The man _____ .

B Pair Work In which sentences in A can you omit the pronoun? Discuss the answer with a partner. Then rewrite the sentences with the pronoun omitted.

3 Nonidentifying Object Relative Clauses

Grammar Presentation

Nonidentifying object relative clauses have the same form as identifying clauses. Unlike identifying clauses, nonidentifying clauses provide additional, not essential, information about the nouns they modify.	*Evidence from crimes, which we call forensic evidence, can help police solve cases.* (*Which we call forensic evidence* is extra information. It is not essential to understanding *Evidence from crimes.*)

3.1 Forming Nonidentifying Object Relative Clauses

A Use *who* or *whom* for people. Use *which* for things. Use *whose* for possessive people and things.	*The Sherlock Holmes stories were written by the Scottish author Arthur Conan Doyle, who / whom many people think was English.*
Do not use *that* in nonidentifying relative clauses.	*Forensic science, which Sherlock Holmes used, has been recognized as science since the 1800s.* NOT *Forensic science, ~~that~~ Sherlock Holmes used, has been recognized as science since the 1800s.*
Do not omit the relative pronoun in nonidentifying object clauses.	*The character Sherlock Holmes, who Arthur Conan Doyle created, was a fictional detective.* NOT *The character Sherlock Holmes, ~~Arthur Conan Doyle created~~, was a fictional detective.*
B Use commas before and after the nonidentifying object relative clause.	*Arthur Conan Doyle, whose medical clinic not many patients attended, had time to write his stories.*

Grammar Application

Exercise 3.1 Nonidentifying Object Relative Clauses

Read part of a presentation on a forensic science program. Underline the nonidentifying clauses. Add commas.

Forensic science, <u>which many of you know about from popular TV shows,</u> has become a popular career. Forensic science courses which many colleges are offering today prepare students for careers in crime scene investigation. The University of Central Florida (UCF) which I attended has a forensic science program. Your area of
5 specialization which you choose during your time here depends on your interests and skills. The area that I chose was forensic biochemistry because I wanted to study

odontology. Forensic odontology which the police use to analyze teeth is challenging and fascinating. Forensic analysis which focuses on chemistry and analysis of different kinds of evidence is also available. Introduction to Forensic Science which you take
10 after other preliminary courses will help you decide on the area of specialty. I wish you all the best of luck!

Exercise 3.2 Using Nonidentifying Object Relative Clauses

Read the sentences about a TV show that popularizes forensics. Combine the sentences with nonidentifying object relative clauses. Add commas when necessary.

1 *NCIS: Naval Criminal Investigative Service* is an American TV series.
Donald Bellisario and Don McGill created it.

NCIS: Naval Criminal Investigative Service, _which Donald Bellisario and_
Don McGill created, is an American TV series. .

2 The program became a hit in 2011. CBS first showed it in 2003.
The program _____ .

3 *NCIS* has been on the air for many years. The entertainment industry has awarded it several awards.
NCIS _____
_____ .

4 The program is shown in Australia, New Zealand, Canada, the UK, and Poland. Over 22 million people watched season 10.
The program _____ .

5 "NCIS Theme" is the show's theme tune. CBS records first released it in 2009.
"NCIS Theme," _____
_____ .

6 *NCIS: The Game* was popular. CBS released it in 2010.
NCIS: The Game _____
_____ .

4 Object Relative Clauses as Objects of Prepositions

Grammar Presentation

The relative pronouns in object relative clauses can be the object of prepositions.	OBJ. OF PREP. *There's the police officer. I spoke to her.* RELATIVE PRONOUN *There's the police officer to whom I spoke.* *There's the police officer who I spoke to.*

4.1 Object Relative Clauses as Objects of Prepositions

A The prepositions in object relative clauses can come at the end of the clause in informal speaking and writing.	The police examined the chair *that/which I was sitting <u>on</u>*. The witness, *who/whom I spoke <u>to</u> yesterday*, will appear in court.
In identifying relative clauses, use the relative pronouns *who*, *that*, or *whom* for people and *that* or *which* for things. You can also omit the relative pronoun.	<div align="right">IDENTIFYING RELATIVE CLAUSE</div>The police examined the chair (<u>that/which</u>) I was sitting on. The police officer (<u>who/that/whom</u>) I met with was robbed.
In nonidentifying relative clauses, use the relative pronouns *who* or *whom* for people and *which* for things. You cannot omit the relative pronoun.	NONIDENTIFYING RELATIVE CLAUSE The door, **which I entered through**, was broken during the crime. The witness, <u>who/whom I spoke to yesterday</u>, will appear in court. NOT The witness, ~~I spoke to yesterday~~, will appear in court.
B In more formal spoken and especially in written English, the preposition comes before the relative pronouns *whom* or *which*. Do not use *that* or *who*.	The police examined the chair <u>on which I was sitting</u>. NOT The police examined the chair on ~~that~~ I was sitting. The witness, <u>with whom I spoke yesterday</u>, will appear in court. NOT The witness, with ~~who/that~~ I spoke yesterday, will appear in court.
You cannot omit the relative pronoun.	NOT The police examined the chair ~~on I was sitting~~. NOT The witness, ~~with I spoke yesterday~~, will appear in court.

Grammar Application

Exercise 4.1 Prepositions and Object Relative Clauses

A Listen to a detective describe a crime scene. Complete the sentences with the words you hear.

I arrived at the crime scene at 11:00 a.m. The crime had taken place in a restaurant. The room __*that*__ the crime occurred __*in*__ was the kitchen.
                                        (1)   (1)
The back door was open. The back wall was covered in graffiti. I found a spray can under a table. The spray can, _____ I found fingerprints _____ , matched
                                                          (2)   (2)
the color of the graffiti. I asked the kitchen staff to talk to me as a group. The group,
_____ the chef was the only one missing, was very nervous. I learned that the
        (3)

chef had a lot of enemies. I spoke to a cleaning person _____ the chef had argued
                                                                    (4)
_____ last week. I also interviewed several waitresses _____ the chef had
   (4)   (5)
gone out _____ . One waitress showed me the chef's locker, _____ I found
            (5)   (6)
more spray cans _____ .
                   (6)

B Listen again and check your answers.

Exercise 4.2 Using Prepositions and Object Relative Clauses

A Combine the sentences from a crime scene investigator. Use identifying object relative
   clauses with a preposition at the end of the clause. Sometimes more than one answer
   is possible.

   1 The room was the office. I found broken furniture in it.

      The room __*which/that I found broken furniture in*__ was the office.

   2 I found fibers on the floor. The broken furniture was lying on the floor.

      I found fibers on the floor _____ .

   3 The neighbors said they heard nothing. I spoke to them.

      The neighbors _____ said they heard nothing.

   4 The house was unlocked. The crime took place in it.

      The house _____ was unlocked.

   5 There were fingerprints on the door. The criminal entered through it.

      There were fingerprints on the door _____ .

   6 The lab matched the fingerprints immediately. I sent the evidence to it.

      The lab _____ matched the fingerprints immediately.

B Rewrite your answers in A as formal sentences.

   1 _*The room in which I found broken furniture was the office.*_

   2 _____

   3 _____

   4 _____

   5 _____

   6 _____

5 Avoid Common Mistakes ⚠

1 **Use *who/whom/that*, not *which*, for people and *which/that* for things.**

who/whom/that
The investigator is someone ~~which~~ he respects.

that/which
NCIS is a crime show ~~who~~ I watch.

2 **Remember to omit the object pronoun after the verb in object relative clauses.**

The evidence that the police found ~~it~~ was used to find the suspect.

3 **Do not use a comma before an identifying object relative clause.**

The TV crime program ~~,~~ that people thought was the most popular ~~,~~ worked closely with the police to develop its stories.

4 **Do not use *what* in relative clauses.**

The crime ~~what~~ I am talking about happened yesterday.

Editing Task

Find and correct six more mistakes in the paragraphs about eyewitness testimony.

A victim who police have taken ~~her~~ to the police station gives testimony. She looks at a man in a police lineup and says, "That's the person which I saw in my car." During the trial, the woman gives her testimony in front of the jury, and the jury makes a decision. Soon, the man goes to jail. However, it is possible the woman whose testimony
5 was used is wrong. Researchers now claim that the eyewitness stories what courts often rely on are not always reliable.

Psychologists have conducted experiments who revealed some surprising results. They played a crime-scene video for participants and then asked the participants to remember details. Results showed that participants often described events, which
10 they knew nothing about and had not seen in the video. Similarly, the suspect what participants chose out of a police lineup was rarely the actual criminal.

Psychologists who courts have hired them have testified that eyewitness testimony is not as accurate as was once assumed. As such, psychologists have developed new rules to guide the use of eyewitness testimony.

23 Relative Clauses with *Where* and *When*; Reduced Relative Clauses

Millennials

1 Grammar in the Real World

A Do you know anyone born after 1995? Some studies suggest that individuals born during this time have similar traits, such as a high level of independence. Read the article about Generation Z, a term for these individuals. How might these people be different from other, older people in the workplace?

B Comprehension Check **Answer the questions.**

1 When was Generation Z born?

2 Why are Gen Zers so hard-working and entrepreneurial?

3 Why is Generation Z so comfortable with technology?

C Notice **Read the sentences. What words could you add to the words in bold to make them relative clauses? Are the new clauses subject or object relative clauses?**

1 David Stillman, **a Generation Z expert**, believes this is the result of the way they were raised.

2 **Gen Zers working a regular job** often have their own income-generating projects on the side.

Generation Z in the Workplace

Generation Z, **also known as iGen or Gen Zers**, are people born between 1995 and 2012. There are over 65 million of them in the United States alone, **where they are now entering the workplace**. It is
5 hard to generalize about such a large group, but these young workers often share certain traits.

This group is hard-working, pragmatic, and entrepreneurial. David Stillman, **a Generation Z expert**, believes this is the result of the way they
10 were raised. They were raised at a time **when many parents lost their jobs in the Great Recession**. Therefore iGen values job security more than previous generations.

In the workplace, their entrepreneurial spirit shows
15 up in several ways. Gen Zers are willing to work very hard, and they prefer to work alone. They also expect to be able to spend time on their own projects at work. **Gen Zers working a regular job** often have their own income-generating projects on the side.
20 These "side hustles" include selling things online and providing services via social media.

Generation Z, **raised in the era of YouTube, social media, and smartphones**, are the first real digital natives. They have never known life without Wi-Fi.
25 They are totally comfortable with technology in the workplace. They are multi-tasking experts. They can watch an online video, comment on Instragram, and listen to music at the same time.

However, their work habits can sometimes serve
30 as distractions. Working on their own side projects can cause moments of inattentiveness, **during which serious errors can occur**. Some members of Generation Z are known for being distracted on the job. Older colleagues may find this trait annoying.

35 This generation of employees will use technology and their own entrepreneurial spirit to make the workplace more efficient. They want to work hard and succeed. Generation Z is ambitious, independent, and tech savvy. These are the traits **already helping them**
40 succeed in workplaces around the country.

2 Relative Clauses with *Where* and *When*

Grammar Presentation

The adverbs *where* and *when* can be used in relative clauses. *Where* is used to modify nouns of place, and *when* is used to modify nouns of time. In these cases, we call these words relative adverbs.

The computer lab is a place where many young students feel comfortable.

Night is a time when many students study for exams.

2.1 Relative Clauses with *Where*

A Use *where* in relative clauses to modify a noun referring to a place. Common nouns include *area, country, house, place,* and *room.*	*This is the only <u>area</u> where you can find Wi-Fi outside of the office.* *The United States is a <u>country</u> where a lot of research on young people is done.* *The office is a <u>place</u> where workers often compete.*
B Do not use a preposition before *where.* Use *which* instead. The use of preposition + *which* is common in academic writing.	*It's a city in which you can find Wi-Fi almost everywhere.* NOT *It's a city ~~in where~~ you can find Wi-Fi almost everywhere.*

▸▸ Relative Clauses: See page A13.

2.2 Relative Clauses with *When*

A Use *when* in relative clauses to modify a noun referring to a time. Common nouns include *day, moment, period, season, time,* and *year.*	*The <u>day</u> when you graduate is the <u>day</u> when you will need to find a job.* *Spring is the <u>time</u> when most students graduate.* *The late 1990s and early 2000s are the years when many young people in the workforce were born.*
B Do not use a preposition before *when.* Use *which* instead. The use of preposition + *which* is very formal.	*Summer is the time during which many jobs become available.* NOT *Summer is the time ~~during when~~ many jobs become available.* *The day on which you start your new job will be very busy.* NOT *The day ~~on when~~ you start your new job will be very busy.*

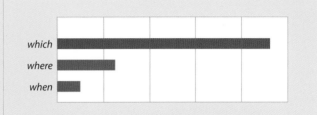

2.2 Relative Clauses with *When* (continued)

C You can omit the relative adverb *when* in identifying relative clauses.	*Ricardo remembered the moment he met his boss.* = *Ricardo remembered the moment* <u>*when*</u> *he met his boss.*

📊 Data from the Real World

Research shows that in writing, nonidentifying relative clauses with *where* and *when* are much less common than nonidentifying relative clauses with *which*. Clauses with *when* are the least common and are used in rather formal writing.

Grammar Application

Exercise 2.1 Object Relative Clauses with *Where* and *When*

Complete the sentences about Generation Z. Circle the correct words. Note Ø means no relative adverb.

1 Gen Zers believe America is a place (**where**)/ **when** anyone can be successful.
2 They were born at a time in **which / where** technology was a part of everyday life.
3 They had childhoods **when / in** which everyone had a smartphone.
4 They are entering the workplace during a period **when / which** Wi-Fi.
5 They expect a work environment **Ø / where** people can work independently.
6 They grew up during a period **when / where** the Great Recession was an issue.
7 The day **Ø / where** they graduate from school is a time of both joy and anxiety.

Exercise 2.2 More Object Relative Clauses with *Where* and *When*

A Listen to an interview with a Millennial who is helping to change the world in a positive way. Circle the answers to the questions.

1 Where did Sean go?

   (**a** To Haiti)   **b** To Florida

2 When did Sean go?

   a After a rainstorm   **b** After an earthquake

3 Why did Sean go?

    a To help people   **b** To take a break from school

4 What did he do there?

    a Work in a large city to   **b** Work in small towns
      give basic medical care   to give basic medical care

 B Listen again. **Complete the interview with the words you hear.**

Interviewer Some people think that members of the Millennial generation only think about themselves, but there are a lot of young people who are making a difference. They are helping others and trying to make the world a better place. One of these young people is Sean Green. Sean is a medical student in Florida. He went to Haiti at a time _*in which*_ they needed him the most.
(1)
Sean, tell us your story.

Sean Sure, I'd be happy to. I went to Haiti at a time _____ many
(2)
people were suffering – right after the 2010 earthquake.

Interviewer Why did you go?

Sean Haiti is a place _____ there aren't enough doctors. I'm in
(3)
medical school now. So it seemed like a good opportunity for me to get experience and to help people as well.

Interviewer What did you do there?

Sean I worked in small towns _____ the earthquake destroyed
(4)
the homes of many people. I lived in a town _____ a lot of
(5)
people were hurt, and helped give basic medical care. It was the season
_____ there is a lot of rain. There was mud everywhere. It was a
(6)
challenge to keep things clean.

Interviewer Tell us a little about the people you worked with.

Sean The people in the town _____ I worked gave us a lot of help.
(7)
They were very friendly and welcoming. It was an amazing experience.

Interviewer Thank you for your time, Sean.

C Listen again and check your answers.

Exercise 2.3 Relative Clauses with *When*

Look at the information in the chart. It shows three important generations in the United States and the major events or influences in their lifetimes. Then write sentences about the years in parentheses. Use relative clauses with *when*, *in which*, and *during which*. Sometimes more than one answer is possible.

	Name of Generation	Years Born	Important Lifetime Events or Influences
	Baby Boomers	1946–1964	President Kennedy dies, 1963 Vietnam War ends, 1975
	Generation X (Gen Xers)	1965–1981	The Berlin Wall falls, 1989
	Millennials	1980–2000	The Great Recession occurs, 2007–2009

1 (1946–1964)

The years 1946–1964 are the years when the Baby Boomers were born.

2 (1963)

_____

3 (1975)

_____

4 (1965–1981)

_____

5 (1989)

_____

6 (1980–2000)

_____

7 (2007)

_____

3 Reduced Relative Clauses

Grammar Presentation

Relative clauses with *be* can often be reduced to phrases. There are three types of reduced relative clauses: participle phrases, prepositional phrases, and appositives.

RELATIVE CLAUSE

The expert *who is giving tomorrow's talk on Generation Z is very well known.*

REDUCED RELATIVE CLAUSE

The expert *giving tomorrow's talk on Generation Z* is very well known.

3.1 Forming Reduced Relative Clauses

A Reduce a subject relative clause by omitting the relative pronoun (*that, which, who*) and *be*.	My brother, *a Gen Zer*, likes a fast-paced environment. = My brother, *who is a Gen Zer*, likes a fast-paced environment.
B Do not shorten a subject relative clause with *be* + a single adjective. Instead, move the adjective before the modified noun.	I know a lot of people *who are self-confident*. I know a lot of *self-confident* people. NOT I know a lot of ~~people self-confident~~.
C Do not reduce object relative clauses.	Our new assistant, *who I am meeting tomorrow*, is a Gen Zer. NOT Our new assistant, ~~meeting tomorrow~~, is a Gen Zer.

3.2 Reduced Relative Clauses with Participle Phrases

A Participle phrases are a reduced form of relative clauses with a verb that includes a form of *be*.	Students *concerned* with the environment should get involved in environmental groups on campus. = Students who *are concerned* with the environment should get involved in environmental groups on campus.
B This verb can be in the form of verb + *-ing* (present participle) or the past participle form. This includes progressive verbs and passive verbs.	VERB + -ING He is the person *designing the best software*. PAST PARTICIPLE She did the things *not expected of her*. This is the intern *known to be the hardest working*.

3.3 Reduced Relative Clauses with Prepositional Phrases

A You can omit the relative pronoun and the verb *be* when they are followed by a prepositional phrase in identifying relative clauses.	PREP. PHRASE *The computers in our classroom are fast.* = *The computers that are in our classroom are fast.*
B An adjective can also come before the prepositional phrase.	ADJ. + PREP. PHRASE *Young workers low in self-esteem are unusual.*

3.4 Reduced Relative Clauses with Appositives

A You can omit the relative pronoun and the verb *be* when they are followed by a noun phrase in nonidentifying relative clauses. This is called an appositive.	*Jan Smith, an expert on Generation Z, will be speaking at noon today.* = *Jan Smith, who is an expert on Generation Z, will be speaking at noon today.*
Often the position of the modified noun and the appositive is interchangeable.	*An expert on Generation Z, Jan Smith, will be speaking at noon today.*
B Appositives begin and end with commas.	*Résumés, brief documents that summarize an applicant's work background, are necessary for all job applications.*
In academic writing, appositives often occur in parentheses, instead of commas.	*Résumés (brief documents that summarize an applicant's work background) are necessary for all job applications.*

Grammar Application

Exercise 3.1 Reducing Relative Clauses

A Read the sentences about different generations. Check (✓) the sentences that can be reduced.

☑ **1** Young people who are entering the workforce are different from other generations.

☐ **2** In general, Millennials, who attentive parents raised, are confident workers.

☐ **3** Gen Zers who are in the workforce tend to be independent and hard-working.

☐ **4** Generation X, which is another large group in the workforce, does not tend to equate age with respect.

☐ 5 Baby Boomers who work with Millennials often think they do not show enough respect.

☐ 6 Baby Boomers, who are loyal employees, have started to retire from their jobs.

☐ 7 Millennials, who were hurt by the recession, still tend to be optimistic.

☐ 8 Baby Boomers who were graduating from college in the 1960s lived in prosperous times.

☐ 9 Most Millennials who are not attending school say they intend to go back.

☐ 10 Many Gen Zers who are in the office also have side jobs.

☐ 11 Gen Zers that dress casually at work sometimes upset older workers.

B Rewrite the sentences in A with reduced relative clauses. If a sentence cannot be reduced, write ✗.

1 _Young people entering the workforce are different from other generations._

2 ✗

3

4

5

6

7

8

9

10

11

C Pair Work Compare your answers with a partner. Discuss what kind of reduced relative clause each sentence is. If a sentence couldn't be reduced, say why not.

A *The reduced relative clause in number 1 is a participle phrase, so it can be reduced.*

B *That's right, but the relative clause in 2 can't be reduced because it is an object relative clause.*

Combine the sentences from a company website about the type of employees it seeks. Use relative clauses. Then rewrite the sentences using reduced relative clauses.

1 People are at JP Corporation. They represent every generation.

People *who are at JP Corporation* represent every generation.

People at JP Corporation represent every generation.

2 People are good with technology. They have an advantage here.

People _____ have an advantage here.

_____

3 Workers are familiar with soical media. They will be able to use these skills here.

Workers _____ will be able to use these skills here.

_____

4 Employees are good at multitasking. They will enjoy our fast-paced environment.

Employees _____ will enjoy our fast-paced environment.

_____

5 Employees are high in self-esteem. They do well here.

Employees _____ do well here.

_____

6 People are interested in advancement. They will find it here.

People _____ will find it here.

_____

7 Employees are in our training programs. They appreciate learning new skills.

Employees _____ appreciate learning new skills.

_____

8 People are accustomed to a dynamic environment. They will be happy here.

People _____ will be happy here.

_____

Read the advice for managers who work with Generation Z. Rewrite the sentences that you can shorten. If you can't shorten the sentence, write ✗.

1 Managers should encourage Gen Zers who are hard-working.

   Managers should encourage hard-working Gen Zers.

2 Workers who are Generation Z seek independence from their managers.

3 Even Gen Zers who are confident appreciate feedback.

4 Gen Zers appreciate work schedules that are flexible.

5 Employees who are Generation Z want their managers to listen to them.

6 It's important to provide challenges for Gen Zers who are successful.

7 Managers must not underestimate GenZers who are self-educated.

8 Managers who are Millenials might expect Gen Zers to work 9 to 5.

9 Employees who are Gen Zers sometimes need less direction than older workers.

10 Gen Zers who are unemployed don't always have a lot of experience in job interviews.

Pair Work With a partner, discuss the work styles of people at your school, such as students, teachers, and administrators. Write five sentences with relative clauses. Then write shortened versions without relative clauses. Use the words in the box or your own ideas.

appreciate feedback	are family oriented	enjoy team work
appreciate work-life balance	are self-assured	have a "can-do" attitude

Students who are at this school tend to have a "can-do" attitude.
Students at this school tend to have a "can-do" attitude.

4 Avoid Common Mistakes ⚠

1 Do not use a preposition before *when*.

There was a period ~~in~~ when people did not change jobs often.

2 In clauses with *where*, remember to use a subject.

                               he
The place where ⌄works is very busy.

3 When shortening relative clauses to appositives, be sure to omit both the pronoun and *be*.

My mother, ~~is~~ an office manager, often works late.

Editing Task

Find and correct eight more mistakes in the paragraphs about the separation between younger and older technology users.

Digital Natives vs. Digital Immigrants

There was a time ~~in~~ when my mother always complained about my use of technology. She did not understand why I had to constantly text friends and go online. My mother, is a digital immigrant, grew up without a lot of tech gadgets. As a result, she is uncomfortable using technology at the office where works. On the other hand, my

5 brothers and I, are all digital natives, are happy to use technology all the time.

Digital natives, are lifelong technology users, use mobile devices instinctively. These people do not remember a time in when they were not connected to the Internet. In fact, they find it annoying when they go to places where cannot connect to the Internet. Digital immigrants, in contrast, remember a time in when there was no Internet.

10 As a result, some of them see the Internet as useful but not essential. In addition, digital immigrants sometimes find it difficult to figure out how to use technology. For example, when my mother first began uploading information, she had to call someone for help. Lately, however, my mother has found a social media site where often goes in her free time to stay in touch with friends and family members.

Real Conditionals: Present and Future

Media in the United States

1 Grammar in the Real World

A Do all the news sources you read (websites, magazines, newspapers, etc.) have similar viewpoints about current topics and issues? Read the article about the news media in the United States. What is the writer's view of the media?

B Comprehension Check **Answer the questions.**

1 How do some political analysts describe the behavior of Americans toward media?

2 What is an example of how media sources reinforce someone's political views?

3 Why might people become even more isolated in their beliefs in the future?

C Notice **Read the sentences from the article. Which sentence describes a present situation? Which sentence describes a future situation?**

1 On the other hand, if people mostly disagree with the president's policies, they often choose to watch news shows that criticize the president.

2 If predictions of increased Internet use are correct, people will likely become even more isolated in their beliefs.

The Influence of **MEDIA** on Public Opinion

The media[1] provide news from a wide of sources with a variety of viewpoints. Some sources provide a more balanced look at the issues than others. These more balanced news sources offer
5 a deeper understanding of the issues without the influence of the views of political parties. This unbiased[2] view of the news may appear to align[3] with the values of Americans, but is it, in fact, what Americans really want? Some political analysts
10 claim that many Americans tend to read, watch, and listen to the news media that reflect their own views. **If people surround themselves with media that reflect only their beliefs,** they may not be exposed to opposing ideas. The media, in
15 this case, are not informing people, but reinforcing that their view of the world is right.

One example of this occurs during an economic crisis. **If people watch certain TV news stations,** they will hear mostly positive things
20 about the president's solutions. **If they support the president's policies,** they may also choose to read online news pages with a similar view. These websites likely explain how the crisis was caused by politicians from the opposing party.
25 **If those people read only these websites,** they might be convinced that the crisis was the fault of the opposing party. They might conclude that the president was doing a wonderful job. On the other hand, **if people mostly disagree with the**
30 **president's policies,** they often choose to watch news shows that criticize the president. They might also visit websites and read blogs that do not support the president's policies. **When they rely only on these news sources,** they come to a
35 different conclusion. They are convinced that the president is failing.

If predictions of increased Internet use are correct, people will likely become even more isolated in their beliefs. This is because links in
40 blogs and web pages will connect people with information that supports only their views. How might this affect politics in the future? **If we don't address this issue today,** could the isolation of beliefs become problematic in our political future?

---

[1]**media:** newspapers, magazines, television, and radio, considered as a group
[2]**unbiased:** not influenced by personal opinion
[3]**align:** agree with and support something or someone

2 Present Real Conditionals

Grammar Presentation

Present real conditionals describe situations that are possible now and their results. They describe general truths, facts, and habits.

If people share beliefs, they often get along better. I usually believe something when I read it in a good newspaper.

2.1 Forming Present Real Conditionals

A Use an *if* clause to describe a possible situation. The *if* clause is the condition. The main clause describes the result. It expresses what happens when the condition exists.

IF CLAUSE (CONDITION)   MAIN CLAUSE (RESULT)
If I like a reporter, I read her articles.

Use the simple present in the *if* clause and in the main clause.

If I <u>have</u> time in the morning, I <u>read</u> the newspaper.

B You can use *when* or *whenever* in the *if* clause. The meaning does not change.

<u>When</u> *you trust people, you tend to believe them.*

= *If you trust people, you tend to believe them.*

C You can put the *if* clause or the main clause first, but the punctuation is different. If the *if* clause is first, a comma follows it. If the main clause is first, do not use a comma. Usually the *if* clause comes first.

        IF CLAUSE   MAIN CLAUSE
<u>If</u> *you control the media, you control public opinion.*

        MAIN CLAUSE   IF CLAUSE
You control public opinion if you control the media.

D You can use conditionals in questions. Use question word order only in the main clause.

        IF CLAUSE   MAIN CLAUSE
If you see something on the news, <u>do you</u> always <u>believe</u> it?

▸▸ Conditionals: See page A15.

2.2 Using Present Real Conditionals

A Use present real conditionals to describe:
Facts and general truths
Habits and routines

If a website is popular, people talk about it.
I always read the news online if I wake up early.

B You can emphasize the result by putting the *if* clause first and using *then* to introduce the main clause. Using *then* is more common in speaking.

If you only read one news website, <u>then</u> you never get the full story.

Grammar Application

Complete the article about news habits. Use present real conditionals with the verbs in parentheses. Add commas when necessary.

CITY VOICES: The News and You

City Voices talked to several area residents. Here's what they had to say.

"When I _____ **am** _____ (be) in the car, I _____ (listen) to the radio.
(1)   (2)

My husband _____ (watch) the comedy news shows if he _____
(3)   (4)

(stay) up late." – Alexa, 28, office manager

"If a friend _____ (text) me about something interesting I generally
(5)

_____ (check) out other websites to find out more information." – Su Ho, 32, engineer
(6)

Complete the interview with a foreign correspondent. Use the conditions and results in the chart.

Condition	Result
1 I hear about a story	I get on the phone
2 I hear about a good story	I try to go beyond the basic facts
3 I feel like I'm getting emotionally involved in a story	I drop it
4 A story is important	Many people talk about it
5 My editor calls and tells me to investigate a story	I move quickly

CAREERS MAGAZINE

Careers Today, we are talking to our foreign correspondent, Mercedes Rivera. Ms. Rivera, how do you get a story?

Mercedes If *I hear about a story, I get on the phone* . I make
(1)
appointments to interview people connected with the story.

| Careers | What makes your reporting special? |
| Mercedes | If _____. I look |

at all the details to give both sides of the story.

| Careers | How do you avoid bias? |
| Mercedes | If _____. I give |

it to another reporter.

| Careers | What is difficult about your job? |
| Mercedes | There's a certain amount of pressure. _____ |

when _____. I have to work fast in the digital

age. _____ if _____ .

| Careers | Well, thank you for talking to us today, Ms. Rivera. |

Exercise 2.3 Emphasizing the Result in Present Real Conditionals

A Read the tips on how to detect bias in the media. Then rewrite the tips as present real conditionals with the words in parentheses and *probably (not) be.* Emphasize the result by using *then.*

How to Detect BIAS in the MEDIA

To detect bias in the media, be aware of the following conditions. These conditions often indicate bias.

1 A newspaper, website, or TV station ignores important stories.

2 A newspaper prints sensational headlines.

3 A newspaper prints an important story in the back of the newspaper.

4 A magazine prints an unflattering[1] photo of a politician.

5 A reporter uses words with negative connotations[2] instead of neutral terms.

[1]**unflattering:** making someone look less attractive or seem worse than they usually do
[2]**connotation:** a feeling or idea that is suggested by a word in addition to its basic meaning

1 (impartial) *If a newspaper, website, or TV station ignores important*

   stories, then it probably isn't impartial.

2 (accurate) _____

3 (balanced) _____

_____

4 (biased) _____

_____

5 (fair) _____

_____

B Pair Work Discuss other ways that the media show that they are biased or fair. Write two sentences using *if* clauses and the expressions with *probably (not) be* in A.

Exercise 2.4 Present Real Conditionals

A Over to You Answer the questions with information that is true for you. Write present real conditionals on a separate piece of paper. Use the phrases in the box or your own ideas.

get the news online	pay attention to the news
know a story is accurate	read a newspaper
listen to news on the radio	watch TV news

■ Do you pay attention to the news?

■ How do you get the news?

■ How do you know a news story is accurate?

If there's a big story in the news, I watch one of the TV news channels, but I don't pay attention to the news much in general.

B Pair Work Interview your partner. Ask and answer the questions in A. Do not look at your sentences when you answer. Look at your partner.

3 Future Real Conditionals

Grammar Presentation

Future real conditionals describe possible situations in the future and the likely results.	*If you don't like a politician, you won't like his or her policies.*

3.1 Forming Future Real Conditionals

A Use the simple present in the *if* clause and a future verb form in the main clause.	*If you arrive early tomorrow at the debate, you will get a good seat.*

3.1 Forming Future Real Conditionals (continued)

| B Use a comma after the *if* clause only when it begins the sentence. | We will have a more balanced view *if we read a variety of news websites*. |
| | *If Sandra doesn't agree with a politician's ideas*, she will not vote for him. |

3.2 Using Future Real Conditionals

| A Use future real conditionals to describe: Plans | *If the TV media don't cover the debate tonight*, I'll read about it online. |
| Predictions | *If you read this article*, you won't be disappointed. |

B Use *even if* when you believe the result will not change. *Even if* means "whether or not."	*Some people will believe the news <u>even if</u> it isn't true.* (The news may or may not be true. Some people will believe it either way.)
Use *unless* to state a negative condition more strongly. It often has the same meaning as *if . . . not*.	*Unless a reporter interviews many people*, she won't find out the truth.
	= *If a reporter does <u>not</u> interview many people*, she won't find out the truth.

| C When an *if* clause has many results, use the *if* clause only once. | *If people believe everything they hear*, they won't know the truth. *They will be easily fooled.* |
| | NOT *If people believe everything they hear, they won't know the truth.* ~~If people believe everything they hear,~~ *they will be easily fooled.* |

Grammar Application

Exercise 3.1 Future Real Conditionals for Predictions

Complete the sentences about being well informed about political viewpoints. Circle the correct verb forms. Add commas when necessary.

1 If a person (studies)/ will study history, she understands /(will understand) political issues better.

2 You **are/will be** a better critical thinker if you **listen/will listen** to opposing viewpoints.

3 You **become/will become** a more informed voter if you **understand/will understand** the issues.

4 You **make/will make** better choices in future elections if you **learn/will learn** about the candidates' voting records.

5 If a person **learns/will learn** about economics he **makes/will make** wiser financial decisions.

6 If people **get / will get** the news from several sources they **have / will have** a more complete picture of an issue.

A A newspaper is having financial difficulties. Write future real conditionals with the information in the chart.

Proposals	Predictions and Plans
1 fire 10 reporters	be able to stay in business
2 stop home deliveries	lose money
3 charge for online access	increase revenue
4 not find new advertisers	not make more money
5 put more articles online	attract new readers

1   *If we fire 10 reporters, we'll be able to stay in busir*

2   _____

3   _____

4   _____

5   _____

B Read what members of the staff have to say about the proposals in A. Circle the correct meaning for each opinion.

1 Even if we fire 10 reporters, we won't be able to stay in business.

   a Firing reporters will help.   **b** Firing reporters won't help.

2 Unless we fire 20 reporters, we'll go out of business.

   a Firing reporters will help.   **b** Firing reporters won't help.

3 Unless we charge for online access, we won't increase revenue.

   a Charging will help.   **b** Charging won't help.

4 Even if we stop home deliveries, we'll lose money.

   a Stopping home deliveries will help.   **b** Stopping home deliveries won't help.

5 Even if we find new advertisers, we won't make more money.

   a Finding new advertisers will help.   **b** Finding new advertisers won't help.

6 Unless we put more articles online, we won't attract new readers.

   a Putting more articles online will help.   **b** Putting more articles online won't help.

Over to You **Complete the sentences about being informed. Write two or more results for the conditions. Don't repeat the *if* clauses for the second or third results. Write sentences that are true for you.**

1 If people stop reading newspapers, *newspapers will go out of business. Many reporters will be unemployed.*

2 If people get only one source of news, _____

_____

3 If you only listen to people you agree with, _____

_____

4 If you are not an informed voter, _____

_____

4 Real Conditionals with Modals, Modal-like Expressions, and Imperatives

Grammar Presentation

Modals, modal-like expressions, and imperatives can be used in the main clause of real conditionals.	*If I watch a lot of TV, I may become more aware of political issues.* *If you have finished reading the paper, put it in the recycling container.*

4.1 Forming Real Conditionals with Modals, Modal-like Expressions, and Imperatives

A In present and future real conditionals with modals and modal-like expressions, use a present form of the verb in the *if* clause. Use a present or future modal or modal-like expression in the main clause.	*If you **haven't heard** the news yet, you should read the newspaper.* *If you **are planning** to vote, you have to register.* *She might learn more about politics if she subscribes to that political magazine.*
B In present and future real conditionals, you can use the imperative in the main clause.	*If you are at home tonight at 7:00 p.m., watch the president's speech.*

▸▸ Modals and Modal-like Expressions: See page A3.

Grammar Application

Complete the sentences about being an involved citizen. Use the words in parentheses.

1 If people don't vote, _they must not be interested in politics_ .
(be interested in politics / not / must)

2 If you haven't registered to vote yet, _____ .
(do it today / should)

3 People _____ if they want to become involved in
(volunteer / ought to)
their community.

4 People _____ if they enjoy teaching.
(tutor children / can)

5 If you want to become informed, _____ .
(watch the news / have to)

6 If people participate in elections, _____ .
(influence the outcome / might)

7 If you aren't happy, _____ .
(change things / could)

8 People _____ if they have not already tried to
(complain / not / should)
find solutions to community problems.

Pair Work Answer the questions about how you think people can be better citizens.
Write real conditionals and share them with a partner. Use *you* in the *if* clause and an
imperative in the main clause. Use the phrases in the box or your own ideas.

be aware of bias in the media	study both sides of an issue
research alternative news sources	volunteer

■ What should people do if they want
to become better informed?

■ What should people do if they want
to become better citizens?

*If you want to become better informed,
research alternative news sources.*

A Listen to an interview about how to be an informed voter. As you listen, complete the chart. Check (✓) *Do* if this is something an informed voter should do. Check (✓) *Don't* if this is something an informed voter should not do.

Action	Do	Don't
1 register early	✓	
2 visit campaign headquarters		
3 visit candidates' websites		
4 rely on campaign ads		
5 pay attention to what media sources say		
6 be influenced by other people's opinions		

B Listen to the interview again. As you listen, complete the sentences with the words you hear.

1 If you __*aren't registered*__ to vote, __*register*__ early so you don't miss the deadline.

2 If you _____ to be an informed voter, _____ the local campaign headquarters for the candidates of both parties.

3 If you _____ to make the right choice, you _____ also _____ the websites of all the candidates.

4 _____ campaign ads for information about the candidates or the issues if you _____ to be an informed voter.

5 _____ attention to what media sources say about a candidate, either, if you _____ the truth.

6 Finally, _____ other people's opinions influence your vote if you _____ to make good choices.

5 Avoid Common Mistakes ⚠

1	**In future real conditionals, use the simple present in the *if* clause.**
	has If my son ~~will have~~ time, he will buy tickets for the show.
2	**Remember that *if* clauses are followed by a comma when they start a sentence.**
	If I get the time off work and the weather looks good‸ I will join you.
3	**Remember to use *if*, not *when*, to describe possible future conditions.**
	if We will cancel the speech ~~when~~ it rains tomorrow.
4	**In questions with *if* clauses, remember to use question word order in the main clause.**
	should If I don't have a signal, what I ~~should~~ do?

Editing Task

Find and correct the mistakes in the paragraphs about the advantages of a campus blog.

   If incoming students want to learn what this college is like, where they *should* ~~should~~ look? If they visit the college website they can learn about sports and campus events. However, incoming freshmen might want a more personal perspective. They may not have the time to attend lectures and other events, or they may want some anonymity. I have decided to start a
5 blog that provides an alternative source of information and help.

   When I want the blog to be successful at helping students, I will need to provide practical suggestions. For example, one concern may be, "If I want to meet people with similar interests, what I can do?" I will tell that person places where he or she can post requests on the school website and how to write his or her requests. I will also include ways to
10 safely respond to queries.

   In addition, if a student will have a problem with a professor, I will write about it in my blog and provide possible ways to solve it. If people want to add advice, how they can do so? They can share advice by commenting. If professors want to comment, they can, too.

   I will not try to write like a journalist and give a lot of facts. If students will want facts,
15 they can go to the college website. In contrast, I will give them personal advice that will help them with everyday problems. If students want real answers to their problems they should try my blog.

25 Unreal Conditionals: Present, Future, and Past

Natural Disasters

1 Grammar in the Real World

A Think of some natural disasters in recent history. Were there any positive effects or changes that resulted from the disasters? Read the article about Hurricane Katrina. What is one positive effect of Hurricane Katrina?

B Comprehension Check **Answer the questions.**

1 Why is Hurricane Katrina considered a catastrophe?

2 What did Paul Vallas do to improve New Orleans's schools?

3 What are charter schools?

C Notice **Read the sentences from the article. Underline the main clause in each sentence.**

1 If they found a strong school superintendent, they could hope for real change.

2 If you had been a public school student in New Orleans prior to 2005, you would have had little hope for the future of your education.

3 Vallas knew that if state exam scores improved, the charter schools would be considered a success.

4 If Katrina hadn't happened, the school might have been closed down.

Is the situation in each main clause real or imaginary?

HURRICANE KATRINA

In 2005, Hurricane Katrina devastated New Orleans, Louisiana. The storm killed over 1,800 people and caused over $75 billion in damages. Certainly, Katrina was a catastrophe.[1] **People wish it had never happened.** Nonetheless, some say Katrina saved the city's schools from failure. In fact, U.S. Education Secretary, Arne Duncan, said, "I think the best thing that happened to the education system in New Orleans was Hurricane Katrina." Although some people thought Duncan's comment was inappropriate, is it possible that the storm did the city a favor and helped its school system?

If you had been a public school student in New Orleans prior to 2005, you would have had little hope for the future of your education. With low test scores and high dropout rates, the New Orleans School District was already in trouble when the hurricane struck. The storm destroyed almost every school in the city. State legislators realized the hurricane was tragic. They also knew it provided a fresh start to rebuild the city's schools. **If they found a strong school superintendent,** they could hope for real change.

[1]**catastrophe:** a sudden event that causes great suffering or destruction

In 2007, Paul Vallas was hired to rescue the poverty stricken and low-performing district. He knew that in order to succeed, he would have to make drastic changes. He hired top teachers and modernized classrooms. Vallas also started several charter schools. Charter schools are independently run public schools. They control their own academics and policies but must show the state how their students have improved. Vallas knew that **if state exam scores improved,** the charter schools would be considered a success.

Vallas received national praise for his experiment with charter schools. Student scores on state tests went up every year that he worked for the district. The Sophie B. Wright Charter School is a good example. It was a failing traditional school before the hurricane. **If Katrina hadn't happened,** the school might have been closed down. Instead, it became a successful charter school.

As for Duncan's comment about Katrina, **some wish he had used a better choice of words.** A number of educational experts disagree. They say that in the end, New Orleans schools are only successful because of the work that Vallas did to rebuild the school system.

2 Present and Future Unreal Conditionals

Grammar Presentation

Present and future unreal conditionals describe imagined situations (situations that are not true).	*If children got better grades on their exams, parents wouldn't be so worried.*

2.1 Forming Present and Future Unreal Conditionals

A Use the simple past or the past progressive in the *if* clause. Use the modals *could*, *might*, or *would* in the main clause.

If I studied every day, I could pass all my tests. (But I don't study every day, so I can't pass all my tests.)

Parents wouldn't worry so much about their children's future if their children's grades were improving. (But the children's grades aren't improving, so their parents are worried.)

B In formal language, use *were* for the verb *be* for all subjects, including *I*. In informal language, native speakers often use *was* for the subject pronouns *I*, *he*, *she*, and *it*.

If I were better at math, I would become an engineer. (formal)

If I was better at math, I would become an engineer. (informal)

▸▸ Conditionals: See page A15.

2.2 Using Present and Future Unreal Conditionals

A The *if* clause describes an imagined condition (something that is not true at the time of speaking or writing). The main clause describes the predicted result or possible outcome.

If all public schools worked well, parents wouldn't choose private schools. (But some public schools don't work well, so parents choose private schools.)

B Use *would* in the main clause to express the predicted result.

If teachers gave students study guides, more students would pass their exams. (Passing is a predicted result.)

Use *could* or *might* in the main clause to express something that is possible or doable.

If students studied more for exams, more of them could/might pass. (Passing exams is doable.)

C Use *could* or the past progressive in the *if* clause to describe an imagined possible situation.

If the city could hire more teachers, we would have smaller classes. (But they can't hire more teachers, so we have large classes.)

We wouldn't feel hopeful if schools weren't improving. (But schools are improving, so we do feel hopeful.)

2.2 Using Present and Future Unreal Conditionals (*continued*)

D Use time words to show present or future time.	*We wouldn't have a place to learn if our school closed next year.* *If classes were smaller today, students might be more motivated.*
E Use unreal conditionals with *If I were you* to give advice. Use *I would* in the main clause.	*If I were you, I'd study harder.* (My advice is to study harder.) *I wouldn't drop out of school if I were you.* (My advice is to stay in school.)

Grammar Application

Exercise 2.1 Present and Future Unreal Conditionals

Complete the sentences about natural disasters. Use present and future unreal conditionals. If you are writing a main clause, use the modals in parentheses.

1 Their house is damaged, so they have to build a new one.

If their house weren't damaged, *they wouldn't have to build a new one* (wouldn't).

2 We don't have flood insurance, so we have to pay for water damage.

If we had flood insurance , we wouldn't have to pay for water damage.

3 There aren't earthquakes here, so we don't need earthquake insurance.

If there were earthquakes here, _____ (might).

4 There's a tsunami[1] warning, so they have to leave the beach.

_____ , they wouldn't have to leave the beach.

5 We don't have a first-aid kit, so we aren't prepared for an earthquake.

If we had a first-aid kit, _____ (would).

6 There's a tornado warning, so José is going into the basement.

_____ , José wouldn't go into the basement.

7 The fire alarm is ringing, so we have to leave the building.

If the fire alarm weren't ringing, _____ (might not).

8 Everyone is worrying about the storm, so we are leaving.

_____ , we wouldn't be leaving.

[1]**tsunami:** an extremely high wave of water that is caused by an earthquake

Complete the statements made by earthquake experts. Use present and future unreal conditionals with *could (not)* in the *if* clause and *would (not)* in the main clause.

Dr. Sarah Green:

1 The government can't repair old bridges. Therefore, people don't feel safe.

If the government __*could repair*__ old bridges, people __*would feel*__ safe.

2 They can't build quake-proof bridges very quickly, so we aren't optimistic.

If the government _____

quake-proof bridges quickly, we

_____ optimistic.

Dr. Joe Wu:

3 Certain regions can build quake-proof buildings. Therefore, they don't suffer a lot of damage.

If certain regions _____ quake-proof buildings, they

_____ a lot of damage.

Dr. Rafael Rodriguez:

4 Some countries often can't avoid contaminated water after an earthquake. Therefore, people get sick.

If some countries _____ contaminated water after an

earthquake, people _____ sick.

5 Engineers aren't able to improve the water systems in all places, so people are not healthy.

If engineers _____ the water systems in all places, people

_____ healthy.

A Over to You Answer the questions with information that is true for you. Write your answers on a separate piece of paper. Use the ideas in the box or your own ideas. Write present and future unreal conditionals.

basement	escape	exit	higher ground
emergency services	evacuate	find shelter	take cover

What would you do if:

- you knew a hurricane were coming?
- an earthquake struck?
- you were driving and heard a tornado warning on the radio?
- you were within a half mile of a wildfire?
- you were at the beach and got a tsunami warning?
- you were in a heat wave?

If I knew a hurricane were coming, I would evacuate the area immediately.

B Group Work **Brainstorm other answers to the questions in A. Share them with another group.**

Exercise 2.4 *If I Were You . . . for Advice*

A Complete the conversations. Write sentences that give advice. Use *If I were you* and the ideas in the box. Sometimes more than one answer is possible.

~~build a new one~~	leave immediately	not go to work
get earthquake insurance	leave the building	stay indoors

1 **A** The house was damaged in the hurricane. What should we do?

 B *If I were you, I'd build a new one.*

2 **A** I live in an earthquake zone. What should I do?

 B _____

3 **A** There's a blizzard warning for tomorrow. What should I do?

 B _____

4 **A** Forecasters are predicting a terrible heat wave for tomorrow. What should we do?

 B _____

5 **A** There's a wildfire three blocks from our house. What should we do?

 B _____

6 **A** The fire alarm is ringing. What should we do?

 B _____

B Pair Work Take turns asking and answering the questions in A. Use your own ideas in your answers.

3 Past Unreal Conditionals

Grammar Presentation

Past unreal conditionals express situations that were not true in the past. They describe something that was possible but did not happen.	*If I had stayed home from school, I would have missed the exam.* (But I went to school, so I didn't miss the exam.)

3.1 Forming Past Unreal Conditionals

A Use the past perfect in the *if* clause. Use *could have*, *may have*, *might have*, or *would have* and the past participle of the verb in the main clause.	*If the city had hired more teachers, the schools might have improved.* (But the city didn't hire more teachers, and the schools didn't improve.)
B The *if* clause typically comes before the main clause, but it may also follow the main clause.	*The schools might have improved if the city had hired more teachers.*

3.2 Using Past Unreal Conditionals

A The *if* clause expresses the past unreal condition (a situation that was untrue in the past). The main clause describes an imagined result.	*If the hurricane had missed our city, the schools wouldn't have received money from the government.* (But it didn't miss our city, so the schools have received money.)
B Use *would have* in the main clause to express a predicted result.	*If you had applied, you would have gotten the job.* (Getting the job was a predicted result.)
C Use *could have* or *might have* in the main clause to express something possible or doable.	*I could have / might have passed the test if I had studied harder.* (Passing the test was doable.)
D You can use past unreal conditionals to express regrets or sadness.	*If I hadn't quit school, I would have become an engineer.* (But I quit school, and I regret it.)
E Use *If I had been you* to give advice indirectly. Use *I would* (*not*) in the main clause. *Had* is often contracted (*'d*).	*If I'd been you, I wouldn't have quit school.*

Grammar Application

Exercise 3.1 Past Unreal Conditionals

Complete the interview with a scientist who studied Mount Vesuvius, a volcano that erupted[1] in 79 CE near Pompeii, Italy. Use past unreal conditionals with the verbs in parentheses.

Reporter Today, I'm talking to Dr. Adam Gannon.

Dr. Gannon, we are all fascinated by Vesuvius, I think, because it practically erased an ancient city.

Dr. Gannon That's correct. If Vesuvius

hadn't erupted (not/erupt), Pompeii
(1)
would not have disappeared
(2)
(not/would/disappear).

Reporter So, Pompeii _____ (would/survived) if Vesuvius
(3)
_____ (not/explode)?
(4)

Dr. Gannon Yes, that's correct. On the other hand, if ash

_____ (not/cover) the city, it
(5)
_____ (not/would/be preserved).
(6)

Reporter The volcano caused other great changes, too, didn't it?

Dr. Gannon Yes. In fact, it completely changed the direction of a nearby river. The Sarno

_____ (would/stay) in the same place if
(7)
Vesuvius _____ (not/change) the course of the
(8)
river. It was a very powerful eruption.

Reporter How do we know so much about the eruption of Vesuvius?

Dr. Gannon We have the writer Pliny the Younger to thank for that. If he and his uncle

_____ (not/be) near Pompeii that day, we
(9)
_____ (not/would/know) much about the
(10)
eruption of Vesuvius. But we still don't know everything.

Reporter Fascinating. Thank you, Dr. Gannon.

[1]**erupt:** throw out smoke, fire, and melted rocks

A Group Work Look at the pictures and discuss these questions in groups: What does a volcanic eruption look like? What are some of the effects of a volcanic eruption?

Mount St. Helens,
Washington State

landslide

ash cloud

B Listen to a man talk about his experience surviving the 1980 Mount St. Helens volcano eruption. Circle *T* if the statement is true. Circle *F* if the statement is false.

1 The speaker and his family were hiking on the mountain the day the volcano erupted. T (F)

2 Falling trees hit the speaker and his friends. T F

3 The speaker thinks it's possible that many people on the mountain survived. T F

4 The speaker's wife wasn't affected by the eruption. T F

5 The sideways eruption of Mount St. Helens caused a lot of damage. T F

6 Ten years after the eruption, the speaker returned to his campsite. T F

7 Scientists didn't learn anything from the eruption. T F

C Listen again and check your answers.

D Complete the statements about the story. Use the words in parentheses to write past unreal conditionals with possible or predicted results.

1 If we hadn't gone camping that day, we *might have avoided the disaster* (**possible:** avoid / the disaster).

2 If we hadn't been in a hole, falling trees _____ (**possible:** hit) us.

3 If people hadn't been on the mountain, they _____ (**predicted:** survive).

4 If his wife had been with him, the eruption _____ (**possible:** affect) her.

5 If Mount St. Helens hadn't been a sideways explosion, it _____ (**predicted:** not / do) so much damage.

6 If the speaker and his friends hadn't returned to the mountain, they _____ (**predicted:** not / see) the site of the destruction.

7 If the eruption hadn't happened, scientists _____ (**predicted:** not / learn) how quickly plant and animal life can return.

4 Wishes About the Present, Future, and Past

Grammar Presentation

Sentences with *wish* express a desire for something to be different, or feelings of sadness or regret.	*I wish (that)* every child could have a better education. (Unfortunately, not every child can have a better education.)

4.1 Wish in the Present, Future, and Past

A *Wish* is followed by a *that* clause. Use a past form of the verb in the *that* clause, similar to conditional sentences. The word *that* is often omitted in informal speaking.	There aren't enough teachers. We **wish that** we <u>could hire</u> more teachers.
B Wishes about the present are followed by *that* clauses with verbs in the simple past or past progressive, or the modal *could*.	*I wish (that)* we <u>had</u> more classrooms. (We don't have a lot of classrooms.) *I wish (that)* my son <u>were doing</u> well in school. (My son is not doing well in school.) *Some people* **wish** *(that)* they <u>could afford</u> to go to college. (They can't afford to go to college.)
C Wishes about the future are followed by *that* clauses with *was / were going to* or the modals *could* or *would*.	*I wish (that)* I <u>were going to have</u> time to meet you tonight. (I'm not going to have time to meet you.) *She* **wishes** *(that)* she <u>could go</u> to class tonight, but she has to work. (She can't go to class tonight.) *We* **wish** *(that)* the school <u>would build</u> a parking lot, but it's too costly. (The school will not build a parking lot.)
D Wishes about the past are followed by *that* clauses with the verb in the past perfect.	*We* **wish** *(that)* we <u>had had</u> more time to study for the test. (We didn't have enough time to study.)

In academic writing, *wish* followed by a singular subject is more commonly followed by *were* than *was*.

| Wish + singular subject + *were* | |
| Wish + singular subject + *was* | |

The president wishes the solution to the problem were *simpler.* (more common in academic writing)

The president wishes the solution to the problem was *simpler.* (less common in academic writing)

▸ Grammar Application

Exercise 4.1 Present and Future Wishes

Complete the sentences about a family's disaster. Write wishes in the present and future. Sometimes more than one answer is possible.

1 There isn't a lot of light. Ben <u>*wishes (that) there was/were more light*</u>.
2 We don't have enough bottled water. We _____.
3 The roof is leaking. Mom _____.
4 We are running out of batteries. Paul _____.
5 The electricity doesn't work. Dad _____.
6 The Internet isn't working. Sue _____.
7 The furniture is going to be ruined. Grandma and Grandpa _____
   _____.
8 We can't go to a hotel. We _____.

Exercise 4.2 Past Wishes

Read the sentences about some past disasters. Then write sentences about the speakers' wishes. Use past wish forms. Sometimes more than one answer is possible.

1 An architect: The 1906 earthquake destroyed a historic building. There wasn't enough money to rebuild it.

   <u>*I wish the earthquake hadn't destroyed the building./I wish*</u>
   <u>*there had been enough money to rebuild it.*</u>

2 A surfer: They closed my favorite beach after the storm. They didn't let people in to clean it up.

3 A historian: A flood destroyed the ancient city. There were no records of what life was like there.

4 A student: A hurricane destroyed my high school. We weren't able to attend graduation.

5 Avoid Common Mistakes ⚠

1 **When forming the present unreal conditional, use the past (not present) form of the verb after *if*.**

          understood
If I ~~understand~~ my teacher, I would enjoy my class more.

2 **Remember to include a subject when forming an *if* clause.**

               she
She would feel safer if ⌄ could stay with us during the storm.

3 **When forming the past unreal conditional, use the past perfect form in the *if* clause.**

        had not ruined
If the flood ~~did not ruin~~ his car, he would have arrived home safely.

4 **When making past unreal wishes, use the past perfect (not the simple past).**

       had not moved
I wish I ~~did not move~~ to such a dangerous place.

Editing Task

Find and correct eight more mistakes in the story about Hurricane Ike.

                    had
    If Hurricane Ike ~~did~~ not come, we would have had an easier time. If the storm missed us, we would not have lived without electricity for two weeks. We would have been able to go to work and school. Our trees would look a lot better if had not been destroyed by the strong winds. For these reasons, some people wish that Hurricane
5 Ike never happened. However, I do not. If the storm did not come to Houston, we would not have learned many valuable lessons.

    First, we learned about our neighbors. We all came together to help each other before and after the storm. If I live in a different place, maybe I would not have gotten to know my neighbors in this way. Second, we learned good emergency survival skills.
10 If we had not learned to boardup our houses, might have been damaged. If another storm comes today, my house would be safe.

    Sometimes I wish that my family did not move to this city. However, I do not feel this way because of the hurricanes. The hurricanes have made our community stronger.

Conjunctions

Globalization of Food

1 Grammar in the Real World

A Have you ever had fast food in a foreign country? Do you think the food looks and tastes the same everywhere that it is sold? Read the article about the globalization of fast-food chains. What do fast-food businesses do to their products to make customers happy?

B Comprehension Check **Answer the questions.**

1 What has Dunkin' Donuts done to succeed globally?
2 How has McDonald's changed its menu to attract vegetarians in India?
3 How is the United States affected by the globalization of fast food?

C Notice **Find the sentences in the article and complete them. What is the function of the missing words? Circle *a* or *b*.**

1 That is not surprising since sweet foods are popular with

Americans, _____ you might not be able to

find that donut in other countries.
   a to add information
   b to show a contrast

2 In Indonesia, they sell donuts filled _____ with

red bean paste _____ with lychee and orange.
   a to emphasize additional negative information
   b to emphasize surprising information

3 Adapting their products to local preferences is a way

to keep customers happy _____ to keep

business booming.
   a to add information
   b to show a contrast

The Globalization of FAST FOOD

Do you want a glazed[1] donut for breakfast? Go to your favorite Dunkin' Donuts in Arizona, New York, **or** almost anywhere in the United States **and** you will find
5 it. That is not surprising since sweet foods are popular with Americans, **but** you might not be able to find that donut in other countries. Instead, in parts of Asia you might find green tea or mango mochi ring donuts. In Korea, they offer kimchi[2] croquettes, donuts filled with
10 pickled[3] vegetables. In Singapore, you would find donuts filled with wasabi[4] cheese **and** seaweed cheese. The wasabi creates a very hot-tasting donut that appeals to people in Singapore. In Thailand, Dunkin' Donuts makes delicious Kai-yong donuts, a combination of
15 glazed donut and shredded chicken that is topped with a spicy Thai chili paste. In Indonesia, they sell donuts filled **not only** with red bean paste **but also** with lychee[5] **and** orange. Thinking globally **but** acting locally has been one of the reasons for Dunkin' Donuts' success in over 32
20 countries **and** over 10,000 restaurants worldwide.

American fast-food chains, like Dunkin' Donuts, seem to be everywhere, **but** these days they are serving **both** food from their U.S. menus **and** food adapted to the tastes **and** customs of other cultures in other countries.
25 McDonald's is another example. In India, there are many people who do not eat meat, **so** McDonald's in India serves only vegetarian burgers **and** prepares non-vegetarian (chicken and fish) meals in a separate area. McDonald's is one of the largest fast-food restaurants
30 worldwide. More than one third of its 33,000 restaurants are located outside the United States. Adapting to local cultures is very important.

The globalization of the fast-food industry is happening with restaurants from all over the world.
35 Pollo Campero, a fast-food restaurant that began in Guatemala in 1971, started adding stores in **both** Europe **and** the Middle East after expanding in Central America. In 2002, it opened its first restaurant in the United States **and** has been growing ever since. In order
40 to appeal to health-conscious consumers in the United States, Pollo Campero decided to offer customers a choice: **either** a healthier, grilled chicken **or** a lightly fried chicken. Grilled **or** fried, the uniquely seasoned chicken has become popular with **both** immigrants from
45 Latin American countries **and** Americans from other cultural backgrounds.

These days, more and more chain restaurants are selling their food in different countries. Adapting their products to local preferences is a way to keep customers
50 happy **and** to keep business booming.[6] It appears to be a strategy for success.

---

[1]**glazed:** covered with a sweet, shiny coating made of sugar

[2]**kimchi:** a Korean dish of pickled vegetables

[3]**pickled:** preserved in a liquid containing salt or vinegar

[4]**wasabi:** a strong-tasting condiment

[5]**lychee:** a sweet, juicy fruit often found in Southeast Asia and other parts of Asia

[6]**boom:** grow rapidly, especially economically

2 Connecting Words and Phrases with Conjunctions

Grammar Presentation

<table>
<tr>
<td>

Conjunctions connect words and phrases.
Coordinating conjunctions include *and*, *but*, and *or*.
Correlative conjunctions include *both . . . and*, *neither . . . nor*, *either . . . or*, and *not only . . . but also*.

</td>
<td>

I love pizza, hamburgers, **and** hot dogs.
I eat **not only** fast food **but also** healthy food.

</td>
</tr>
</table>

2.1 Coordinating Conjunctions

<table>
<tr>
<td>

A Use coordinating conjunctions to link two or more nouns, gerunds, verbs, or adverbs.

Use the same part of speech in linked words or phrases to create parallel structure. This makes speech and writing clearer.

</td>
<td>

*Have you ever eaten pizza with <u>shrimp</u> **or** <u>olives</u>?* (nouns)
*I've been to fast-food restaurants in <u>Asia</u>, <u>Europe</u>, <u>Africa</u>, **and** <u>North America</u>.* (proper nouns)
*I don't like <u>cooking</u> **or** <u>baking</u>.* (gerunds)
*The meal is <u>unhealthy</u> **but** <u>delicious</u>.* (adjectives)

</td>
</tr>
<tr>
<td>

B Use *and* to add information.

</td>
<td>

*There are many vegetarians in India **and** the U.K.*

</td>
</tr>
<tr>
<td>

Use *but* to show a contrast.

</td>
<td>

*This food is cheap **but** very good.* (*But* contrasts the price of the food and the quality.)

</td>
</tr>
<tr>
<td>

Use *or* to connect related ideas or items in a negative statement or to show alternatives.

</td>
<td>

*I <u>don't like</u> hamburgers **or** pizza.*
*Do you want to eat at a restaurant **or** at home?*

</td>
</tr>
<tr>
<td>

C When you connect three or more words or phrases, use a comma between each one.

Put the conjunction before the last word or phrase.

</td>
<td>

*I select my food based on taste, nutritional value, **and** price.*
*Would you like to have juice, milk, **or** water with your meal?*

</td>
</tr>
</table>

2.2 Correlative Conjunctions

<table>
<tr>
<td>

A Correlative conjunctions have two parts. They often emphasize equality between the words or phrases they connect.

</td>
<td>

Both fried foods and grilled foods are served here.
Fast food is neither delicious nor healthy.

</td>
</tr>
</table>

2.2 Correlative Conjunctions (continued)

B Use *both . . . and* to add information. When connecting two subjects, use a plural verb.	*Both* the food *and* the atmosphere are wonderful.
Use *either . . . or* to emphasize alternatives. The verb agrees in number with the noun that is closest to it.	*Either* potatoes *or* rice is fine with me. (Use a singular verb with *rice*.) *Either* rice *or* potatoes are fine with me. (Use a plural verb with *potatoes*.)
Use *not only . . . but also* to emphasize surprising information. The verb agrees in number with the noun that is closest to it.	*Not only* two drinks *but also* dessert comes with this entree. (Use a singular verb with *dessert*.) *Not only* dessert *but also* two drinks come with this entree. (Use a plural verb with *drinks*.)
Use *neither . . . nor* to emphasize additional information in negative statements. The verb agrees in number with the noun that is closest to it.	*Neither* my parents *nor* my brother wants to try eel. (Use a singular verb with *brother*.) *Neither* my brother *nor* my parents want to try eel. (Use a plural verb with *parents*.)

Grammar Application

Exercise 2.1 Coordinating Conjunctions

Combine the sentences about global food. Use the coordinating conjunctions in parentheses. Sometimes more than one answer is possible.

1 There's a Taco Bell in Iceland. There's a Taco Bell in India. (and)

   There's a Taco Bell in Iceland and in India.

2 Starbucks operates in Asia. It operates in Europe. It operates in Latin America. (and)

   _____ and _____

3 The U.S. branch doesn't have vegetarian burgers. It doesn't have lamb burgers. (or)

   _____ or _____

4 Would you prefer to try something unusual? Would you prefer to try something familiar? (or)

   _____ or _____

5 Vegans don't eat eggs. Vegans don't eat cheese. Vegans don't eat yogurt. (or)

   _____ or _____

6 The food is cheap. The food is very healthy. (but)

   _____ but _____

7 The coffee is expensive. The coffee is very popular. (but)

   _____ but _____

A Read the monthly sales report from Branch #345. Then complete the report to headquarters. Circle the correct correlative conjunctions.

Branch #345 – Shanghai, China – June

PRODUCTS

Frozen Yogurt and Smoothies	Drinks	Snacks
frozen yogurt: **55%** smoothies: **45%**	coffee: **50%** tea: **43%** mineral water: **5%** milkshakes: **2%**	chips: **59%** cookies: **41%**

FLAVORS OF FROZEN YOGURT AND SMOOTHIES

Western Flavors	chocolate: **3%**	
	vanilla: **2%**	
Asian Flavors	dragon fruit: **55%**	
	lychee: **40%**	

Report to Headquarters on Branch #345

This branch offers (**both**)/ **neither** Western (**and**)/ **or** Asian flavors. Asian flavors seem to be
⎣__(1)__⎦ ⎣__(1)__⎦
more popular. For example, dragon fruit and lychee are the most popular flavors this month.

Most customers tend to choose **neither** / **either** dragon fruit **nor** / **or** lychee yogurt. Therefore,
⎣__(2)__⎦ ⎣__(2)__⎦
please note that **both** / **neither** chocolate **and** / **nor** vanilla is selling well at this branch.
⎣__(3)__⎦ ⎣__(3)__⎦

Neither / **Not only** frozen yogurt **nor** / **but also** smoothies are popular at this branch.
⎣__(4)__⎦ ⎣__(4)__⎦
Either / **Neither** mineral water **or** / **nor** milkshakes sold well this month. The reason is that
⎣__(5)__⎦ ⎣__(5)__⎦
most customers prefer **neither** / **either** coffee **nor** / **or** tea. **Both** / **Neither** coffee **and** / **nor**
⎣__(6)__⎦ ⎣__(6)__⎦ ⎣__(7)__⎦ ⎣__(7)__⎦
tea are selling well. It is interesting to note that customers are buying snacks. Surprisingly,

neither / **not only** chips **nor** / **but also** cookies are selling well.
⎣__(8)__⎦ ⎣__(8)__⎦

I recommend that we create more locally flavored products to offer at this location.

B Group Work In groups, choose a country that you know well. Discuss possible frozen yogurt flavors and types of drinks and snacks that you think would or would not sell well in this country. Then write five sentences about your choices with correlative conjunctions.

Both chocolate and vanilla would sell well in Mexico.

Exercise 2.3 More Correlative Conjunctions

Combine the sentences about the availability of items in a Latin American coffee chain's global locations. Use the correlative conjunctions in parentheses.

1 Milk is available in the United States. Juice is available in the United States. (both . . . and)

   Both milk and juice are available in the United States.

2 Tea is inexpensive in Egypt. Tea is very popular in Egypt. (both . . . and)

3 You can use your own mug at coffee shops in the U.K. You can use a store cup at coffee shops in the U.K. (either . . . or)

4 Donuts are available in the United States. Muffins are available in the United States. (not only . . . but also)

5 Recycling is encouraged in China. Reusing cups is encouraged in China. (not only . . . but also)

6 Generally, forks are not available in Chinese restaurants. Generally, knives are not available in Chinese restaurants. (neither . . . nor)

7 Hot dogs are not typically eaten for lunch in the Dominican Republic. Pizza is not typically eaten for lunch in the Dominican Republic. (neither . . . nor)

3 Connecting Sentences with Coordinating Conjunctions

Grammar Presentation

| The coordinating conjunctions *and*, *but*, *or*, *so*, and *yet* can connect independent clauses. | Kevin doesn't eat meat, **but** he eats fish.
Jennifer is a vegetarian, **so** we shouldn't put meat in the lasagna. |

3.1 Connecting Sentences with *And*, *But*, and *Or*

A Use a comma before the coordinating conjunction when you connect two complete sentences. The comma implies a pause.	Starbucks opened in 1971, **and** it has become an international success. The café sold muffins, **but** it did not sell sandwiches. Consumers liked the food, **so** sales were good.
B When you connect sentences with the same subject with *and* or *or*, you do not need to repeat the subject. The result is a compound verb. Do not use a comma with compound verbs. If the modals or the auxiliary verbs are the same, you do not have to repeat the modals or auxiliaries.	CLAUSE, + AND + CLAUSE We ate at that restaurant last week, **and** we really liked it. VERB + AND + VERB We ate at that restaurant last week **and** really liked it. Karen can ride with us, **or** she can meet us at the restaurant. Karen can ride with us **or** meet us at the restaurant. My brother has visited India, **and** he has eaten fast food there. My brother has visited India **and** eaten fast food there.
C In some writing, such as in newspapers and magazines, sentences begin with conjunctions like *and* and *but* to emphasize information. Do not do this in academic writing.	The changes to the menu attracted many new customers. **And** the company's profits rose significantly.

3.1 Connecting Sentences with *And*, *But*, and *Or* (continued)

D Use *and* to connect an independent clause that adds information. You can also use *and* to show a sequence of events.	He is an excellent cook, **and** I love his recipes. This restaurant changed its chef, **and** now it is very popular.
Use *but* to introduce contrasting or surprising information.	This is supposed to be a good Mexican restaurant, **but** my Mexican friends don't like it.
Use *or* to introduce a choice or alternative. It is often used in questions or statements with modals of possibility.	We could have seafood, **or** we could make pasta. Could you prepare the meal, **or** should I ask Sam to prepare it?

3.2 Connecting Sentences with *So* and *Yet*

A Use *so* to connect a cause and its result.	CAUSE RESULT Henry doesn't like pizza, **so** we ordered pasta. That spice is rare in my country, **so** I substitute a different one.
Use *yet* to connect contrasting ideas or surprising information. *Yet* sometimes expresses a stronger contrast than *but*.	Cathy doesn't eat clams, **yet** she eats oysters. The restaurant serves wonderful food, **yet** it is known more for its music.
B Use a comma to combine sentences with *so* and *yet*. Do not use a compound verb.	Mary is a vegetarian, **so** she eats tofu. NOT ~~Mary is a vegetarian so eats tofu.~~

Grammar Application

Exercise 3.1 Connecting Sentences with *And*, *But*, *Or*

Complete the sentences about a European supermarket chain that opened stores in the United States. Circle the correct conjunctions. Add commas when necessary.

1 FoodCo opened 100 stores in the United States in 2008, **(and)**/but the managers expected to have great success in certain areas.

2 First, they studied the new market but/**(and)** they even sent anthropologists to study U.S. eating and shopping habits.

3 They opened stores in wealthy neighborhoods or/**(and)** they also opened some in low-income neighborhoods.

4 The trend in the United States is toward "big box" stores[1] and/**(but)** FoodCo decided to open small, convenience-type stores.

[1]**"big box" store:** a very large store that sells almost everything, including food

5 Convenience stores in the United States usually do not sell fresh produce ~~but~~ / or FoodCo has changed the definition of *convenience store* with its new stores.

6 FoodCo has positioned itself as a healthy convenience store (and) / or it provides high-quality groceries and produce at reasonable prices.

7 Customers can use FoodCo's shops to pick up last-minute items, but / (or) they can do their weekly shopping there.

8 Now shoppers in low-income neighborhoods have a choice. They can buy junk food at a convenience store but / (or) they can buy healthy products at a FoodCo shop.

Exercise 3.2 Connecting Sentences with *So* and *Yet*

Complete the article about Chinese-American dishes. Use *so* or *yet*. Add commas when necessary.

Many Chinese restaurants serve dishes that are not authentic. Chinese restaurant owners wanted to be successful in foreign countries **, _SO_** they adapted
(1)
dishes to local tastes. Here are some examples: Fortune cookies are popular desserts in many Chinese restaurants **_yet_** they were never popular in China. In
(2)
fact, the cookies were actually invented in Japan and then introduced to the United States by an immigrant in the early 1900s (although some people dispute this and say that a Chinese immigrant invented them first). General Tso's Chicken is another example. No one is absolutely certain of its origin **_yet_** it appears on many
(3)
U.S. Chinese restaurant menus. It's fried chicken with a sweet sauce. Fried chicken is a traditional American dish **, _So_** a clever Chinese restaurant owner probably
(4)
invented it to appeal to American tastes for sweet sauces. Chop suey is another Chinese-American invention. There are many legends about its creation **, _Yet_**
(5)
no one really knows for sure how it came about. In one story, a Chinese-American dishwasher created the dish from leftover bits of meat and vegetables. The man received part of his pay in food **, _so_** he took what he could find at the end
(6)
of the day. Customers asked about the delicious-smelling creation **, _so_** the restaurant manager put it on the
(7)
menu. Some of these dishes may seem inauthentic **, _yet_** they have been extremely popular in the
(8)
United States since the 1900s.

Exercise 3.3 Combining Sentences

[handwritten: abroad 4 autros Baises]

Combine the sentences about the localization of food. Use the conjunctions in parentheses. Omit the subject and use a compound verb when possible. Add commas when necessary.

1 You can travel to many countries. You can still find dishes from home. (and)

   You can travel to many countries and still find dishes from home.

2 I have eaten tacos in China. ~~I have~~ ordered kimchi in France. (and) *[handwritten: and / or]*

   _____ *[handwritten: , and I have ...]*

3 You might get an authentic dish abroad. ~~You might~~ find a local version of it. (or) *[handwritten: or]*

   _____

4 I often find international dishes abroad. They are usually adapted to local tastes. (but) *[handwritten: but]*

   _____

5 Beef isn't eaten in some countries. A fast-food chain might sell lamb burgers. (so) *[handwritten: so]*

   _____ *[handwritten: , so a Fast ....]*

6 I travel constantly. I never miss food from home. (yet) *[handwritten: yet]*

   _____ *[handwritten: , yet I never ...]*

Exercise 3.4 Using *So* and *Yet*

Over to You On a separate piece of paper, complete the answers about local food tastes. Write sentences that are true for you. Discuss your ideas with a partner.

1 How do supermarkets in your neighborhood address local tastes?

   Supermarkets in my neighborhood want to address local tastes, so

   they have an imported-food section .

2 How might an international food company adapt a product to local tastes?

   People in _____ like _____ , so _____ .
        (name a country)   (food or taste)

3 What inauthentic ethnic dishes are sometimes very popular?

   _____ is inauthentic, yet _____ .
    (name of dish)

4 Reducing Sentences with Similar Clauses

Grammar Presentation

When you connect sentences that have similar clauses, you can often reduce the words in the second clause.	*Shrimp is one of my favorite foods. Chicken is one of my favorite foods.* *Shrimp is one of my favorite foods, **and** chicken is, **too**.*

4.1 Reducing Sentences

A In sentences with *be* as the main verb, use the *be* verb in the reduced clause.

*Their Chinese food isn't very good, **but** their Thai food is.*

B For other verb forms with auxiliaries, you can reduce the verb form in the reduced clause.

*My brother didn't eat fast food in college, **and** I didn't, **either**.*

For the present progressive or past progressive, keep the form of *be* and omit verb + *-ing*.

*The price of beef was rising last month, **but** the price of chicken wasn't.*

For simple verb forms, use *do / does* (not) or *did* (not).

*I don't like this restaurant, **and** Lisa doesn't, **either**.*
*We went out to eat, **and so** did Victor.*

For the present progressive or past perfect, use *have / has* or *had* and omit the past participle.

*The cost of eating out has risen, **and** the cost of cooking at home has, **too**.*

For modals or future forms, use the modal or future form by itself.

*Jason can join us for lunch, **and** Liz can, **too**.*
*I won't eat fried food, **and** Greg won't, **either**.*

C Use *and . . . too* or *and so* to combine two affirmative sentences. Use:

- *and* + subject + auxiliary + *too*
- *and so* + auxiliary + subject

Note that the order of the auxiliary and subject are reversed in *and so* reduced clauses.

We usually use a comma before *too*.

AFFIRM. SENT. + AFFIRM. SENT.
I ate there yesterday. She ate there yesterday.

AND + SUBJ. + AUX. + TOO
*I ate there yesterday, **and** she did, **too**.*

AND SO + AUX. + SUBJ.
*I ate there yesterday, **and so** did she.*

4.1 Reducing Sentences (continued)

D Use *and . . . not, either* or *and neither* to combine two negative sentences. Use:

- *and* + subject + auxiliary + *not, either*

- *and neither* + auxiliary + subject.

NEG. SENT. + NEG. SENT.
I don't have any coffee. Kim doesn't have any coffee.

AND + SUBJ. + AUX. + NOT, EITHER
*I don't have any coffee, **and** Kim doesn't, **either**.*

AND NEITHER + AUX. + SUBJ.
*I don't have any coffee, **and neither** does Kim.*

E Use *but* to combine an affirmative and a negative sentence.

AFFIRM. SENT. + NEG. SENT.
The beef is dry. The chicken isn't dry.

AFFIRM. CLAUSE + BUT + NEG. CLAUSE
*The beef is dry, **but** the chicken isn't.*

NEG. CLAUSE + BUT + AFFIRM. CLAUSE
*The chicken isn't dry, **but** the beef is.*

F You can also use *too, so, either,* and *neither* in separate sentences in speaking and less formal writing.

Use *too* and *so* for two affirmative sentences. Use *either* and *neither* for two negative sentences.

*Japanese food is delicious. Korean food is, **too**.*
*Japanese food is delicious. **So is** Korean food.*
*The coffee isn't warm. The tea isn't, **either**.*
*The coffee isn't warm. **Neither is** the tea.*

Exercise 4.1 Reducing Sentences with Similar Clauses

Combine the sentences about food localization in India. Use coordinating conjunctions. If there are two lines, write the sentence in two different ways.

1 Americans like fast food. Indians like fast food.
   Americans like fast food, and Indians do, too.
   Americans like fast food, and so do Indians.

2 Some U.S. food companies are successful in India. Some U.S. food companies aren't successful in India.

_____

3 Beef isn't popular in India. Pork isn't popular in India.

_____

_____

4 McDonald's adapts its menu to local tastes. Pizza Hut adapts its menu to local tastes.

_____

_____

5 Pizza Hut doesn't serve meat in some regions. McDonald's doesn't serve meat in some regions.

_____

_____

A Group Work Match the words with pictures of food. Tell the group which foods you have eaten raw.

_b_ **1** eel

_____ **2** jellyfish

_____ **3** sea urchin

_____ **4** seaweed

_____ **5** tuna

a

b

c

d

e

B Listen to the interview with the chef of a restaurant. Circle *T* if the statement is true. Circle *F* if the statement is false.

1 The chef is talking about Asian dishes that he serves at his restaurant. (T) F

2 All the dishes he offers are popular with his customers. T F

3 The chef has adapted some dishes to local tastes. T F

4 The chef does not plan to make any changes to his menu. T F

C Listen again. Rewrite the statements to match what the chef says. Use reduced forms.

1 Raw fish is getting more popular. Seaweed salad is getting more popular.

Raw fish is getting more popular _, and so is seaweed salad_ .

2 Tuna has been selling well. Eel hasn't been selling well.

Tuna has been selling well, _____ .

3 Jellyfish didn't sell well last month. Sea urchin didn't sell well last month.

Jellyfish didn't sell well last month, _____ .

4 Spicy noodles have sold well. Cold noodles have sold well.

Spicy noodles have sold well, _____ .

5 This restaurant can't get customers interested in Thai dishes. Our other restaurants can't get customers interested.

This restaurant can't get customers interested in Thai dishes,

_____ .

6 We'll probably stop offering Thai dishes. The other branches will probably stop offering Thai dishes.

We'll probably stop offering Thai dishes, _____ .

7 We won't serve that. Most other Asian restaurants won't serve that.

We won't serve that, _____ .

8 The ice cream has been selling well. The cake has been selling well, too. The ice cream has been selling well, _____ .

5 Avoid Common Mistakes ⚠

1   **Use *or* to connect ideas in a negative sentence.**

                                 or
There were no nuts in the vegetarian ~~and~~ the meat dishes.

2   **Use *both*, not *either*, when joining ideas with *and*.**

            both
They use ~~either~~ butter and oil for cooking.

3   **Use *either*, not *too*, after a negative verb.**

                            either
They do not eat pork, and we don't, ~~too~~.

4   **Do not use a comma when a conjunction joins two phrases.**

Most local people love durian fruit~~,~~ but dislike the smell.

Editing Task

Find and correct eight more mistakes in the paragraphs about food.

Intercultural Dinners

                                                                both

My roommate and I come from different cultures, so ~~either~~ our eating habits and food preferences differ. Fortunately, we have some food preferences in common. I do not eat junk food, and he does not, too. There are no cookies and other desserts in our house. Instead, we have either fresh fruits and nuts for snacks.

5   However, we have some differences. I eat either rice and pasta every day. My roommate, however, thinks meals with rice, and dishes with pasta will make him gain weight, so he does not want to eat them often. Likewise, I do not like to eat a lot of meat and dairy products because I believe they are not healthy. Fortunately, I do not complain about his tastes, and he does not complain about mine, too. When we

10   cook, we try to make food that represents either his culture and mine.

Adverb Clauses and Phrases

Consumerism

1 Grammar in the Real World

A What are some normal behaviors that can become problems under certain circumstances? Read the web article about shopping addiction. When is shopping an addiction?

B Comprehension Check **Answer the questions.**

1 Why aren't shopping addictions considered a serious problem by most people?

2 What problems can a shopping addiction lead to?

3 What are two ways in which shopaholics can treat their problem?

C Notice **Find the sentences in the article and complete them. Then circle the meaning of the words.**

1 _____ these people do not need more clothes or electronics, they keep buying them.
   a The words introduce contrasting ideas.   b The words give a reason.

2 _____ shopping may be seen as an amusing addiction, society does not always consider it a serious problem.
   a The word introduces contrasting ideas.   b The word gives a reason.

3 _____ shopaholics enjoy the excitement, they often feel depressed or guilty after a shopping trip.
   a The words introduce contrasting ideas.   b The words give a reason.

SHOPPING ADDICTION:
When Spending Hurts

Some people have closets filled with new clothes that they do not wear. Others have desks covered with electronics that they
5 never use. **Even though these people do not need more clothes or electronics,** they keep buying them. They cannot help themselves. **Although many**
10 **people like to shop,** some people shop too much. If someone is unable to control spending, he or she may be a shopping addict, or "shopaholic." **Because**
15 **shopping may be seen as an amusing addiction,** society does not always consider it a serious problem. As a result, many people do not recognize they have a
20 problem that needs treatment. However, if this addiction is not treated, it can ruin a person's life.

Shopping can activate[1] chemicals in the brain associated
25 with pleasure, **so some people get a natural "high"[2] while** shopping. Also, some people shop **because it makes them feel in control.** This often happens
30 **when they face difficulties in their personal or professional lives.** These feelings could be signs of shopping addiction. **While it may appear to some that**
35 **many more women than men are affected by this addiction,** current statistics show that this is not true. The percentage of men addicted to shopping is about the
40 same as the percentage of women (around 5 percent).

Like most addictions, a shopping addiction can cause serious problems. First of all,
45 it is difficult for addicts. **Even though shopaholics enjoy the excitement,** they often feel depressed or guilty after a shopping trip. **Spending**
50 **more money than they have,** many shopaholics have financial problems. **As they spend,** they may lie to their families about their spending habits. These lies are
55 almost always hurtful and can even destroy the family.

Fortunately, shopping addiction can be treated. **In order to change their behavior,**
60 shopping addicts must admit that they have a problem and then seek help. In addition, shopping addicts should always take a friend along **when they need to** buy
65 something. Most shopping addicts only overspend when they shop alone.

While shopping is usually a harmless activity, an addiction
70 to shopping can cause financial and personal problems. Therefore, people should understand the signs of a shopping addiction **so that they can get help.** Shopping
75 should be a constructive activity, not a destructive one.

[1]**activate:** cause something to start

[2]**high:** a feeling of being excited or full of energy

2 Subordinators and Adverb Clauses

Grammar Presentation

[handwritten: Despite + noum / noun phrase / gerund (Ving)]

Adverb clauses show a relationship between ideas in two clauses. They begin with subordinators, such as *although* and *because*.	*Although she enjoys wearing new clothes, she doesn't enjoy shopping.* *Eric doesn't go shopping often because he doesn't like to spend money.*

2.1 Forming Adverb Clauses

A An adverb clause has a subject and a verb, but it is a dependent clause. It is not a complete sentence.	MAIN CLAUSE DEPENDENT CLAUSE *She shops because it makes her feel good*
B In general, use a comma when an adverb clause begins the sentence.	*Although I sometimes buy things I don't need, I'm not a shopping addict.*

2.2 Using Adverb Clauses

A Use *because* and *since* to give reasons. *Because* is more common.	<u>*Because*</u> *shopping is necessary, shopping addicts aren't easily recognized.* *Treatment is important for shopping addicts* <u>*since*</u> *it is very difficult to overcome this problem on one's own.*
B Use *although*, *even though*, and *though* to show a contrasting idea or something unexpected. *Although* is a little more formal. Use a comma with adverb clauses that include these subordinators, whether they begin or end the sentence.	*[handwritten: Despite]* <u>*Even though*</u> *shopping addicts enjoy shopping, they feel depressed afterward.* *She spends a lot on clothing,* <u>*though*</u> *she doesn't make much money.* *[handwritten: despite not]*
C Use *while* to show contrasting ideas. Use a comma whether the adverb clause begins or ends the sentence.	*Shopping addicts buy things they don't need,* <u>*while*</u> *nonaddicts tend to buy mostly things they need.*
D You can use *as, since, when,* and *while* in adverb clauses to express time relationships.	*It has been six weeks* <u>*since*</u> *he went shopping.* <u>*While*</u> *she was at the mall, she bought many useless things.*

Grammar Application

Exercise 2.1 Adverb Clauses

Combine the sentences about shopping addiction. Use the subordinators in parentheses. Add commas when necessary. Sometimes more than one answer is possible.

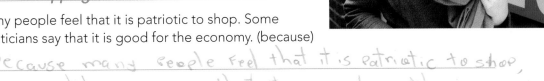

1 We are surrounded by advertising messages. It is often difficult to avoid shopping. (since)

Since we are surrounded by advertising messages, it is often difficult to avoid shopping.

2 Many people feel that it is patriotic to shop. Some politicians say that it is good for the economy. (because)

Because many people feel that it is patriotic to shop, some politicians say that it is good for the economy.

3 We may not need items. We sometimes want what others have. (even though)

We may not need items, even though we sometimes want what other have.

4 Shopping addiction seems to be a recent problem. It has almost certainly existed for centuries. (although)

Shopping addiction seems to be a recent problem, although it has almost certainly existed for centuries

5 Addicts may shop to escape negative feelings. Normal people shop to buy things they need. (while)

While addicts may shop to escape negative feelings, normal people shop to but things they need

6 Normal shoppers use the items they buy. Compulsive shoppers often do not use them. (while)

Normal shoppers use the items they buy, while compulsive shoppers often do not use them.

A Complete the interview with a shopping addict. Rewrite each pair of sentences as one sentence. Use one of the subordinators in parentheses.

Jane So, Claire, how did you know you were a shopping addict?

Claire I saw a show on TV. I realized I was an addict. (when/since)

    1   *When I saw a show on TV, I realized I was an addict.*

Jane I understand that you're getting help.

Claire Yes. My insurance pays for it. I was able to sign up for therapy. (because/although)

    2 _____

Jane Is your therapy helping?

Claire Definitely. I've only been in therapy a short time. I'm feeling better already. (although/when)

    3 _____

Jane How are things different now?

Claire I only buy what I really need. I'm spending much less money. (since/although)

    4 _____

Jane Describe a recent shopping trip.

Claire I was at the mall yesterday. I only went to one store. (even though/since)

    5 _____

    I had a list. I only bought things I truly needed. (since/while)

    6 _____

Jane Good for you! Thank you for sharing your story with us.

B Listen to the interview and check your answers.

Group Work What are some ways to avoid bad shopping habits? Write five sentences using adverb clauses. Use the ideas in the unit and your own ideas.
Decide as a group which two ideas are the most effective and give reasons.

You should take a friend with you when you shop.

3 Reducing Adverb Clauses

Grammar Presentation

Sometimes you can reduce adverb clauses to *-ing* forms. The subject of the main clause must be the same as the subject of the adverb clause.	*While he was shopping*, he bought things he didn't need. *While shopping*, he bought things he didn't need.

3.1 Reducing Adverb Clauses

In many cases, you can reduce adverb clauses. Omit the subject, and use the verb + *-ing*.	*While he was shopping*, he bought a jacket. *While shopping*, he bought a jacket.

3.2 Reducing Clauses That Give Reasons

You can reduce clauses that give reasons when the verb is in the simple past, present perfect, or past perfect.	
For the simple past, omit the subordinator and the subject, and use the verb + *-ing*.	*Because he was cautious*, he didn't spend much money. *Being cautious*, he didn't spend much money.
For the present perfect and past perfect, change *have* to *having*. The *-ing* forms usually begin the sentences.	*Since she has gotten help*, she no longer shops so often. *Having gotten help*, she no longer shops so often.

3.3 Reducing Time Clauses

A You can reduce a time clause when the verb is in the present progressive or past progressive. Omit the subject and the form of *be*.	*You can save money while you are going to college.* *You can save money while going to college.* *While he was shopping*, he bought a jacket. *While shopping*, he bought a jacket.
B You can also reduce a time clause with a verb in the simple present or simple past. Omit the subject, and use the verb + *-ing*.	*She started shopping at malls before she realized that shopping was addictive.* *She started shopping at malls before realizing that shopping was addictive.*

Grammar Application

Complete the sentences about Mike and Eric, two hoarders.[1] Rewrite the reason clauses in parentheses as reduced clauses.

1 _Buying new things all the time_ , Mike filled his apartment with useless items.
    (because he bought new things all the time)

2 _____ , he took action.
          (because he understood that he had a problem)

3 _____ , he had no savings.
          (because he had spent so much money on clothes)

4 _____ , Eric is now able to keep his
              (since he has received treatment)
apartment much cleaner.

5 _____ , he no longer feels anxious.
          (because he has worked with a therapist)

6 _____ , he no longer hoards useless items.
              (since he has gotten help)

[1]**hoarder:** a person who collects large supplies of things, usually more than he or she needs

Complete the sentences about a compulsive spender. Rewrite the time clauses in parentheses as reduced clauses.

1 _While shopping online_ , Amy was ecstatic.
    (while she was shopping online)

2 _____ , she was in an altered state.
    (while she was spending money)

3 Amy had spent over $30,000 _____ .
                          (before she got treatment)

4 _____ , Amy decided to join Debtors
    (before she spent more money)
   Anonymous (DA).[1]

5 _____ , Amy learned how to budget.
    (after she joined DA)

6 She also got help with her credit _____ .
                                    (after she started DA)

7 Amy has changed her behavior _____ .
                                (since she received treatment)

[1]**Debtors Anonymous (DA):** an organization that helps compulsive spenders

4 Subordinators to Express Purpose

Grammar Presentation

Some subordinators can express a purpose.	*He got help for his shopping addiction **so that** he could feel better.* (= He got help for the purpose of feeling better.)

4.1 Using Subordinators to Express Purpose

A Use *so* or *so that* to show a reason or purpose. Clauses with *so that* usually come after the main clause.	*People go to psychologists **so that** they can talk about their problems.* *I keep track of my money **so** I don't spend too much.*
B You can also show a reason or purpose with *in order to* or *to* when the subject of the main clause and the adverb clause are the same. Do not repeat the subject.	*Shopping addicts buy things they don't need **to** feel good.* (= Shopping addicts buy things they don't need so that they feel good.) *Shopping addicts may get help **in order to** stop shopping.* (= Shopping addicts may get help so that they stop shopping.)

A Complete the sentences from the book *Consumer World*. Put the subordinators in parentheses in the right place in the sentences.

in order to

1 Psychologists have shown that we actually need very little feel happy. (in order to)

2 Some people buy things feel good about themselves. (to)

3 Some people acquire things they have a sense of who they are. (so that)

4 It's also possible that people acquire things feel secure. (in order to)

5 They buy a lot feel that they are financially secure. (in order to)

6 They buy a lot they are prepared for any emergency. (so that)

7 Find out how little you really need, think about what you would do if you had to move. (to)

8 I think that have true peace of mind, you should have as little as possible. (in order to)

B Group Work Discuss the questions with your group. Use *in order to, so, so that,* and *to* in your discussion.

■ Does owning things make people happy?

■ What are some of the problems that owning things can cause?

■ What do people have to do to be truly happy?

■ What are some ways to live with less?

A *In order to be truly happy, you should focus on people, not things.*
B *I agree, but to have a happy life, you need some possessions.*

C Write sentences about your five best ideas in B. Use subordinators to express purpose.

In order to be truly happy, you should focus on people, not things.
Pretend you are moving so you can decide what to get rid of.

5 Avoid Common Mistakes ⚠

1 **Remember that *even though* is two words, not one.**

                            even though

I bought a computer bag ~~eventhough~~ I do not own a computer.

2 **Use *even though*, not *even*, to create an adverb clause.**

Even though

~~Even~~ it was late, the store was open.

3 **Do not start a new sentence with *because*, *whereas*, or *although* when the clause refers to the previous sentence.**

                              store because

I returned the camera to the ~~store. Because~~ I did not really need it.

4 **Remember to use the verb + *-ing* in reduced clauses after words like *after*, *before*, *while*, and *when*.**

               watching

When ~~watch~~ ads on TV, some people feel a strong urge to buy the products.

Editing Task

Find and correct eight more mistakes in the paragraphs about addictions.

                  looking

After ~~look~~ at research, we see clearly that alcohol and drug addictions are serious physical conditions. Psychologists are now considering adding shopping to the list. Eventhough these experts say that shopping is as addictive as drugs, I disagree that it should be considered a serious addiction.

5   People who argue that shopping is addictive have good reasons. While shop, many people get a good feeling. They like spending money even they may not need to buy anything. However, after go home, they feel regret. They have spent money on something they did not want or need. Because buying something makes them feel a sense of power.

10   However, after examine the situation of over-shopping closely, one can see that many people are victims of advertising. Even they may not plan to buy something, a powerful advertisement can change their mind. If people did not watch so much TV, they would not feel the urge to shop as strongly. In this way, shopping addiction differs from drug and alcohol addictions, which create a chemical change in the body that is very difficult to resist.

15   Eventhough shopping too much is a serious problem, it should not be considered an addiction. If advertisements disappeared, society would not have this problem called shopping addiction.

Connecting Information with Prepositions and Transitions

Technology in Entertainment

1 Grammar in the Real World

A How are video games today different from the games of 5 or 10 years ago? Read the article about a kind of animation technology that is being used in games today. How has it changed the look of video games?

B Comprehension Check **Answer the questions.**

1 What is "mocap"?

2 In what areas is mocap used?

3 Why isn't mocap used more often in movies and video games?

C Notice **Match the words in bold with their meaning.**

1 **Because of** the realism that mocap gives its animated figures, a common use for mocap is in video games. __b__

2 **Furthermore,** mocap can be used in training for jobs such as firefighting. __a__

3 **Despite** the expense, mocap technology is becoming more popular in many different areas. __c__

a introduces additional information

b introduces a reason

c introduces contrasting information

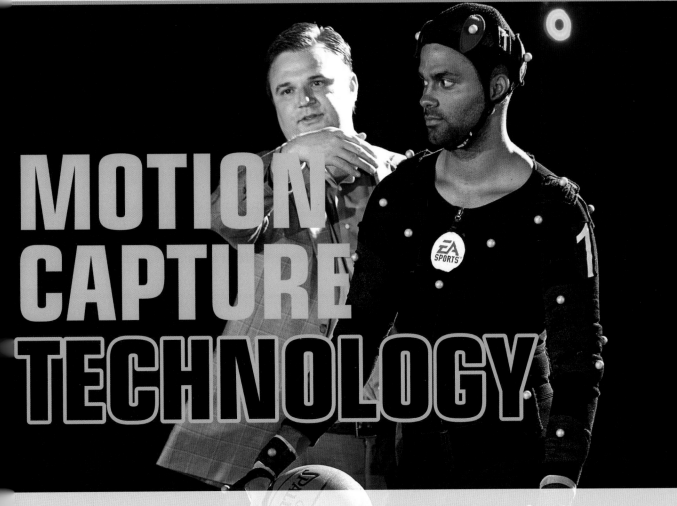

MOTION CAPTURE TECHNOLOGY

Computer animation was first introduced in the late 1970s; **however**, today's animation is much more realistic than it was then. While the first animated video game characters moved in only two directions, today's animated
5 game heroes can jump, kick, and spin. The use of sensors[1] to record these movements is called motion capture, or "mocap."

Because of the realism that mocap gives its animated figures, a common use for mocap is in video games.
10 Video game creators use real people to help create their characters. With sports video games, for example, famous athletes are used **instead of** actors. **Consequently**, the games can feature each athlete's unique moves. How does it work? **First**, the athlete puts on a tight suit
15 that has special markers[2] all over it. **Next**, he or she performs a sequence of actions. Video cameras record these movements using the markers. **Finally**, digital information is collected from the markers and the video. This information is used to create the movements of the
20 video character.

Another common use of mocap is in movies. The makers of *Titanic* needed characters that could move realistically in a situation that would have been much too dangerous for a real actor. **As a result**, they used mocap.
25 **Besides being** completely safe, it was a lot cheaper and easier than filming people falling off a sinking ship!

In addition to these uses, motion capture technology is used in medicine. **For instance**, doctors have patients in mocap suits walk on treadmills. The mocap information
30 helps doctors diagnose problems such as weak bones. **Furthermore**, mocap can be used in training for jobs such as firefighting. New firefighters can use mocap games to practice moving through virtual[3] house fires. **Instead of** taking risks in a real setting, they can practice in a virtual
35 reality.

Despite the expense, mocap technology is becoming more popular in many different areas. **Due to** its success so far, who knows what it will be used for next?

---

[1]**sensor:** a device that discovers and reacts to changes in such things as movement, heat, and light

[2]**marker:** a small, reflective dot that is taped to a figure

[3]**virtual:** created by a computer

2 Connecting Information with Prepositions and Prepositional Phrases

Grammar Presentation

Some prepositions and prepositional phrases can connect information to an independent clause. Like subordinators, these prepositions can be used to add information, give reasons, show contrasts, present alternatives, or give exceptions.

Video games look realistic today **because of** improvements in computer animation.

Despite the popularity of animation, most people prefer to watch live-action movies.

2.1 Using Prepositions and Prepositional Phrases to Connect Ideas

A One-word prepositions, such as *besides* and *despite*, and multi-word prepositions, such as *as well as*, *because of*, *in addition to*, and *in spite of*, are followed by nouns, noun phrases, or gerunds.

Besides being very expensive, animated movies can take a long time to produce.

Some animated movies are also popular with adults *in spite of* their appeal to kids.

B Prepositional phrases, like adverb clauses, can come before or after the main clause. Use a comma when the prepositional phrase comes first.

Video games usually use athletes *instead of actors*.

Instead of actors, video games usually use athletes.

2.2 Meanings of Prepositions Used to Connect Ideas

A Use *as well as*, *besides*, and *in addition to* to emphasize another idea.

I enjoy animated movies *as well as* live-action movies.

This TV has 3D technology *in addition to* high definition.

Besides being a talented director, he is an excellent actor.

B Use *as a result of*, *because of*, and *due to* to give reasons.

Because of the high cost of tickets, many people don't go to the movies.

As a result of voters' opinions, the director was nominated for an Academy Award.

The movie's appeal is *due to* its special effects.

2.2 Meanings of Prepositions Used to Connect Ideas *(continued)*

C Use *instead of* to give alternatives.	*Let's see a drama instead of a comedy.* *Instead of going out, they watched TV at home.*
D Use *except* or *except for* to give exceptions. When the main clause is a negative statement, you can also use *besides* to mean "except for."	*This composer wrote the music for all the Alien Adventures movies except the first one.* *Except for their parents, the audience was mostly children.* *Besides the parents of the children, there weren't any adults in the audience.*
E Use *despite* and *in spite of* to show contrasting ideas.	*Despite being made for children, this movie is enjoyed by adults.* *In spite of its short length, the movie was very powerful.*

Grammar Application

Exercise 2.1 Prepositional Phrases to Connect Ideas

Complete the paragraphs about one use of motion capture technology. Use the words in the box. Sometimes more than one answer is possible.

as well as	because of	due to	in addition to	instead of	~~in spite of~~

In spite of the high cost of mocap, its use is expanding. For example, Ford
(1)
Motor Company, a car manufacturer, is using mocap technology to create digital
humans.[1] _because of_ their human-like behavior, digital humans are used to
(2)
study people's behavior in cars. _in addition to_ studying driver behavior, engineers
(3)
are also studying ways to make passengers feel more comfortable. For example,
instead of using a real human, the company uses a short digital female to test
(4)
a short driver's ability to reach the gas pedal.

   Motion capture technology helps the company improve worker safety
as well as driver safety. _Due to_ the technology's ability to
(5)   (6)
replicate workers' movements, the company has reduced the number of assembly
line accidents.

[1]**digital human:** an electronic representation of a person

Complete the sentences about using mocap technology to help athletes recover from injuries and improve their speed. Circle the correct prepositions.

1 (In addition to) / Because of filmmakers, physical therapists are using motion capture technology to help injured athletes.

2 As a result of / Instead of an injury, athletes could lose their careers.

3 An athlete's career could be destroyed (because) of / instead of injuries.

4 Analyzing an injury without motion capture technology is not always accurate, due to / besides being time-consuming.

5 With motion capture technology, therapists accurately see the problem in spite of / instead of guessing where the problem is.

6 The success of motion capture technology with Olympic athletes is in spite of / due to its ability to analyze the athletes' movements at high speeds.

7 Except for / Despite the success of motion capture technology with athletes, it cannot replace the hours of practice that athletes need to succeed.

A Combine the ideas about the use of technology in health care. Use the prepositions in parentheses and the underlined words to create prepositional phrases.

1 Many hospitals are no longer using <u>paper medical records</u>. They are using electronic medical records. (instead of)

   Instead of paper medical records, some hospitals are using electronic records.

2 Everyone has <u>quick access to your records</u>. Doctors can share information with each other more easily. (Due to)

_____

3 There are <u>many advantages to electronic records</u>. Some doctors still have serious concerns. (in spite of)

_____

4 There should be <u>accurate information in the records</u>. The information could contain data input errors. (instead of)

_____

5 There will be <u>a lot of security</u>. Hackers could still steal information from hospitals. (despite)

_____

B Group Work Choose an area that is changing because of technology. Use one of the ideas below or your own idea. As a group, write statements that explain the technology, its effects, and the possible advantages and disadvantages of using it. Use prepositional phrases.

- high speed trains
- online learning
- use of cell phones instead of money to purchase products

3 Connecting Information with Transition Words

Grammar Presentation

Transition words are words or phrases that connect ideas between sentences. They are frequently used in academic writing and formal situations.	*It's important not to judge a movie's quality by whether it is animated or not.* **Furthermore,** *you should not assume that a movie with human actors is superior to an animated movie.*

3.1 Using Transition Words

A Transition words join the ideas in two sentences.	*Movie stars often do the voices in animated movies.* **However,** *their fans don't always recognize them.*
Coordinating conjunctions (*but*, etc.), subordinators (*although*, etc.), and prepositions (*in spite of*, etc.) combine two different sentences into one new sentence.	*Music in movies is very important for setting the tone,* **but** *most people don't pay attention to it.* **Although** *animated movies sometimes win the best picture award, they also have their own category.* **In spite of** *having a lot of famous actors, the movie did not get very good reviews.*
B Most transition words occur at the beginning of the second sentence and are followed by a comma. You can also use a semicolon between the two sentences that you combine.	*The studio executives choose a script.* **After that,** *they select a director.* *She is a very talented artist;* **moreover,** *her use of color is exceptional.*
Many – but not all – transition words can go in the middle of the sentence or at the end. When the transition word comes at the end, it is preceded by a comma.	*Most people,* **however,** *associate animation with movies.* *Most people associate animation with movies,* **however.**

3.1 Using Transition Words *(continued)*

C The short transition words *so*, *then*, and *also* are often used without a comma. *So* is used at the beginning of a sentence only in informal writing.

Use more formal transition words with the same meanings in academic writing: *afterward, in addition, therefore*.

My daughter enjoys animated movies a lot. *So* we take her to them pretty often. *Then* she usually wants to stop for a snack on the way home. I am *also* usually hungry after a long movie.

Children often enjoy animated movies. *Therefore*, their parents often take them to the movies. *Afterward*, it is not unusual to stop for something to eat. *In addition*, parents often buy a book or souvenir connected to the movie for their children.

3.2 Meanings of Transition Words

A To show a sequence or the order of events or ideas, use *first, second, then, next, after that*, and *finally*.

How do animators capture an athlete's movement? *First*, the athlete puts on a special suit. *Then* the athlete performs the action. *Next*, the computer collects digital information.

B To summarize ideas, use *in conclusion, to conclude*, and *to summarize*.

In conclusion, technological innovations will change many fields, including animation.

C To give additional information, use *also, furthermore, in addition*, and *moreover*.

Animation is used in movies, video games, and other entertainment industries. *In addition*, it is used in sports medicine.

D To give alternatives, use *instead*.

I had expected the movie to be boring. *Instead*, I thought it was quite entertaining.

E To give contrasting ideas, use *on the other hand* and *in contrast*.

The story was not very original. *On the other hand*, the animation was impressive.

F To give a result, use *as a result, consequently, therefore*, and *thus*.

The game was designed with animation. *Therefore*, the characters were very lifelike.

G To give examples, use *for example* or *for instance*.

Many animated movies are very popular. *For example*, Kung Fu Panda and Despicable Me were huge box office hits.

📊 Data from the Real World

The most common transition words in writing are:	The most common transition words in conversation are:
however, so, then, therefore, thus	anyway, so, then, though

Grammar Application

Exercise 3.1 Transition Words to Show Sequence

A Pair Work Look at the steps involved in computer game design. Can you put them in the correct order? Make guesses with your partner and try to number the steps in order from 1 to 6.

_____ a Make a prototype (a model or "first draft") of the game and test it.

_____ b Work with the marketing team to get the game ready to sell.

_1_ c Decide on the theme and environment of the game.

_____ d Do research on the theme.

_____ e Figure out the goal of the game and the rules.

_____ f Make any necessary changes to the game.

B Now listen to a game designer describing her job. Were your answers correct?

C Listen again and complete the sentences. Use the sequence words in the box. Add commas when necessary.

after that	finally	~~first~~	next	second	then

1 _____*First,*_____ I decide on an overall concept for a game.

2 _____ I figure out the goal of the game and the rules.

3 _____ I do research on the theme.

4 _____ I use software to make a prototype of the game.

5 _____ I go back to the computer and make any necessary changes.

6 _____ I work with the marketing people.

Exercise 3.2 Transition Words for Academic Writing

Complete the paragraph about the differences between computer animation and traditional animation. Circle the correct transition words.

Computer-generated animation (CGA) is very popular today. The spectacular effects of CGA in big-budget movies impress many people. Therefore /(However), in my opinion, CGA is not as pleasant to
                    (1)
look at as traditional animation (TA). First /(Afterward), CGA does not
                                            (2)
require the same skill as TA. Traditional animators draw by hand, and the resulting images look complex and rich in style. Instead / To summarize,
                                                                    (3)
computer animators use software to produce images. These images often

Computer-Generated
Animation

have a cold, hard look to them. **To conclude** / **Furthermore** ,
(4)
with CGA, objects are often overly bright. This adds to the
unnaturalness of their appearance. **In contrast** / **Thus** , the
(5)
images from TA are often soft and appear more natural.
In conclusion / **Moreover** , TA produces better-looking
(6)
images that have more style as well as a lifelike appearance;
on the other hand / **therefore** , it is better than CGA.
(7)

Traditional
Animation

Exercise 3.3 Using Transition Words

A Look at the brainstorming notes a student made for a paragraph comparing two movies.
Use the words to write sentences to summarize the ideas. Use the notes to help you.

War of the Aliens	The Magical Forest
excellent computer graphics dull plot[1] unappealing characters bad dialog	poor animation interesting story likeable characters good dialog

[1]**plot**: story

1 excellent computer graphics / in contrast / poor animation

   War of the Aliens had excellent computer graphics. In contrast,
   The Magical Forest had poor animation.

2 excellent computer graphics / however / dull plot

   _____

3 furthermore / unappealing characters

   _____

4 on the other hand / interesting story

   _____

5 in addition / likeable characters

   _____

6 moreover / good dialog

   _____

7 in contrast / bad dialog

   _____

8 in conclusion / a better movie than

   _____

B Over to You Think of two movies you have seen that have animation or special effects. Which one was better? Why? Write four to six sentences comparing the two movies. Use transitions to add ideas and show contrasts.

Cowboys in Space was very popular. On the other hand, Cowboys in Space II didn't do very well.

4 Avoid Common Mistakes ⚠

1 The prepositional expressions *as well as, in spite of, despite,* and *in addition to* are followed by a noun phrase or a gerund, not a subject + verb.

         the high costs

Despite ~~the costs are high~~, 3D TVs are becoming very popular.

                     using

The filmmakers used mocap in addition to ~~they used~~ digital technology.

2 Use *on the other hand*, not *in the other hand*, when contrasting points of view.

                       on

The movie industry has many career opportunities; ~~in~~ the other hand, it is very competitive.

Editing Task

Find and correct four more mistakes in the paragraph about the filmmaking industry.

          the slow economy

     Filmmaking is a durable industry. Despite ~~the economy is slow~~, the movie industry is doing well. People always seem to find money for entertainment. As a result, movie production companies often hire people because it takes many professionals to create a movie. In addition to they hire actors and directors, they hire tens of thousands of other professionals that are

5 not well known – for example, grips (people who set up and tear down the sets), production assistants, and camera operators. The jobs can be exciting and challenging; in the other hand, some can be low paying. As with most other careers, it is necessary to work hard and be ambitious to succeed. The work can also be especially tough for production crews – for example, camera operators, production assistants, and makeup artists – who work up to 18

10 hours a day. Despite they have long hours, these jobs can be difficult to find because there is a lot of competition for them. In general, moviemaking is seen as a glamorous profession, and some people want to be a part of that glamor more than anything else. Movies often require celebrities and artists; in the other hand, they also rely on many people with other skills. It is a growing industry, too. The Bureau of Labor Statistics states that employment opportunities for

15 people in the filmmaking industry will increase 12 percent between now and 2016. In short, this industry is competitive, but young people should pursue it if they have an interest in movies.

Appendices

1 Irregular Verbs

Base Form	Simple Past	Past Participle	Base Form	Simple Past	Past Participle
be	was/were	been	hide	hid	hidden
become	became	become	hit	hit	hit
begin	began	begun	hold	held	held
bite	bit	bitten	hurt	hurt	hurt
blow	blew	blown	keep	kept	kept
break	broke	broken	know	knew	known
bring	brought	brought	leave	left	left
build	built	built	lose	lost	lost
buy	bought	bought	make	made	made
catch	caught	caught	meet	met	met
choose	chose	chosen	pay	paid	paid
come	came	come	put	put	put
cost	cost	cost	read	read	read
cut	cut	cut	ride	rode	ridden
do	did	done	run	ran	run
draw	drew	drawn	say	said	said
drink	drank	drunk	see	saw	seen
drive	drove	driven	sell	sold	sold
eat	ate	eaten	send	sent	sent
fall	fell	fallen	set	set	set
feed	fed	fed	shake	shook	shaken
feel	felt	felt	show	showed	shown
fight	fought	fought	shut	shut	shut
find	found	found	sing	sang	sung
fly	flew	flown	sit	sat	sat
forget	forgot	forgotten	sleep	slept	slept
forgive	forgave	forgiven	speak	spoke	spoken
get	got	gotten	spend	spent	spent
give	gave	given	stand	stood	stood
go	went	gone	steal	stole	stolen
grow	grew	grown	swim	swam	swum
have	had	had	take	took	taken
hear	heard	heard	teach	taught	taught

Irregular Verbs (*continued*)

Base Form	Simple Past	Past Participle	Base Form	Simple Past	Past Participle
tell	told	told	wake	woke	woken
think	thought	thought	wear	wore	worn
throw	threw	thrown	win	won	won
understand	understood	understood	write	wrote	written

2 Stative (Non-Action) Verbs

Stative verbs do not describe actions. They describe states or situations. Stative verbs are not usually used in the progressive. Some are occasionally used in the present progressive, but often with a different meaning.

Research shows that the 25 most common stative verbs in spoken and written English are:

agree	dislike	hope	love	see
believe	expect	hurt	need	seem
care (about)	hate	know	notice	think
cost	have	like	own	understand
disagree	hear	look like	prefer	want

Other stative verbs:

appear	deserve	mean	smell
be	feel	owe	sound
belong	forgive	recognize	taste
concern	look	remember	weigh
contain	matter		

Stative verbs that also have action meanings:

be	have	look	taste
expect	hear	see	think
feel	hope	smell	weigh

Using the present progressive form of these verbs changes the meaning to an action.
*Can you **see** the red car?* (= use your eyes to be aware of something)
*I **'m seeing** an old friend tomorrow.* (= meeting someone)
*I **think** you're right.* (= believe)
*Dina **is thinking** of taking a vacation soon.* (= considering)
*I **have** two sisters.* (= be related to)
*We**'re having** eggs for breakfast.* (= eating)
*He **is** in his first year of college.* (= exist)
*She **is being** difficult.* (= act)

3 Modals and Modal-like Expressions

Modals are helper verbs. Most modals have multiple meanings.

Function	Modal or Modal-like Expression	Time	Example
Advice less strong	*could* *might (not)*	present, future	He **could** do some puzzles to improve his memory. You **might** try some tips on improving your memory.
stronger	*ought to* *should (not)*	present, future	We **ought to** take a memory class next month. Greg **should** improve his memory.
	had better (not)	present, future	You**'d better** pay attention now.
Past Advice, Regret, or Criticism	*ought to have* *should (not) have*	past	She **ought to have** tried harder to improve her memory. You **should have** made an effort to improve your memory. He **shouldn't have** taken that difficult class.
Permission	*can (not)* *may (not)*	present, future	You **can** register for the class next week. You **may not** register after the first class.
	could (not)	past	You **could** ask questions during the lecture yesterday, but you **could not** leave the room.
formal →	*be (not) allowed to* *be (not) permitted to*	past, present, future	He **was not allowed to** talk during the test, but he **was allowed** to use his books. Students **will not be permitted to** refer to notes during examinations.
Necessity / Obligation	*have to* *need to* *be required to* *be supposed to*	past, present, future	I **have to** study tonight. She **needs to** quit her stressful job. You **won't be required to** take a test. He **is supposed to** tell you his decision tomorrow.
	must (not)	present, future	You **must** have experience for this job.
Obligation not to / Prohibition	*must not* *be not supposed to*	present, future	You **must not** talk during the exam. Students **are not supposed to** take their books into the exam room.

Modals and Modal-like Expressions (*continued*)

Function	Modal or Modal-like Expression	Time	Example
Lack of Necessity / Choices or Options	not have to not need to be not required to	past, present, future	You **didn't have to** bring your notes. You **don't need to** study tonight. You **are not required to** bring your books.
Ability	can (not)	present, future	We **can** meet the professor at noon tomorrow.
	could (not)	past	I **could** understand the lecture, but I **could not** remember it.
	be (not) able to	past, present, future	She **wasn't able to** see very well from her seat.
	could have	past	I **could have** done well on that memory test.
	could not have	past	I **couldn't have** taken the test yesterday. I was in another state!
Probability	can't could (not) (not) have to must (not)	present	Hackers **can't** be interested in my data. He **could** be online now. She **has to** be at work right now. He **must not** be worried about data security.
	may (not) might (not) ought to should (not)	present, future	Your computer **may** be at risk of hacking. That software **might not** be good enough. That password **ought to** be strong enough. It **shouldn't** be difficult to find good software.
	could will (not)	future	The company **could** start using cloud computing next month. My sister **will** probably get a new computer soon.
	can't have could (not) have may (not) have might (not) have must (not) have	past	I **can't have** entered the wrong password! The expert **could not have** given you good advice. The company **may have** been careless with security. I **might have** written the wrong password down. Someone **must have** stolen all the passwords.

4 Noncount Nouns and Measurement Words to Make Noncount Nouns Countable

Category of Noncount Noun	Noun Examples	Measurement Words and Expressions
Abstract concepts	courage, luck, space, time	a bit of, a kind of You had **a bit of** luck, didn't you?
Activities and sports	dancing, exercise, swimming, tennis, yoga	a game of, a session of They played **two games of** tennis.
Diseases and health conditions	arthritis, cancer, depression, diabetes, obesity	a kind of, a type of She has **a type of** diabetes called Type 2.
Elements and gases	gold, hydrogen, oxygen, silver	a bar of, a container of, a piece of, a tank of We have **tanks of** oxygen in the storage room.
Foods	beef, broccoli, cheese, rice	a bottle of, a box of, a bunch of, a can of, a grain of, a head of, a loaf of, a package of, a piece of, a pinch of, a serving of, a slice of, a wedge of I'll take **a serving of** rice and beef.
Liquids	coffee, gasoline, oil, tea	a bottle of, a cup of, a gallon of, a glass of, a quart of I would like **a cup of** tea.
Natural phenomena	electricity, rain, sun, thunder	a bolt of, a drop of, a ray of There hasn't been **a drop of** rain for three months.
Particles	pepper, salt, sand, sugar	a grain of, a pinch of My food needs **a pinch of** salt.
Subjects and areas of work	construction, economics, genetics, geology, medicine, nursing	an area of, a branch of, a field of, a type of There are a lot of specialty areas in **the field of** medicine.
Miscellaneous	clothing, equipment, furniture, news	an article of, a piece of I need **a piece of** furniture to go in that empty corner.

5 Order of Adjectives Before Nouns

When you use two (or more) adjectives before a noun, use the order in the chart below.

Opinion	Size	Quality	Age	Shape	Color	Origin	Material	Nouns as Adjectives
beautiful	big	cold	ancient	oval	black	American	cotton	computer
comfortable	fat	free	antique	rectangular	blue	Canadian	glass	evening
delicious	huge	heavy	new	round	gold	Chinese	gold	government
expensive	large	hot	old	square	green	European	leather	rose
interesting	long	safe	young	triangular	orange	Japanese	metal	safety
nice	short				purple	Mexican	paper	software
pretty	small				red	Peruvian	plastic	summer
rare	tall				silver	Thai	silk	training
reasonable	thin				yellow		silver	
shocking	wide				white		stone	
special							wooden	
ugly							woolen	
unique								

Examples:
*That was a **delicious green Canadian** apple!* (opinion before color before origin)
*I saw the **shocking government** report on nutrition.* (opinion before noun as adjective)
*Wei got a **small oval glass** table.* (size before shape before material)

6 Verbs That Can Be Used Reflexively

allow oneself	challenge oneself	hurt oneself	remind oneself
amuse oneself	congratulate oneself	imagine oneself	see oneself
ask oneself	cut oneself	introduce oneself	take care of
be hard on oneself	dry oneself	keep oneself (busy)	talk to oneself
be oneself	enjoy oneself	kill oneself	teach oneself
be pleased with oneself	feel sorry for oneself	look after oneself	tell oneself
be proud of oneself	forgive oneself	look at oneself	treat oneself
behave oneself	get oneself	prepare oneself	
believe in oneself	give oneself	pride oneself on	
blame oneself	help oneself	push oneself	

7 Verbs Followed by Gerunds Only

admit	keep (= continue)
avoid	mind (= object to)
consider	miss
delay	postpone
defend	practice
deny	propose
discuss	quit
enjoy	recall (= remember)
finish	risk
imagine	suggest
involve	understand

8 Verbs Followed by Infinitives Only

afford	help	pretend
agree	hesitate	promise
arrange	hope	refuse
ask	hurry	request
attempt	intend	seem
choose	learn	struggle
consent	manage	tend (= be likely)
decide	need	threaten
demand	neglect	volunteer
deserve	offer	wait
expect	pay	want
fail	plan	wish
forget	prepare	would like

9 Verbs Followed by Gerunds or Infinitives

begin	like	regret*
continue	love	start
forget*	prefer	stop*
get	remember*	try*
hate		

*These verbs can be followed by a gerund or an infinitive, with a difference in meaning.

10 Expressions with Gerunds

Use a gerund after certain fixed verb expressions.

Verb expressions	
spend time / spend money waste time / waste money have trouble / have difficulty / have a difficult time	I **spent time helping** in the library. Don't **waste time complaining**. She **had trouble finishing** her degree.

Use a gerund after certain fixed noun + preposition expressions.

Noun + preposition expressions	
an excuse for in favor of an interest in a reason for	I have **an excuse for not doing** my homework. Who is **in favor of not admitting** him? He has **an interest in getting** a scholarship. He has **a reason for choosing** this school.

11 Verbs + Objects + Infinitives

advise	force	remind	ask*
allow	get	request	choose*
cause	hire	require	expect*
challenge	invite	teach	help*
convince	order	tell	need*
enable	permit	urge	pay*
encourage	persuade	warn	promise*
forbid			want*
			wish*

* These verbs can be followed by an object + infinitive
or an infinitive only, with a difference in meaning.

Examples:
My boss **advised me to go** back to school.
They **urged the advertisers not to surprise** people.
My department **chose* Sally to create** the new ads.
My department **chose* to create** the new ads.

12 *Be* + Adjectives + Infinitives

be afraid	be delighted	be encouraged	be lucky	be sad
be amazed	be depressed	be excited	be necessary	be shocked
be angry	be determined	be fortunate	be pleased	be sorry
be anxious	be difficult	be fun	be proud	be surprised
be ashamed	be easy	be happy	be ready	be upset
be curious	be embarrassed	be likely	be relieved	be willing

13 Verbs + Prepositions

Verb + *about*
ask about
care about
complain about
be excited about
find out about
forget about
hear about
know about
learn about
read about
see about
talk about
think about
worry about
be worried about

Verb + *against*
advise against
decide against

Verb + *at*
look at
smile at
be successful at

Verb + *by*
be affected by
be raised by

Verb + *for*
apologize for
apply for
ask for
care for
look for
pay for
be responsible for
wait for

Verb + *from*
graduate from

Verb + *in*
believe in
find in
include in
be interested in
involve in
result in
show in
succeed in
use in

Verb + *of*
be afraid of
approve of
be aware of
consist of
dream of
be guilty of
hear of
know of
take care of
think of
be warned of

Verb + *on*
concentrate on
count on
decide on
depend on
insist on
keep on
plan on
rely on

Verb + *to*
admit to
belong to
confess to
listen to
look forward to
refer to
talk to
be used to

Verb + *with*
agree with
argue with
bother with
deal with
start with
work with

14 Adjectives + Prepositions

Adjective + about
concerned about
excited about
happy about
nervous about
pleased about
sad about
sorry about
surprised about
upset about
worried about

Adjective + at
amazed at
angry at
bad at
good at
successful at
surprised at

Adjective + by
amazed by
bored by
surprised by

Adjective + for
bad for
good for
ready for
responsible for

Adjective + from
different from
safe from
separate from

Adjective + in
high in
interested in
low in

Adjective + of
accused of
afraid of
ashamed of
aware of
capable of
careful of
full of
guilty of
sick of
tired of
warned of

Adjective + to
accustomed to
due to
similar to

Adjective + with
bored with
content with
familiar with
good with
satisfied with
wrong with

15 Verbs and Fixed Expressions that Introduce Indirect Questions

Do you have any idea ...?
Can you tell me ...?
Do you know ...?
Do you remember ...?
Could you explain ...?
Would you show me ...?

I'd like to know ...?
I wonder / I'm wondering ...?
I want to understand ...?
Let's find out ...?
Let's ask ...?
We need to know ...?

I don't know ...?
I'm not sure ...?
I can't imagine ...?
We don't understand ...?
It doesn't say ...?
I can't believe ...?

16 Tense Shifting in Indirect Speech

Direct Speech	Indirect (Reported) Speech
simple present *She said, "The boss is angry."*	**simple past** *She **said** (that) the boss **was** angry.*
present progressive *He said, "She **is enjoying** the work."*	**past progressive** *He **said** (that) she **was enjoying** the work.*
simple past *They said, "The store **closed** last year."*	**past perfect** *They **said** (that) the store **had closed** last year.*
present perfect *The manager said, "The group **has done** good work."*	**past perfect** *The manager **said** (that) the group **had done** good work.*
will *He said, "The department **will add** three new managers."*	***would*** *He **said** (that) the department **would add** three new managers.*
be going to *She said, "They **are going to hire** more people soon."*	***be going to** (past form)* *She **said** (that) they **were going to hire** more people soon.*
can *The teacher said, "The students **can work** harder."*	***could*** *The teacher said (that) the students could work harder.*
may *Their manager said, "Money **may not be** very important to them."*	***might*** *Their manager **said** (that) money **might not be** very important to them.*

* Note: *should, might, ought to,* and *could* do not change forms.

17 Reporting Verbs

Questions	Statements				Commands and Requests	
ask	admit	convince	notify	show	advise	request
inquire	announce	exclaim	observe	state	ask	say
question	assert	explain	promise	suggest	command	tell
	assure	find	remark	swear	demand	urge
	claim	indicate	remind	yell	order	warn
	comment	inform	reply			
	complain	mention	report			
	confess	note	shout			

18 Passive Forms

	Active	Passive
present progressive	*People are speaking English at the meeting.*	*English is being spoken at the meeting.*
simple present	*People speak English at the meeting.*	*English is spoken at the meeting.*
simple past	*People spoke English at the meeting.*	*English was spoken at the meeting.*
past progressive	*People were speaking English at the meeting.*	*English was being spoken at the meeting.*
present perfect	*People have spoken English at the meeting.*	*English has been spoken at the meeting.*
past perfect	*People had been speaking English at the meeting.*	*English had been spoken at the meeting.*
simple future	*People will speak English at the meeting.*	*English will be spoken at the meeting.*
future perfect	*People will have spoken English at the meeting.*	*English will have been spoken at the meeting.*
***be going to* (future)**	*People are going to speak English at the meeting.*	*English is going to be spoken at the meeting.*
Questions	*Do people speak English at the meeting?* *Did people speak English at the meeting?* *Have people spoken English at the meeting?*	*Is English spoken at the meeting?* *Was English spoken at the meeting?* *Has English been spoken at the meeting?*

19 Relative Clauses

	Identifying	Nonidentifying
Subject Relative Clauses	Many people **who/that support the environment** recycle.	My sister, **who lives in Maine**, loves being outside.
	Electricity **that/which saves energy** is a good thing.	People power, **which is a way to create energy**, is popular.
	They are the scientists **whose research has won awards**.	Brad Pitt, **whose movies are well known**, gives a lot of money to environmental causes.
Object Relative Clauses	Detectives are people (**who/whom/that**) **I respect tremendously**.	The character Sherlock Holmes, who/**whom Arthur Conan Doyle created**, was a fictional detective.
	Evidence (**which/that**) **criminals leave at the crime scene** is called forensic evidence.	Evidence from criminals, **which we call forensic evidence**, can help police solve cases.
	The person **whose car the thieves stole** was a friend of mine.	Arthur Conan Doyle, **whose medical clinic not many patients attended**, had time to write his stories.
Object Relative Clauses as Objects of Prepositions	There's the police officer (**that/who/whom**) **I spoke to**. (informal) There's the police officer **to whom I spoke**. (formal)	There's Officer Smith, **who/whom I spoke to yesterday**. (informal) There's Officer Smith, **to whom I spoke yesterday**. (formal)
	Police found evidence from the crime scene under the chair (**that/which**) **I was sitting on**. (informal) Police found evidence from the crime scene under the chair **on which I was sitting**. (formal)	The door, **which I entered through**, had been broken during the robbery. (informal) The door, **through which I entered**, had been broken during the robbery. (formal)

Relative Clauses (*continued*)

	Identifying	Nonidentifying
Relative Clauses with *Where* and *in Which*	It's a city **where you can find Wi-Fi almost everywhere**. It's a city in **which you can find Wi-Fi almost everywhere**.	The city of Atlanta, **where my sister lives**, is very large. The city of Atlanta, **in which my sister lives**, is very large.
Relative Clauses with *When* and *During Which*	Night is a time **when many students study for exams**. Night is a time **during which many students study for exams**.	Joe prefers to study at night, **when his children are asleep**. Joe prefers to study at night, **during which his children are asleep**.
Participle Phrases	Students **concerned with the environment** should get involved in environmental groups on campus.	Millennials, **raised in the era of technology, cell phones, and the Internet**, understand technology very well.
	The expert **giving tomorrow's talk on Millennials** is very well known.	The movie Twilight, **starring Millennials**, is based on a book by Gen Xer Stephenie Meyer.
Prepositional Phrases	The computers **in our classroom** are fast. Young workers **low in self-esteem** are unusual.	
Appositives		Jan Smith, **the president of Myco**, will be speaking at noon today. Jan Smith (**the president of Myco**) will be speaking at noon today. (formal writing)

20 Conditionals

Situation	Tense	*If* clause	Main clause	Example
Real Conditionals	present	simple present	simple present	*If a website **is** popular, people **talk** about it.*
	future	simple present	future	*If you only **listen** to one station, you **will hear** only one opinion.*
Unreal Conditionals	present	simple past or past progressive	*would, could, might* + base form of verb	*If I **studied** every day, I **would pass** all my tests.* *If I **weren't dreaming** all day, I **would pass** all my tests.*
	future	simple past	*would, could, might* + base form of verb	*If our school **closed** next year, we **wouldn't have** a place to learn.*
	past	past perfect	*would have, could have, might have* + past participle	*If the city **had hired** more teachers, the schools **might have improved**.*

Wishes	Tense	*that* clause		Example
	present	simple past, past progressive, could		*I wish (that) schools **were improving**.*
	future	*were going to, would, could*		*I wish (that) the teachers **were going to** give us a party.*
	past	past perfect		*I **wish** (that) I **had studied** more.*

Index

Art Credits

Student Book Level 3

The authors and publishers acknowledge the following sources of copyright material and are grateful for the permissions granted. While every effort has been made, it has not always been possible to identify the sources of all the material used, or to trace all copyright holders. If any omissions are brought to our notice, we will be happy to include the appropriate acknowledgements on reprinting and in the next update to the digital edition, as applicable.

The following images are sourced from Getty Images.

U1: Jose Luis Pelaez Inc/Blend Images; Jacqueline Veissid/DigitalVision; Ajr_images/iStock; XiXinXing; U2: Nikada/E+; Universal Images Group; Jose Luis Pelaez Inc./Blend Images; U3: Dinodia Photos/Hulton Archive; Michael Gottschalk/Photothek; Jetta Productions/Blend Images; Benoist SEBIRE/Moment; Tim Robberts/The Image Bank; Jon Kopaloff/FilmMagic; View Pictures/Universal Images Group; Paul Morigi/WireImage; U4: Strickke/E+; Aaron Mccoy/Photolibrary; Stephen Simpson/The Image Bank; Newton Daly/DigitalVision; Andrew Brookes/Cultura; Deborah Kolb/Image Source; Blend Images - KidStock/Brand X Pictures; Hero Images; U5: Tim Robberts/The Image Bank; Cosinart/iStock; Guvendemir/iStock Unreleased; Image Source/DigitalVision; U6: Westend61; Hinterhaus Productions/DigitalVision; U7: Tonivaver/iStock; Phil Boorman/Cultura; Westend61; Hero Images; U8: Bill Hinton/Moment; Hero Images; Kali9/E+; U9: Alexander Spatari/Moment; Bluestocking/iStock; Monticelllo/iStock; Yevgen Romanenko/Moment; Paci77/iStock; Enter89/iStock; Kolesnikovserg/iStock; Pearleye/E+; U10: Gchutka/iStock; KatarzynaBialasiewicz/iStock; U11: Vgajic/E+; U12: Alejandrophotography/E+; Klaus Vedfelt/DigitalVision; U13: Sam Mellish/In Pictures; U14: Monkeybusinessimages/iStock; PhotoAlto/Eric Audras/Brand X Pictures; U15: MPI/Archive Photos; Darren pearson (dariustwin)/Moment; Seb_ra/iStock; U16: H. Armstrong Roberts/ClassicStock/Archive Photos; Hulton Archive; U17: Jon Feingersh/Blend Images; Monkeybusinessimages/iStock; Jacoblund/iStock; U18: Hero Images; Vm/E+; Caiaimage/Agnieszka Olek; U19: Caiaimage/Caiaimage/Robert Daly; U20: Jose A. Bernat Bacete/Moment; Istanbulimage/E+; Kosamtu/E+; NoDerog/iStock; U21: Echo/Juice Images; Photobalance/iStock; Maciej Lulko/Moment; U22: Steve Allen/Stockbyte; Monty Rakusen/Cultura; Stephen Chernin; Andersen Ross/Blend Images; U23: PeopleImages/E+; JGI/Tom Grill/Blend Images; Johnny Greig/E+; Juanmonino/E+; Juanmonino/E+; Simon Marcus Taplin/Corbis; U24: Bloomberg Creative Photos; Skynesher/iStock; Franckreporter/E+; U25: 1001nights/E+; Huntstock/Brand X Pictures; Kickstand/iStock; Joshuaraineyphotography/iStock; Stocktrek Images/Richard Roscoe; U26: Lew Robertson/Photolibrary; Will Heap/Dorling Kindersley; ilietus/iStock; SolStock/E+; Cgissemann/iStock; chengyuzheng/iStock; MIXA Co. Ltd.; LUNAMARINA/iStock; Troscha/iStock; GlobalP/iStock; U27: Csondy/E+; Michaelpuche/iStock; Carlos Ciudad Photography/Moment; Gavin Jackson/ArcaidImages; U28: Handout; BSIP/Universal Images Group; Scibak/iStock.

Images from other sources

U3: Jackie ellis/Alamy Stock Photo; U9: Jose Luis Stephens/Alamy Stock Photo; yronovych/Shutterstock; U15: ClassicStock/Alamy Stock Photo; U19: Keith Crowley/Alamy Stock Photo; U21: WENN Ltd/Alamy Stock Photo; U24: Artur Marciniec/Alamy Stock Photo; U25: FEMA/Alamy Stock Photo; U26: Catinsyrup/Shutterstock; U28: Everett Collection Inc/Alamy Stock Photo.